# Inside Relationships

## Dedication

To MMF and JDA,
my favorite and fierce companions who give good advice.
Mom, if you blink too much,
your eyeball will fall out.
(Mimi, age 3)

# Inside Relationships

## A Creative Casebook in Relational Communication

Sandra L. Faulkner
Editor

Left Coast
Press Inc.

Walnut Creek, California

LEFT COAST PRESS, INC.
1630 North Main Street, #400
Walnut Creek, CA 94596
www.LCoastPress.com

**Left Coast Press** Inc.

ISBN 978-1-61132-270-5 hardback
ISBN 978-1-61132-271-2 paperback
ISBN 978-1-61132-273-6 consumer eBook

Library of Congress Cataloging-in-Publication Data

Inside relationships : a creative casebook on relational communication / Sandra L. Faulkner (editor).
    pages cm
  Includes bibliographical references.
  ISBN 978-1-61132-270-5 (hardback : alk. paper) — ISBN 978-1-61132-271-2 (pbk. : alk. paper) — ISBN 978-1-61132-273-6 (consumer ebook)
  1. Interpersonal communication—Case studies. 2. Interpersonal relations—Case studies. I. Faulkner, Sandra.
  HM1166.I67 2013
  302—dc23
                              2013003888

Printed in the United States of America

♾™ The paper used in this publication meets the minimum requirements of American National Standard for Information Sciences—Permanence of Paper for Printed Library Materials, ANSI/NISO Z39.48–1992.

**green press** INITIATIVE

Left Coast Press, Inc. is committed to preserving ancient forests and natural resources. We elected to print this title on 30% post consumer recycled paper, processed chlorine free. As a result, for this printing, we have saved:

4 Trees (40' tall and 6-8" diameter)
2 Million BTUs of Total Energy
298 Pounds of Greenhouse Gases
1,616 Gallons of Wastewater
108 Pounds of Solid Waste

Left Coast Press, Inc. made this paper choice because our printer, Thomson-Shore, Inc., is a member of Green Press Initiative, a nonprofit program dedicated to supporting authors, publishers, and suppliers in their efforts to reduce their use of fiber obtained from endangered forests.

For more information, visit www.greenpressinitiative.org

Environmental impact estimates were made using the Environmental Defense Paper Calculator. For more information visit: www.papercalculator.org.

# Contents

List of Illustrations                                                                 7

Preface: How To Use This Book                                                          9

Introduction: An Argument for Creative Approaches                                     15
    to Relationships

Chapter 1:  What Is a Relationship?                                         25
    Case 1:  Body of Work by Sheila Squillante           29
    Case 2:  The Person in the Moon by Gabriel Welsch     36
    Case 3:  Life After Death: Continuing Close Relationships   48
        in New and Different Ways by Tiffani Baldwin

Chapter 2:  Relationship Metaphors and Forms                                55
    Case 4:  Migration Patterns by Kimberly Dark          61
    Case 5:  Doing Valentine's Day Differently by Meg Barker   65
    Case 6:  Twenty-One-Year-Old Virgin by Malorie Palma    69

Chapter 3:  Uncertainty, Information Management, and                          75
    Disclosure
    Case 7:  BIRTHing ARTiculations by Erin K. Willer       80
    Case 8:  Storying Mindfulness, (Re)imagining Burn by     86
        Keith Berry
    Case 9:  "Are You Calling Me a Slut?" Sharing Personal    97
        Information in Close Relationships by Kate
        Magsamen-Conrad

Chapter 4:  Friendship                                                      103
    Case 10:  Our Choice without a Choice: Similarities in   107
        Friendships and Romantic Relationships by
        Lindsey T. Boyd
    Case 11: Goodbye Friend by Julia A. Galbus                  116
    Case 12: Friendships and Social Support in Coping with      123
        Illness Diagnosis: The Story of Sherry and the
        Martha's Vineyard Communication Association
        by Sherry Shepler and Ashley Duggan

Chapter 5:  Family Communication                                           133

Case 13:  Is God like My Father? Exploring Abusive Family      137
          Relationships through Sibling Narratives by
          Ellen Leslie and Frances Spaulding
Case 14:  Diary of Anorexia by Marne Austin                   151
Case 15:  That Baby Will Cost You: An Intended                161
          Ambivalent Pregnancy by Sandra L. Faulkner

Chapter 6:  The Social Self                                                 177

Case 16:  (Not Remotely) Hot Online Action! by Jenn McKee     181
Case 17:  Thank You for Not Asking by Suzanne V. L. Berg      188
Case 18:  Transforming Vignettes of NonBeing into            195
          Life Affirming (M)Otherhood by Ellen Gorsevski

Chapter 7:  Gender and Culture                                              207

Case 19:  Seven Tattoos: A Personal History by               213
          Cynthia Nicole
Case 20:  The Conversation about Gender and Culture that      220
          I Would Have with You by Manda V. Hicks
Case 21:  Sticks and Stones: Dealing with Discrimination      225
          by Lisa K. Hanasono

Chapter 8:  Relationship Maintenance                                        233

Case 22:  Comfort by Camille-Yvette Welsch                   237
Case 23:  Tell Me About Love by Paul D. Ruby                 239
Case 24:  The Onion by Abigail Lea Van Vlerah                242

Chapter 9:  The Dark-Side: Conflict, Dissolution and Other    247
            Difficult Conversations

Case 25:  Falling Spell/Spelling Fail: Examining a History of  254
          Physical and Emotional Abuse by Dessa Anderson
Case 26:  Frogging It: A Poetic Analysis of Relationship      263
          Dissolution by Sandra L. Faulkner
Case 27:  Institutionalized by Wonda Baugh                   276

Index                                                         283

About the Authors                                            291

# Illustrations

**Figures**

| | | |
|---|---|---|
| 3.1 | Robin with Babies | 81 |
| 3.2 | The Gift | 82 |
| 4.1 | The Make Up to Break Up | 109 |
| 4.2 | The On Again, Off Again | 110 |
| 4.3 | The Should Have, Could Have | 111 |
| 4.4 | The Love To Hate | 112 |
| 4.5 | The Harshman Boys | 113 |
| 4.6 | Slob Squad | 114 |
| 5.1 | Dear Pregnant Body | 164 |
| 7.1 | Tattoo One | 213 |
| 7.2 | Tattoo Two | 214 |
| 7.3 | Tattoo Three | 215 |
| 7.4 | Tattoo Four | 216 |
| 7.5 | Tattoo Five | 217 |
| 7.6 | Tattoo Six | 218 |
| 7.7 | Tattoo Seven | 218 |
| 8.1 | Tell Me About Love | 240 |
| 8.2 | The Onion | 242 |

**Table**

| | | |
|---|---|---|
| 6.1 | Chart of NonBeing | 204 |

# Preface

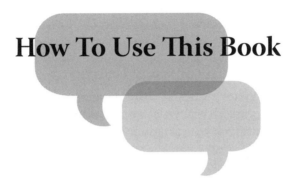

## How To Use This Book

### Why This Book

Using cases studies in the classroom is an accepted, and increasingly ubiquitous, teaching model designed to enhance student learning through the principle of active engagement. We respond to well-told stories and recognize them as part of our everyday communication landscape. With this aim, *Inside Relationships* uses creative case studies that pay careful attention to and explore critical issues of narrative aesthetics concomitant with interpersonal and relational theory and skill building. Using creative writing from both academics and writers promises to engage the student in all of us through the use of literature. I put together this book because of my experience teaching interpersonal and relational communication. When I have used literature such as blogs, short stories, and poetry in the classroom, it has promoted dialogue and skill building in ways that solely academic writing has not. Students have responded better to the story than the theory, so I decided I needed to collect theoretical stories. This is a book I want to use in my relational communication courses. This is a book that my fall 2012 relational communication students piloted for all of us. They made sure the stories were believable and engaging, the discussion questions and activities useful for promoting lively class dialogue.

This book contributes to interpersonal pedagogy through a focus on the aesthetic/creative dimensions of readings. Relational theory is implicitly and explicitly engaged through the use of stories of everyday relational life and the challenges inherent in the relating process (for example, identities, monogamy, self-image, conflict). This book makes an excellent text in relational and interpersonal courses by asking and answering the following overarching questions: How do we initiate difficult conversations in our close relationships? How do we maintain our close relationships through the use of effective communication? What constitutes effective relational communication? How does writing about our relationships contribute to relational health and satisfaction?

## Features and Benefits

This book contributes to the teaching of interpersonal and relational communication in several ways. First, the book tackles what many would consider difficult conversations in close relationships. The topics of infidelity, self-image, abuse, sexuality, death and dying, relational expectations, and conflict are part of our mundane everyday relational worlds, but the skills to contend with these challenges to promote relationship health and satisfaction require reflection and practice.

Second, this book demonstrates the use of effective relational communication through the reflective practice of writing about difficult relational situations and conversations. This writing is an important therapeutic and theoretical practice. Narrative theory instructs us that the process of storytelling is part of our sense making and an important part of our everyday communication practice. The text will serve as an extended example of how one can use creative writing to reflect on relationship practices.

Third, this book also offers an aesthetic contribution through the case study writing. We need well-written depictions of relational challenges. The focus on the craft of creative writing equal to a focus on the craft of relationship theory is a major benefit. The use of a variety of forms (blogs to poetry to photo-essays to short stories) adds interest, kind of like annual *Best Stories of Relationships 20XX*.

This book contains 27 case studies arranged in 9 chapters according to themes and keywords. You will notice that the case studies have overlapping concepts threading through the entire book, thus I focus in on what I consider to be the predominant themes in each section in the chapter introductions, letting you discover the connections as you use the book. The vitality of using creative cases for teaching relational and interpersonal theory and skills is demonstrated at the end of each case with a list of questions and writing activities for discussion and references for further reading and research. At the beginning of each chapter, I provide a brief summary of important relational and interpersonal concepts to give you a context and a way to frame your reading of the case studies that follow. Also use the keywords at the opening of each case and the ending discussion questions and activities as a reading guide. The creative cases encourage you to reflect on and write about your own relationships and relationship practices.

Chapter 1 asks about the components we think are necessary in our close relationships: Must an individual be alive to exert influence on us? Do all romantic relationships presume sexual activity? How does relationship history influence our needs? A poetic meditation on sexual talk and body image demonstrates how our self-concept develops from our interactions with significant others. Welsch's short story about a failed marriage proposal highlights the concept of intimacy readiness and the interaction of lifespan communication, and Baldwin's personal essay on the death of grandparents investigates the need for and difficulty of final conversations.

Chapter 2 contains three essays on what we mean when we use the word "relationship" and the metaphors about relationships we use and see every day. Dark challenges us to define family beyond a nuclear conception of mom, dad, and child. Barker asks in a blog whether pop-culture representations of couple-hood, such as Valentine's Day, limit our understanding of relationships. In "Twenty-One Year Old Virgin," Palma explains the connection between religious values and upbringing and the pressure to be sexually active in romantic relationships.

Chapter 3 details how expectations, situation, and uncertainty influence our disclosure decisions in close relationships. Willer uses painting and blogging to share feelings of loss and forgiveness surrounding infertility and miscarriage. Berry reflects on how mindfulness can ease difficult disclosures about identity, and Magsamen-Conrad presents a fictionalized text message in which a woman expresses concern about her friend's partying behavior.

Chapter 4 concerns what we mean by friendship, how we develop and maintain friendships, and the role they play in our relational lives. In a photo-essay, Boyd represents interviews with friends about how situation, environment, and personal dispositions influenced the formation of romantic relationships and friendships. Galbus's meditation on the lack of scripts for the ending of friendships asks us to consider what friends mean in the context of our lives, and MVCA gives us a story of how a group of friends and colleagues contend with illness in their friendship circle.

Chapter 5 explores family communication through work that queries how family dynamics contribute to and hinder relational health.

Leslie and Spaulding ask questions about how a religious response could help the challenge of physical and emotional abuse in religious households. Using a diary format, Austin presents a mother-daughter story of anorexia and why family communication is part of the healing process. Faulkner's personal narrative about an intended ambivalent pregnancy addresses dialectics of work-life issues, certainty and uncertainty, and family decision-making.

Chapter 6 details how others and our social worlds, including our computer-mediated communication, shape our relationship expectations and experiences. McKee's blog about an unexpected online encounter highlights the role of framing and expectations in infidelity. Berg's chronicle of (in)fertility represents Facebook posts about pregnancy and conversations with relatives and medical personnel as contributing to feelings of isolation and confusion in her marriage. Gorsevski details seemingly innocuous daily conversations about parenthood that serve to stigmatize women without children.

Chapter 7 contains three cases that (de)construct gender and culture in our relationships. Nicole maps the tattoos on her body as geographic representations of gender and surviving in close relationships. Hicks defines culture and gender through a musing about how daily interactions at work and on vacation personalize these concepts. Hanasono's personal narrative of others' reactions to her being American as a third generation Japanese woman demonstrate the process of how telling one's story can be a form of social support.

Chapter 8 uses poetic and visual representations to demonstrate how we maintain our relationships. Welsch wrote a poem about her aunt's cancer to ask if lying to a dying loved one, as a form of comfort, is justifiable. Ruby visualizes a dialogue between a romantic couple about meanings of love, lust, and romance in a photo-poem, and Van Vlerah uses a diagram of frustrations about communication with a lover to demonstrate the importance of talking about interaction expectations.

Chapter 9 highlights cases with darker concepts like mental illness, verbal and physical abuse, and the breakdown of relationships. Anderson's personal essay on multi-generational abuse in her family reveals the normalization of family violence. Faulkner's performance poetry piece shows the breaking down process of romance and friendships. In a series of poems about being institutionalized for mental illness, Baugh discusses the importance of social support for helping with healing and the sting of stigma.

# Acknowledgments

I want to express my appreciation to Xiao Hu, my research assistant during fall 2012, for helping me find references.

The students in Bowling Green State University's Communication 4070: Relational Communication (Fall 2012) piloted the case studies for all of us: Don Bonesteel, Kristen Boyd, Shaylyn Galley, Lindsay Garwood, Erique Geiger, Kara Leonard, Sarah Martinelli, Chase McCune, Bridget Mendyuk, Alex Novack, Eric Olson, Jason Thayer, and Matt Williams made thoughtful suggestions about the relationship processes described in the cases, the discussion questions, and the activities to make this a better book.

Portions of the material in Case 26 appeared in my article: Faulkner, S. L. (2012). Frogging it: A poetic analysis of relationship dissolution. *Qualitative Research in Education, 1*(2), 202–227. doi:10.4471. qre.2012.08 Copyright © QRE.

Portions of the material in Case 15 appeared in my article: Faulkner, S. L. (2012). That baby will cost you: An intended ambivalent pregnancy. *Qualitative Inquiry, 18*(4), 333–340. doi:10.1177/1007800411431564 [qix.sagepub.com/] Copyright © Sage.

Case 13 appeared originally in the *International Review of Qualitative Research* (vol. 2, no. 1, 2012) and is included here by permission of Left Coast Press, Inc.

# Introduction

# An Argument for Creative Approaches to Relationships

## Creative Approaches

In the introduction, I craft an argument for the study of close relationships using a creative lens, in particular the use of arts based methods. The cases presented in this book can be considered arts based research (ABR), which is a systematic process of using art, "the actual making of artistic expressions in all of the different forms of the arts, as a primary way of understanding and examining experience by both researchers and the people that they involve in their studies" (McNiff, 2008, p. 29). The most distinguishing feature of ABR is the use of aesthetic qualities to illuminate often unseen/unspoken situations and experiences, things that we can't talk about in other forms (Eisner, 2006, 2008). ABR includes the types of cases presented in the book-narrative inquiry, fiction, poetry, and visual arts. It is useful for the study of many of the concepts and experiences discussed in the following pages: identity, subjugated perspectives, difficult experiences not easily talked about, multiple meanings and dialogue (Leavy, 2009). For instance, I use video and poetry to talk about the often invisible gender socialization at school, work, and in parenting (see Faulkner, 2011).

ABR offers us a means to understand in more imaginative ways by allowing for personal, emotional, experiential, and embodied

*Inside Relationships: A Creative Casebook in Relational Communication*, edited by Sandra L. Faulkner, 15–24. © 2013 Left Coast Press, Inc. All rights reserved.

expressions of knowledge that value alternative, participatory, and indigenous ways of knowing. It can even be "a methodology for radical, ethical, and revolutionary research that is futuristic, socially responsible, and useful for addressing social inequities" (Finley, 2008, p. 71). The arts address the qualitative nuances of situations by addressing what is subtle but significant, by developing dispositions and habits of mind that reveal to the individual a world he or she may not have noticed. There is a shift away from the conventional assumption that all research is meant to bring us closer to a definitive understanding of various dimensions of the social world. It means abandoning the notion that the research process should always result in a more persuasive argument or interpretation of how social and cultural phenomena are best perceived or conceptualized. The goal is to re-present meaning and make that meaning-making process explicit to an audience (Leavy, 2009).

Arts based inquiry also implies a shift from relying on cognitive processes to create knowledge, and focuses on the use of the imagination through feeling and form to create new concepts of the world in a quest to reveal truth (Eisner, 2008). Some of the present book's case studies use photos to describe relationship processes, such as Paul Ruby's photo poem about romance and Lindsey Boyd's photo essay about how situation, environment and individual characteristics interact in our friendships and romantic relationships. Most of the case studies use poetry and fictional devices, so I will discuss the benefits and features of poetry and fiction, in particular.

## Poetic Inquiry as Interpersonal Research

Many researchers consider poetry an excellent means to (re)present data, to analyze and create understanding of human experience, to capture and portray the human condition in a more easily "consumable," powerful, emotionally poignant, and open-ended non-linear form compared with prose research reports (Prendergast, 2009). Poetry constitutes a way to say things evocatively and to say those things that may not be presented at all. Researchers use poetry throughout the research process: as a method of inquiry, as (re)presentation, as qualitative data, and as a means of data analysis (for example, Faulkner, 2009; Pelias, 2011).

Because poetry focuses on the minutiae of language use and form to not only present but also create an experience for the reader, it makes a valuable contribution to our understanding of personal relationships. Poetry matters because it is powerful, the fact that it "serves up the substance of our lives, and becomes more than a mere articulation of experience—although that articulation alone is part of its usefulness... it allows us to see ourselves freshly and keenly. It makes the invisible world visible" (Parini, 2008, p. 181). The poet's focus on form is important for meaning making in poetry.

> Form is the visible side of content. The way in which the content becomes manifest. Form: time turning into space and space turning into time simultaneously....We name one thing and then another. That's how time enters poetry. Space, on the other hand, comes into being through the attention we pay to each word. The more intense our attention, the more space, and there's a lot of space inside words. (Simic, 1990, p. 85)

Form and language are also intimately connected. Pelias (2011) eloquently stated that "constituted in interaction, I am formed by the language that passes between me and others. And I make sense of my relationships by finding a language that provides some account of my personal observations and feelings" (p. 17). The language of poetry demonstrates how communication is relational, how we create identities, and how we feel our way through our relationships.

The use of poetry to examine relational processes can be categorized as performative writing because the personal experiences of the researcher are connected to the ethnographic project (Denzin, 1997), the writing takes shape through observation and field experience to bring the audience the most interesting and complex moments of our lived experience (Pelias, 2005). Performative writing is evocative because it brings the reader in contact with other worlds (Pollock, 1998). Using writing that is both performative and poetic allows us to represent relational experiences in a "messy" format that speaks to representational issues of empowerment and disempowerment (Alcoff, 2003), the perspectives of everyone in relationships. Denzin (1997) describes narratives of the self as messy texts because they are multi-voiced and no one interpretation is privileged. "The poetic self is simply willing to put itself on the line and to take risks...predicated on a simple proposition: This writer's personal experiences are worth sharing with others. Messy texts make the writer a part of the writing project" (p. 225). The writing vacillates between description and interpretation, using voice as a means to write *for* those studied rather than *about* them. Poetry as an experience can create empathy in audience members by allowing them to see and feel what the writer does (Pelias, 2005).

Leslie Baxter and Dawn Braithwaite (2008) contend that interpersonal research and theory is biased toward post-positivist methods. They content analyzed published studies in two popular relational journals from 1990–2005 and discovered that 83.3% took a post-positivist stance, with 13.9% adopting an interpretive stance and 2.9% a critical perspective. This suggests to me that there exists room for poetry as/in relational research. Prendergast (2009) argued that the best poetic inquiry is that which concerns itself with affect as well as intellect and deals with topics grounded in the "affective experiential domain." The use of relationship processes as a basis for poetry represents human thought in an affective context (McAdams, 1993). We create stories or narratives about our relationships to provide the closure we, and those in our social networks, need (Kellas & Manusov, 2003). Therefore, the impulse to create poetry is the impulse toward narrative. McAdams (1993) believes that our narratives provide, at least in part, a window into our thoughts, behavior, and experiences. Narratives allow a way to examine identities, the communicative behavior that externalizes our thoughts about identity (Faulkner & Hecht, 2011), how we make sense of our cultural and social worlds, and how we try to create coherence (Lieblich, Tuval-Mashiach, & Zilber, 1998). In many instances, we narrate particular life experiences where there is a rift between a real and ideal self or between the self and society (Riessman, 1993). For example, the end of a relationship, and the shifting of it into another form, entails a threat to our social and personal order (Duck, 2011). Our personal order contains our preferences, experiences, and identities (e.g., being part of a couple, being nice, discovering a partner's affair), and the social order references cultural context (e.g., being in a romantic relationship is often viewed as better than not being in a romantic relationship).

The goal of the poetry pieces in this book is "freedom for personal resonance," for you to experience the poetry as "evocative mediators" of painful and joyful relational experiences (Todres & Galvin, 2008, p. 571). Using performative writing, specifically poetry, to examine relational processes like breaking up and mental illness provides insight into underlying values of how to do relationships, and in this case, how communication plays a role before, during, and after they end (Pelias, 2011). Many poets assert that all good poetry addresses large issues—death, silence, absence, and loss—all reasons for why relationships end (see Faulkner, 2009). The power of poetry to reconnect our selves to loss, conscious and unconscious hurts that manifest in our relational interactions, offers interpersonal scholars, educators, and those in relationships other ways of understanding. Pelias (2011) noted that he used poetry in a collection of essays about personal relations because, "I want the poetic to discover how meaning feels and how feeling means" (p. 12).

## Fiction in Social Research

"Each different form of knowledge calls for a different set of criteria for judging it, and likewise, each different form of knowledge allows for different types of claims to be made" (Krizek, 2003, p. 145).

The ontological question of what constitutes fact in research using fiction as data, analytic tool, and representation is best posed as a dialectical continuum representing degrees of truth. The question posed is "But is this true?" I demonstrate this fact/fiction dialectic using two cases presented in this book that employ fictional devices as analytical tools and representations illustrative of this continuum. In each of these examples, the question of fact is contingent on the goals of the research/representation, the politics of evidence debate, and resulting criteria.

For me, the tired argument that social research is based on "facts" with a capital T TRUTH rather than multiple little t truths needs to be put to rest, especially because fiction *is in* social research and has been for some time (see, for example, A. Banks & S. Banks, 1998; Leavy, 2013). Watson (2011), however, argues that acceptance of narratives does not extend to widespread support for creative nonfiction and fictional narratives due to "a deeply felt need for research to be grounded in an empirical reality of something that really happened" (Watson, 2011, p. 396). The counter claim that to at least some extent all narratives are made up rankles because the implication is that it may be impossible to determine fact from fiction. I ask why should it matter if interpretivist and critical research goals focus more on understanding and change than validity? "By declaring ones work simultaneously fiction and social science, the researcher runs the risk, through disturbing the pact between author and reader, of not having [his or her] work read as social science (or indeed at all) and therefore dismissed" (Watson, 2011, p. 396). Let's talk about the cases here that we can label social science *and* fiction to demonstrate the tensions of claims and criteria (Richardson, 1997).

## Example 1: The Person in the Moon

Welsch's short story presents themes of relational redefinition, rejection, and communication across the lifespan. We can argue that a fictional mode of representing relational hurts is more effective for inside and outside of the classroom if it brings the audience more fully into the research through the experience of feeling the character's struggle (Bochner, 2000), a kind of ekphrastic teaching (Watson, 2011). Kiesinger (1998) points out that evocative narratives allow "researchers to transform collected materials into vivid, detailed accounts of lived experience that aim to show how lives are lived, understood, and experienced" (p. 129). She asks the following: "As a form of reporting, are evocative narratives fact or fiction? If as researchers we become so engaged and involved in the experiences of those we study, can we accurately portray our subject's experiences? Are writers of evocative narrative producing scholarship, literature, or something else all together?" (p. 129). The fact that transcripts are not stories and are themselves a kind of fiction (Hammersley, 2010) makes writing a short story a way to offer some cogent account, a reconstruction of participants' understanding of their relational struggles in a meaningful form to speak to transferable authenticity. Or to put it another way, if a reader feels the characters' struggles, cares about the characters, and/ or learns (in)appropriate patterns of response in close relationships, then the short story works to show how we can *do* and *think* about our relationships better.

## Example 2: That Baby Will Cost You
### An Intended Ambivalent Pregnancy

This personal narrative highlights an intended ambivalent pregnancy, speaking to Sotirin's (2010) call for radical specificity in mother-writing. The use of creative nonfiction frames the story as a series of marginalized discourses from a relational dialectics perspective, in particular ambivalence (versus certainty), bodily knowledge (versus medicalization, versus middle class pregnancy), and flux (versus cost-benefit ratios). The problem is that these marginalized discourses are not well represented in the totalizing picture of the *pregnant lady*. The story works as a performance text to transform totalizing oppressive discourse into a restructured aesthetic moment (Denzin, 2003). The reader and author rewrite and reread the script together. Lee Gutkind (2012) argues that creative nonfiction with a focus on story is more memorable and persuasive for readers than a series of presented facts.

Personal narratives in the form of creative nonfiction can counter Krizek's (1998) observation that "we often render our research reports devoid of human emotion and self-reflection. As ethnographers we experience life but we write science" (p. 93). There is no other representation. It was vital in this project that the voice of ambivalence be experiential because "our understandings must be at least partially in the voice of those under study so that a true evocation can be achieved, rather than some distancing authoritative rendition of a culture" (Krizek, 1998, p. 94). Telling about ambivalence is not as effective as showing it. Goodall (2000) asserts that good writing achieves what it sets out to do by posing interesting, important questions, being informed by current literature, helping readers learn, and fulfilling the writer's purpose. "If the question we ask is worthy enough, if the issue if compelling enough, then whatever story form that evokes or answers it should be good enough, too" (p. 194). Fiction is qualitative research. Fiction, creative non-fiction, and the cases presented in this book are theoretical depictions and explorations of relationship processes in useful and evocative forms.

# References

Alcoff, L. M. (2003). Introduction. In L. M. Alcoff (Ed.), *Singing in the fire: Stories of women in philosophy* (pp. 1–13). Lanham, MD: Rowman & Littlefield.

Banks, A., & Banks, S. P. (Eds.). (1998). *Fiction & social research: By ice or fire.* Walnut Creek, CA: AltaMira Press.

Baxter, L. A., & Braithwaite, D. O. (Eds.). (2008). Engaging theories in communication: Multiple perspectives. Thousand Oaks, CA: Sage.

Bochner, A. P. (2000). Criteria against ourselves. *Qualitative Inquiry, 6,* 266–272.

Denzin, N. K. (1997). *Interpretive ethnography: Ethnographic practices for the 21st century.* Thousand Oaks, CA: Sage.

Denzin, N. K. (2003). *Performance ethnography: Critical pedagogy and the politics of culture.* Thousand Oaks, CA: Sage.

Duck, S. (2011). *Rethinking relationships.* Thousand Oaks, CA: Sage.

Eisner, E. (2006). Does arts-based research have a future? *Studies in Art Education, 48*(1), 9–18.

Eisner, E. (2008). Art and knowledge. In J. G. Knowles & A. L. Cole (Eds.), *Handbook of the arts in qualitative research: Perspectives, methodologies, examples, and issues* (pp. 3–12). Thousand Oaks, CA: Sage.

Faulkner, S. L. (2009). *Poetry as Method: Reporting Research through Verse.* Walnut Creek, CA: Left Coast Press, Inc.

Faulkner, S. L. (2011). Hello Kitty does Gender in Four Scenes. *Women and Language.* Visual and Performance. Available at www.womenandlanguage.org/category/alternative-scholarship/

Faulkner, S. L., & Hecht, M. L. (2011). The negotiation of closetable identities: A narrative analysis of LGBTQ Jewish identity. *Journal of Social and Personal Relationships, 28*(6), 829–847.

Finley, S. (2008). Arts-based research. In G. J. Knowles & A. L. Cole (Eds.), *Handbook of the arts in qualitative research: Perspectives, methodologies, examples, and issues* (pp. 71–81). Thousand Oaks, CA: Sage.

Goodall, H. L. (2000). *Writing the new ethnography.* Walnut Creek, CA: AltaMira Press.

Gutkind, L. (2012). *You can't make this stuff up: The complete guide to writing nonfiction from memoir to literary journalism and everything in between.* Boston, MA: Lifelong Books.

Hammersley, M. (2010). Reproducing or constructing? Some questions about transcription in social research. *Qualitative Research, 10*(5), 553–569.

Kellas, J. K., & Manusov, V. (2003). What's in a story? The relationship between narrative completeness and adjustment to relationship dissolution. *Journal of Social and Personal Relationships, 20*(3), 451–466.

Kiesinger, C. E. (1998). Portrait of an anorexic life. In A. Banks & S. P. Banks (Eds.), *Fiction & social research: By ice or fire* (pp. 115–136). Walnut Creek, CA: AltaMira.

Krizek, R. L. (1998). Lessons: What the hell are we teaching the next generation anyway? In A. Banks & S. P. Banks (Eds.), *Fiction & social research: By ice or fire* (pp. 89–113). Walnut Creek, CA: AltaMira Press.

Krizek, R. L. (2003). Ethnography an excavation of personal narrative. In R. P. Clair, *Expressions of ethnography: New approaches to qualitative methods* (pp. 141–151). Albany: State University of New York Press.

Leavy, P. (2009). *Method meets art: Arts-Based research practice.* New York: Guilford.

Leavy, P. (2013). *Fiction as research practice: Short stories, novellas, and novels.* Walnut Creek, CA: Left Coast Press, Inc.

Lieblich, A., Tuval-Mashiach, R., & Zilber, T. (1998). *Narrative research: Reading, analysis, and interpretation.* Thousand Oaks, CA: Sage.

McAdams, D. P. (1993). *The stories we live by: Personal myths and the making of the self.* New York: William Morrow.

McNiff, S. (2008). Art-based research. In J. G. Knowles & A. L. Cole (Eds.), *Handbook of the arts in qualitative research: Perspectives, methodologies, examples, and issues* (pp. 29–40). Thousand Oaks, CA: Sage.

Parini, J. (2008). *Why poetry matters.* New Haven, CT: Yale University Press.

Pelias, R. J. (2005). Performative writing as scholarship: An apology, an argument, and anecdote. *Cultural Studies ↔ Critical Methodologies, 5*(4), 415–424.

Pelias, R. J. (2011). *Leaning: A poetics of personal relations.* Walnut Creek, CA: Left Coast Press, Inc.

Pollock, D. (1998). Performative writing. In P. Phelan & J. Lane (Eds.), *The ends of performance* (pp. 73–103). New York, New York University Press.

Prendergast, M. (2009). *"Poem* is what?": Poetic inquiry in qualitative social science research. In M. Prendergast, C. Leggo, & P. Sameshima (Eds.), *Poetic inquiry: Vibrant voices in the social sciences.* Rotterdam, Netherlands: Sense.

Richardson, L. (1997). *Fields of play: Constructing an academic life.* New Brunswick, NJ: Rutgers University Press.

Riessman, C. K. (1993). *Narrative analysis.* Newbury Park, CA: Sage.

Revell, D. (2007). *The art of attention: A poet's eye.* Minneapolis, MN: Graywolf Press.

Simic, C. (1990). *Wonderful words, silent truth: Essays on poetry and a memoir.* Ann Arbor: University of Michigan Press.

Sotirin, P. (2010). Autoethnographic mother-writing: Advocating radical specificity. *Journal of Research Practice, 6*(1), Article M9. Retrieved from jrp.icaap. org/index.php/jrp/article/view/220/189

Todres, L., & Galvin, K. T. (2008). Embodied interpretation: A novel way of evocatively re-presenting meanings in phenomenological research. *Qualitative Research, 8*(5), 568–583.

Watson, C. (2011). Staking a small claim for fictional narratives in social and educational research. *Qualitative Research, 11*(4), 395–408.

# Chapter 1

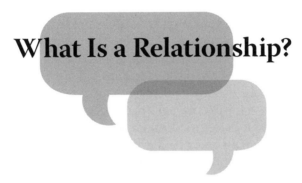

# What Is a Relationship?

What is a relationship? A relationship is _____ (fill in the blank). Yes, really, what do you regard as essential features before you count an interaction as a relationship? The cases here ask you to think about the necessary components in our close relationships: Must an individual be alive to exert influence on us? Do all romantic relationships presume sexual activity? How does relationship history influence our needs? How do you differentiate a relationship from a series of interactions? Sheila Squillante's poetic meditation on sexual talk and body image demonstrates how our self-concept develops from our interactions with significant others. Gabe Welsch's short story about a failed marriage proposal highlights the concept of intimacy readiness and the interaction of lifespan communication, and Tiffani Baldwin's personal essay on the death of grandparents investigates the need and difficulty of final conversations.

When I ask students to define *close relationship*, they look puzzled at first and then laugh because this is something we don't usually define. We just know. However, it is important to think about the characteristics, qualities, and interaction patterns that make up relationships before we talk about quality in subsequent chapters. What I hear from students most often and see in relationship research is

*Inside Relationships: A Creative Casebook in Relational Communication*, edited by Sandra L. Faulkner, 25–28. © 2013 Left Coast Press, Inc. All rights reserved.

that a close relationship displays the following: self-disclosure, intimacy, a sense of history, loyalty, similarities, companionship, trust, affection, and respect. I like defining a close relationship as a judgment we make based on specific interactions and behaviors sustained over time; relationships are cognitive assessments based on repeated interaction (Sillars & Vangelisti, 2006). This seems especially true because communication is relational; action is the basis of our relationships (Duck, 2011). Even the idea of the *self* is constructed from communication we have with others about individual and cultural expectations, in addition to our material circumstances. We can strengthen our self-concepts through positive and supportive interaction with family and peers (Dailey, 2010).

*Intimacy* is a perception of cohesiveness determined by our interactions with another, the amount and quality of self-disclosure, feeling close, and how responsive we consider our partner to be (Laurenceau & Kleinman, 2006). We may have different motivations to form, maintain, and end intimate relationships contingent on our life circumstances, resources, and personal characteristics. For instance, I hear students talk about not wanting to be in a romantic relationship because of a need to focus on schoolwork. I also hear students talk about wanting to be in a romantic relationship because they have been in one in the past, they want to settle down and get serious about the future, and they need the companionship. The importance of sex, particularly in marriage and committed dating relationships, is also something that often arises in our conversations (Hinchliff & Gott, 2004).

When we study relationships, assumptions about competent ways of relating are rife; we assume that there are good and bad ways to relate, that certain relationships are appropriate and others are inappropriate (Duck, 2011). In part, these assumptions are rooted in *relationship schemas*—cognitive structures that help us process and organize information (Anderson, 1993). They provide us with ways to make sense of relationships. We hold and create prototypes of people, such as characteristics of professors (absent-minded, awesome) or best friends (loyal, funny) and make comparisons. Think of other assumptions we make: romantic relationships are sexual ones. Romantic relationships are the pinnacle of our relational lives and perhaps more important than friendships. Individuals should go to school, get a job, get married, and then have children. Magazine advice columns tell us how to make our relationships better. Talk shows provide us opportunities to comment on (and scream at) how others are doing their relationships.

Our schemas involve comparisons, which we can consider to be the way we do relationships, and our enactments of these schemas. What we think about marriage can influence whether we get divorced (see, for example, Yoseefi et al., 2010). Or whether we even get married at all. Or whether we are allowed to get married. Children's experiences with maltreatment and abuse influence their conceptions of interpersonal relationships and later perpetration of aggression (Crawford & Wright, 2007). Having positive schemas of interpersonal power, the ability to influence a partner's actions, can improve relationship functioning (Smith, Welsh, & Fite, 2010). The limitations of our schema may be obvious given the implication that relationships exist solely in the mind, rather than an emphasis on relating as communication and the influence of culture, situation, and environment in the creation and recreation of our relationship schema.

# References

Andersen, P. A. (1993). Cognitive schemata in personal relationships. In S. W. Duck (Ed.), *Individuals in relationships [Understanding relationship processes 1]* (pp. 1–29). Newbury Park, CA: Sage.

Dailey, R. M. (2010). Testing components of confirmation: How acceptance and challenge from mothers, fathers, and siblings are related to adolescent self-concept. *Communication Monographs, 77*(4), 592–617.

Duck, S. (2011). *Rethinking relationships.* Thousand Oaks, CA: Sage.

Crawford, E., & Wright, M. O. (2007). The impact of childhood psychological maltreatment on interpersonal schemas and subsequent experiences of relationship aggression. *Journal of Emotional Abuse, 7*(2), 93–116.

Hinchliff, S., & Gott, M. (2004). Intimacy, commitment, and adaptation: Sexual relationships within long-term marriages. *Journal of Social and Personal Relationships, 21,* 595–609.

Laurenceau, J. P., & Kleinman, B. M. (2006). Intimacy in personal relationships. In A. L. Vangelisiti & D. Perlman (Eds.), *The Cambridge handbook of personal relationships* (pp. 637–648). New York: Cambridge University Press.

Sillars, A. L., & Vangelisti, A. L. (2006). Communication: Basic properties and their relevance to relationship research. In A. L. Vangelisiti & D. Perlman (Eds.), *The Cambridge handbook of personal relationships* (pp. 331–351). New York: Cambridge University Press.

Smith, J. D., Welsh, D. P., & Fite, P. J. (2010). Adolescents' relational schemas and their subjective understanding of romantic relationship interactions. *Journal of Adolescence, 33*(1), 147–157.

Yoosefi, N., Etemadi, O., Bahrami, F., Fatehizade, M. A., & Ahmadi, S. A. (2010). An investigation on early maladaptaive schema in marital relationship as predictors of divorce. *Journal of Divorce & Remarriage, 51*(5), 269–292.

# Case 1

# Body of Work

## Sheila Squillante

*Keywords:* aging, body image, identities, self-image, sexual talk, sexuality

Thursday, October 7, 2010

### *The Bird Sisters*
A blog dedicated to artists and writers

thebirdsisters.blogspot.com/2010/10/body-of-work-by-sheila-squillante.html

1.

I have never seen myself naked.

This is not a metaphor; I mean that I have truly never in my life really looked carefully at, pondered or appreciated my body—my actual, physical form—in its own skin and nothing more. I never stood in front of a mirror as a teenager, monitoring my developing curves, nor as a grown woman, assessing changes to the landscape after childbirth. While I have a general sense of the shape of things—I have caught glimpses, accidentally—I have no clear knowledge of what I would see if I *really* looked.

Sunday was my 40th birthday and I have been writing *this* piece in other essays, poems, and in my head since I was at least 13 years old. In my diary that year, the one with the blue gingham cover pocked with pen marks and scratches, puffy hearts drawn all over the inside pages, there are only three entries, written over and over again: I Love a Boy Who Thinks I'm Stupid; Something Bad is Going on With My Parents; I Am

*Inside Relationships: A Creative Casebook in Relational Communication*, edited by Sandra L. Faulkner, 29–35. © 2013 Left Coast Press, Inc. All rights reserved.

So Disgusting That I Can't Even Look at Myself. It's become part of my identity: "the girl who has never beheld her own naked shape," in one poem, the one who cannot "imagine the unseen surface" of her own back in another. In each, a tone of disapproval, admonishment, an unspoken *knock-it-off-already-you-know-better.*

Though I announce my ignorance here—in public, on a blog, which will perhaps be read by my friends and family, colleagues and readers—with what might seem like confidence and naked (ha.) bravery, I am not proud of this. In fact, as a woman, a mother, a feminist, and, it turns out, a writer, it is one of my greatest shames.

It's probably obvious why a poor body image would be concerning for the first three of those selves, and I could offer far too many theories (most predictable) about how I ended up so impressively wacked out about this. But what interests me at the moment is a strong sense that my corporal alienation is also tied inextricably to my writing self. It's a nagging kind of sensation, and one I've long wanted to work out on the page, shifting the pieces around to see how they might connect, what they might offer up.

So I'm grateful for this space.

I am also feeling incredibly, painfully naked right about now, tinkering endlessly with each word, each sentence, delaying sending it, dreading seeing it go live.

2.

*David wants to kiss me. He mumbles this sort of in my direction, eyes anywhere but on my face. I am twelve years old, and in my memory we are sitting, for some reason, on the floor of my parents' bedroom, our backs nervous-stiff and aching against the bed. I have never been kissed before, though many of the girls in my seventh grade class are already playing Two Minutes in the Closet with boys at parties to which I am not invited.*

*I can see David in my periphery, turning his head and leaning in. I keep my back straight and turn my head too; it doesn't occur to me yet to move my whole body toward a kiss.*

*I don't remember the kiss beyond that moment of decision and approach, have no memory of skin or lips or tongue. What I remember—what I will transcribe into countless diary entries, free-writes and onto the blank page of my self for years to come—is what he said after: "You know, you are really beautiful from the waist up."*

3.

I live in my own periphery, my full-length reflection a thin sliver of only one side of me. My approach to mirrors, windows, the shine off of cars in the parking lot purposefully avoidant, my image askew. Head, hair, face, eyes, shoulders, sometimes breasts, those are easier, acceptable even to me. Those I can look at. Otherwise, I either view myself in sections, incoherent parts of a whole, or not at all.

4.

Open on my desktop at this moment are two files, each containing a full-length manuscript of poetry—my poetry. I have been tending, polishing, readying them for the endless contest circuit. I have read them each countless times, and I quite like them both. I think there are readers who will respond to them, should I be lucky enough to get published. These manuscripts could not be more aesthetically different from one another. One is firmly narrative, largely auto-biographical, shot through with longing and nostalgia and loss. The other is more deeply rooted in language and the beautiful and perplexing shapes it can make. It is fragmentary, associative, a little surreal. I joke that in the unlikely event that these books showed up next to each other on a reader's shelf, that reader would be very confused indeed about who the writer is.

Though I have long espoused a philosophy of both/and, rather than either/or in poetry—I read work from both traditions—confessional and language, have obviously written in both, and hear my voice naturally in both— the idea of claiming them both publically makes me more than a little anxious.

5.

*After my divorce, I enroll in a writing workshop at my local university. There, I enter into dalliance with a fellow writer. He is, like most of the other men in my life to this point, confident, assured, opinionated and searingly intelligent. For months he keeps me at arm's length physically. The night we finally fall into bed, our pillow talk turns to poems. To my poems—the ones about my father's death—which he has read and about which he has readied the following commentary: "You know, no one really wants your emotional baggage." I don't remember responding; I don't think I could have. I remember putting my clothes back on quickly and then driving him home.*

6.

A poem should look
Poems should face each other
Poems should echo
Poems should or shouldn't be poking you in your eye
A poem should sit a while
A poem should ride on its own
A poem should be different from your expectations
A poem should be on the moon
A poem should always have birds in it
Poems should radiate lots of affection
Poems should do without any comment
Poems should be in plain text
Poems should include a baby girl
Poems should be *I'm in love, damn it!*
Poems should progress
Poems should be read aloud to children
Poems should be lingered over
Poems should move
Poems should not be relied upon too heavily

7.

*My lover and I kneel facing each other on the floor of my college dorm room, running our hands frantically over exposed flesh. I am so caught up in his body, in mine, that I have forgotten the full-length mirror hanging on the inside of the door. I turn my head to allow him better access to my neck and accidentally see myself—the curves of my breasts and hips, thighs, knees, slope of calves, feet. I make myself look for a long, shocked moment and think, is that really what I look like? Is that woman really me?*

8.

If I publish manuscript #1, some of the confident, assured, opinionated men in my life will continue to pat me on the head and send me on my quaint, confessional way. They will not want my "baggage."

If I publish manuscript #2, some of the others will roll their writerly eyes and use words like "pedantic," and "pretentious." They will wonder where I went, why I have eschewed the world of the body.

When I worry over this, one man—a friend and himself a poet—will ask (again), "Why do you care so much about the opinions of men who really don't matter?"

9.

[insert death of confident assured, etc. father here]

10.

My favorite poems are simple and direct, glittery gems hand-hewn from mineral rock, grounded in the sensual world, in human relationships. I roll them between my teeth and tongue.

11.

My favorite poems are painterly abstractions, elliptical gestures, unfinished thought. They invite me in and then inflate with impossible language, float above me, just at the limit of my reach.

12.

*I am nine months pregnant with my first child, my son. I step out of a hot shower, hotter than I'm supposed to take, and reach for a towel. As always, I stare straight ahead at the towel bar opposite the tub, perpendicular to the sink and the mirror. But something moves in the corner of my eye, and before I realize, before I remember not to look, I have turned to follow it. Through the humidity and behind the scrim of steam I see my belly, breasts, hips, mouth. Eyes filled with relief and bright wonder.*

13.

Here is what I want:

I want to look directly into the mirror and learn my shape, begin to know it first without

judgment, then with appreciation.

With praise.

I want to spend this decade unafraid and unashamed.

I want to knock it off, already.

I want to throw out the Book of Poetic Shoulds. Open my arms wide.

I want to walk into my 40s full-ready to embrace every line, every lump, every word:

*I lived it. I made it. I claim it.*

14.

My naked body is pretty much like any other naked body

My naked body is a humiliating example

My naked body is unlikely, thrilling

My naked body is sensual in the extreme

My naked body is not what it was in pre-baby days

My naked body is an affront

My naked body is a participant

My naked body is these potato chips

My naked body is now hidden under the table

My naked body is as beautiful as my naked thoughts

My naked body is the least of your concerns

My naked body is the blank page

## Questions and Activities for Discussion

1. Squillante discusses different identities and the ways identities can conflict with one another. What are these identities? How do multiple identities tie into our self-image? Into our close relationships? How do you contend with multiple, and at times, conflicting identities?

2. How does one "throw out the Book of Poetic Shoulds?" What does this mean for the self and one's relationships?

3. Discuss the link between body image and sexuality. How do time, values, and experience influence this link?

4. Write your own ode to self like Squillante's #14. What does it tell you? Now, write what you want for yourself as in #13. Are there differences between your ode to self and what you want? If so, what are the differences and what do they tell you about your self-image?

## For Further Reading and Reference

Anderson, M., Kunkel, A., & Dennis, M. (2011). 'Let's (not) talk about that': Bridging the past sexual experiences taboo to build healthy romantic relationships. *Journal of Sex Research, 48*(4), 381–391.

Faulkner, S. L., & Lannutti, P. J. (2010). Examining the content and outcomes of young adults' satisfying and unsatisfying conversations about sex. *Qualitative Health Research, 20,* 375–385.

Hesse-Biber, S. N., & Leavy. P. (2006). *The cult of thinness* (2nd ed.). New York: Oxford University Press.

Manzi, C., Vignoles, V. L., & Regalia, C. (2010) Accommodating a new identity: Possible selves, identity change and well-being across two life-transitions. *European Journal of Social Psychology, 40*(6), 970–984.

Rahav, G., & Baum, N. (2002). Divorced women: Factors contributing to self-identity change. *Journal of Divorce & Remarriage, 37*(3–4), 41–59.

# Case 2

# The Person in the Moon

## Gabriel Welsch

*Keywords:* intimacy, intimacy readiness, marriage proposal, rejection, relationship history, relationship trajectories

After eight months together, Irvin proposes to Andy while they are watching his favorite juggling troupe, but not before he takes a moment to memorize the details he knows he will want to remember later: they are lofting glass rods through the air, each rod catching light for an instant of refraction, each release timed to a note in the "Moonlight Sonata," played on a piano at stage left. The tune is the most impossibly romantic one he knows, and although he had not planned to deliver the ring at that moment, the notes moved him, the perfect reflection of sound in the light of the jugglers, the crisp ease of their tuxedos, the perfect solitude of a darkened theater, her ear so near his lips when he turns his head. The baubles of light from the stage drift over them, the music resonant and growing beyond its notes and through the crowd, and he is suspended for a moment when he breathes, "Marry me."

She looks at him, then follows his eyes to his hand, where the ring box is open. When she finally looks back up and smiles, it is the type of smile as if he had just done a trick, and he is surprised.

The way her face softens, he assumes his own face must have fallen to pieces.

She whispers, "It's not really the right time, is it?" and he wonders if she means the right time for a proposal or the right time for marriage. He lets the ring box snap shut, and he replaces it in the left pocket of

*Inside Relationships: A Creative Casebook in Relational Communication,* edited by Sandra L. Faulkner, 36–47. © 2013 Left Coast Press, Inc. All rights reserved.

his corduroy sport coat, the pocket without the hole, and crosses his legs again as the flurry of notes is lightly tapped out with the sound of the jugglers' hands clapping onto their rods. Before long, he is in repose, his breathing matched to the measures of the music, his reflex for counting taken over his attention, and he figures out the number of days they've known one another, the number of hours spent together, what the percentage of intimate time they owned, what part they had carved out of their lives specifically for one another, and as the music reaches an intensity that has the foreheads of the jugglers in front of him beginning to glisten, he wonders why the time they've had together so far is not enough for her to say yes directly, in the dark, within and away from the world at the same time.

He loved that they had met in the February of a leap year, even though they did meet at a supermarket as the result of his shopping ineptitude. For six years, he hadn't purchased groceries, and as he was only in his fourth month A.D. (after Delia), he still didn't have the instincts to stroll through aisles and figure out what he would eat. He deliberated endlessly. Standing before a full blush of spaghetti sauce jars, he was suddenly knocked off balance by a stout boy careening into his legs. As he stood, the boy's mother appeared at his side, her noisy raincoat swishing against his sweatpants. After apologies, she introduced herself, and then grinned at his name. She asked him, "Well, are you an Irvin or an Irv?"

"An Irvin,"—he remembered the silliest things, the taunts, *you've got a lot of Irv, am I gettin' on your Irvs?* the girl who told him she couldn't dance with someone named Irv because she thought about butchers, that butchers were named Irv, and they wore bloody aprons, and she couldn't hold a man if she thought about bloody aprons—"definitely an Irvin."

The pause must have given his comment some charm, weight beyond the importance he felt for his name, because she smiled then. He remembers thinking, *she likes decisiveness*, and just as quickly taking it back. He knew nothing about her; she wore a bit too much Chanel, her son had all the jitters of any eight-year-old, and she had a purse half her size. More like a backpack with a shoulder strap. Her hair was always in her eyes, bangs long grown out, and during a conversation she would curl her lips at points to blow the strands back. In the months they got to know each other, that gesture had become a small joke; when he saw her do it, he would do the same thing. On good days, she laughed. When she was angry with him and he did it to try and cheer her, she pretended to ignore it.

For three consecutive evenings after the supermarket toppling, they dated. The first night, Irvin suggested dinner and they ate at an inn down in Cape May, tidy tables with candles, pinpoint centers of conversation dotting the dining room, a tired place that had its chic point sometime in the 1970s. The next night, the Cape May County Zoo, where Andy confessed an aversion to birds as she was a light sleeper. They had strolled the wooden walkway above the grounds, their casual stride matched in the ponderous steps of the rhinoceros, giraffe, and elephant that roamed freely below them. The third night she accompanied him to his school's production of *Arsenic and Old Lace*, and didn't once complain about the actors, as Irvin expected she might. Each evening, as Irvin sought to wear something that hadn't been frayed by the routine of chalk and lunch monitoring, to disguise the fact that he owned only three sport coats, he wondered what would happen, what she saw in him, apart from his fluorescent skin and chalk dried hands, receding hair, and the distracting point of his Adam's apple.

For weeks, the whole thing felt to Irvin wonderfully clandestine; that it happened in the cold months when the entire eastern half of New Jersey shut down; when vans, RVs, and campers no longer rumbled through Rio Grande on Route 45; when stores boarded up, hotels darkened, and ice cream shops sat in their windblown parking lots, as if bundled for the weather. Even the kids in his classes were calmer, nearly losing their tans, the talk of surfing and boardwalks down, their parents not as hectic, the sand and trees edged in salt and gray of the season. Most locals talked about it as somewhere between a reprieve that lingers too long and an outright curse, but Irvin always wished it would go on forever, this time when a person felt he might slip into a quieter routine, where people would not be passing his window from elsewhere, curious about all the lights at the side of the street. Love could work in private, slowly, unnoticed.

Another of the math teachers noticed though. Mrs. Snoeyenbos, crotchety but unusually talkative, announced to him between drags on a Virginia Slim behind the gymnasium that he seemed lighter of foot since he'd been dating. Had she been ten years younger, he'd have taken it as an insult. He still wasn't sure how he took it, but as she had lit his cigarette so often when he left his lighter back in his brief case, he figured he'd let it slide. It would not be good, he thought, to alienate the one person left to smoke with behind the school.

Andy didn't smoke, and for the first few weeks he worried that when she found out that he did, that would be it. She learned late in the spring, at one of her son's ball games. Irvin took off his coat and a pack of Winstons fell out. He was surprised at how embarrassed he was. "Haven't really sustained a try at quitting," he offered, trying to smile the moment away. She patted him on the knee and looked out at the field. Her gaze followed her son. "Just don't let Stuart see, okay?"

After that Irvin felt the need to be an example. He felt drawn to and almost responsible for the portly kid perpetually on the verge of exasperating Andy. Often he would show up at their apartment and hear them arguing through the door as he came to the top of the stairs. When she opened the door, despite her smile for him, he could see the wear in her eyes, and he wondered if he looked that way to her after bad days at school. In the old days, Delia had never come home before 4 p.m. because she didn't want to be around Irvin for that hour after he got home. One of her favorite remarks to him was, "Good thing teaching pays well enough to offset the moods."

In his adopted role of example, their outings grew more wholesome and educational through the summer and into the fall. Bookstores for coffee, museums, and often just simple dinners at Irvin's, after which they would aim his telescope at the brightest clusters of stars on a given evening, chart and learn the names of constellations, and Stuart would scribble things down on a clipboard as if it were the most important thing he had ever done. On nights when the moon was out, they would gaze at its craters and valleys, and Irvin would ask Stuart how he thought such formations had arrived there, and on nights when he felt talkative, the boy would hold forth.

Once, Irvin started the tale about the man in the moon, and Andy laughed so loud he stopped. "What?"

She shook her head. "I just remembered the dumbest thing from when I was a kid."

Irvin sniffed, looked at his shoes to wait for her to continue.

"I never used to be able to find the man in the moon," she said. "I just wasn't convinced, you know? How could you tell? But I liked that idea, that someone was looking out for me. So I convinced myself that there was simply a person up there, a person in the moon keeping an eye out, and that way if I said person I didn't get on the bad side of whoever was really up there."

"Well what exactly did you expect, a mustache?" he said.

She shook her head, laughing into her sweater. "No, of course not."

She tossed her head back, reborn after the comment. "But now, of course, I am convinced it's a woman."

Irvin noticed that he was not the only one staring at her at this point; Stuart's fingers fidgeted near his pockets as he looked at his mother. Irvin wasn't sure how often, if ever, the boy had heard his mother speak too much like an adult. Sympathy welled in Irvin, at the boy who didn't understand his mother's sudden force, Irvin's quiet, the joke in it all, the context. Irvin excused himself to go in the house for a moment.

In the dark of his kitchen, he lit a cigarette, and between inhales, he kept the end below the level of his window, so neither would see the red glow. Blued by the moon, pushing shadows about in his yard, the two of them came together in a hug at once, their soft huddle a small shudder against the stillness of the chain link fence of the other yards, the tall cypresses in back, against the noise of the highway. They were denser matter, he mused, drawing in the light from the moon that landed on them. A surface so dense that light could not escape it. In the airless kitchen, the smoke a nebula before the window, he felt their pull, wanted to orbit and protect them, know the closeness of a family again, know the perfection of sleep with another, of the rooms in his house full, all the chairs properly worn.

Just down the road from his yard, the Cape butted into the water, and the waves that crashed against it were pushed by the same moon that lit them all now. People would be walking that beach, under the moon, many on honeymoons or anniversaries, claiming the moon as their own, something so distant that felt so personal. Something that drew such feelings out of them just as it drew shore and ocean closer for part of every day. Normally, Irvin would latch on to such an idea and contemplate the force of the moon to move things, but that night, standing in his kitchen and feeling want seize him, he felt her to be the moon, laughed at his own cliché, resolved to begin referring to her secretly as Juliet.

Once again, the cold keeps Irvin's car from starting easily, chugging in the parking garage outside the Civic Center. He can feel Andy being patient, even though she is shivering. He can see her movement in his periphery, and she is silent, surprising him as he leans over the wheel as if praying, working the key and the gas at once, give and take. He thinks of time, baby-sitters, the sluggish movement of cold grease, gas flooding into reluctant valves, and he is ready to curse when the car spits a gob of black smoke out its tail pipe and rumbles to life. As he backs up, a drop of sweat stings his eyes.

They talk about the show on the way home, on the juggling matched with the music, about resonance and how one of the performers said that music is a metaphor of notes placed over the medium of time. If a person could throw the notes out on a musical staff as she played them, the burly juggler had said, they would show how the experience of the music is one dependent wholly on time, and you can see the arrangement and feel the expression of its power even better.

"That part made my head hurt," Andy says. "I don't really like my head hurting. I just enjoyed the juggling and kinda ignored them when they spoke."

"Mmm. Jugglers shouldn't speak."

"I didn't say *that*," she says, laughing. "I just, you know, if I want depth I'll go back to school, thank you very much."

"Funny, you were talking about your head hurting, and I remembered the last time my head really hurt was in an astronomy class in college, the same kind of concept stuff. This professor, a British guy, was talking about planetary resonance."

"What's that?"

He realizes he can't explain it well, so he bluffs. "It's complicated, but it basically has to do with light and our ability to predict the orbits of planets, I think. But it works the same way that music does, and to illustrate, he brought in bagpipes and played them, and I got it, just from his goofy bagpipes."

"So it lets you know where a planet is?"

"Yes. You look for the light, I guess."

The first day it snowed, Irvin met Snoeyenbos behind the cafeteria for their standard third period smoke. This time, it was he who remembered the lighter, and was noble in his gesture, cupping his hand at the end of her smoke so she might avoid the wind. She remarked that on major weather events, it was the smokers who were most lucky, privy through their habits to the changes of seasons. He smiled and leaned back against the bricks, letting his head go lighter with each inhale. That day, he didn't even bother to remove the cigarette from his lips. So what if he ended up talking out one side of his mouth.

"You seem to be enjoying these breaks more lately," she said, hugging herself and shivering among the fat flakes.

"Yeah, well, Andy doesn't want me to let her son see me smoking," he said, "so the only time I can really relish a cigarette is in the mornings, in my car, or at work."

"You two are pretty serious about one another?"

He looked at her, a roll of his head against the bricks. He didn't want to answer her for so many reasons, and she might have sensed it, because they stood silently, but for the snap of their lips at the end of an inhale. The moon was visible at midday, in plain view in a corner of the sky. He wondered if this was the dark time in Sweden and as he stood against the bricks computing months, a tire screech jolted him, and a dozen yards away, a young man crumpled and slid back over the hood of a rocking Volkswagen Beetle.

For the next several moments, his mind drew back from the present, and every step he took across the wiry, frost-rimed lawn was involuntary, his voice calling out to the driver, his notice of the large tears running down her face, the sick bend at the knee in the boy's right leg, the way his screams stopped abruptly, his pale face seeming to sink into the pavement as if it were a pillow, Irvin's own hands frisking the boy's legs for the press of off-kiltered bone, for blood, for wetness, and then he held the girl, pulled her into his arm, toward the curb, away from the still running car that he went back to shut off. By then other teachers had run across the lawn, students milled out of the cafeteria and gathered in groups about the lot, and he was surprised to hear at one point a laugh titter up over the assembled, the last sound he had expected to hear, and suddenly he was returned to himself, and his fists went to balls, suddenly looking for the laughter, and he saw it had been the girl, crouched at the curb, a bit undone, and it may even have been a shrill part of laughter, but she looked so small to him then, insubstantial, barely more than bones inside a husk of a dress, calico and faded, more artifice than clothing, and in a moment he was glad: when she lit a cigarette, no one said a thing.

After the paramedics set the boy's leg and took him to the hospital, after the parents and police and administrators had heard his story, and when the parking lot was calm again, empty but for the familiar constellation of headlights, Irvin went to the pay phone by the cafeteria and tried to reach Andy on her car phone. It was off. He wasn't to see her that night; she and Stuart had to shop for new shoes. But he still wanted to see her. The accident had not totally undone him, but he loved that Andy had a practical ability to manage emotion, to remind him of where he and everything else stood.

He was in Cape May the next morning by seven, parked on Ocean Street, looking at the cold character of the waves against the warmth of the Victorian porches. The front doors stood open on all of them, and the owners strolled out one by one, windbreakers buttoned up against the salt air, each with a steaming mug, and before too long, the minivans turned the corner and started to park in a line, three of them. The doors slid open, a whisper on the street that morning, and with silent steps the women emerged with buckets, bandanas over their heads, in sweats and sneakers, and drifted in a rush of laughing and crushing out cigarettes, into the open doors of the houses after a nod and smile at the owners. Andy stepped out of the driver's seat of her van and started to write on her clipboard when she saw Irvin's car.

Looking at her, he felt a little foolish then, driving down there, risking being late for his morning class, just to see her. Perhaps if he had driven down the afternoon before, or had been able to find her or contact her, he would have felt different then. Once he had crossed the street, she asked him almost in a whisper what he was doing there.

"I don't know," he said. "Had a hairy day yesterday. Just wanted to see you."

"Like this?" she gestured down at her Faith Hill t-shirt and old jeans.

"Yeah," he poked her in the shoulder, "like this, in the flesh."

She smirked and surprised him. "Maybe later."

"That's not what I meant."

She tossed her clipboard back through the window and took his hands. "What's the matter?"

"Nothing. Really. I'm just being a little silly, I think."

"Are you in there?" she said, then rolled her eyes up at the sky, "Or are you out there?"

"I'm here." He paused. "I bought some tickets to a juggling show tomorrow night, I figured you and I and Stuart could go. I think he'd really enjoy it."

"Juggling?"

"Well, juggling and more," he said. "They do stuff with music, other tricks. They're good. They've been on *Seinfeld*."

"Well, okay, I guess."

"And then you and I should go to dinner the next night. And you should get a baby-sitter."

"And I should also get to work, and you should get to school."

He had only ever seen one other car accident in his life. He had been in college at the time. A man in a green station wagon attempted a left turn from the far right lane of a four lane highway. Another man, going too fast and too angrily in a blue Buick, hit him hard in the door directly behind the driver's seat. He knew the accident would happen several seconds before it did, and while others honked their warnings, he simply kept driving, and the cars slowed to an impossible crawl just before they hit, bounced away from a splash of glass and skid noise, the sound hollow like a punch to the body. He stopped to help, and as he approached the man from the station wagon, he heard him saying again and again, in a staccato Indian accent, "I did not know where I was. I did not know where I was." The woman with him knelt inside the car, her sari bunched around a bundle from the car seat, her face louder than anything she was saying. In the coming year he would meet Delia, lose his mother, and graduate, but that moment he remembers best, shaken by the near loss, by the consequences of losing location, by how many ways a person could become lost.

He could not get those thoughts out of his head at the jewelry store, and the young woman in teased hair and a pants suit didn't know it, but those thoughts kept him from making up his mind about a ring, began to frustrate her, until at once he stared at her and said, finally, "Which one of these would you want to get?"

She read it wrong. "Look mister, I have a boyfriend."

"What?" he said. Then, "No, no. Not that. I'm just not good at this. Suggest one for me."

"Well, you know, there are a lot of women that think the size of the stone is most important."

"She wears gloves a lot, and has her hands in some pretty foul stuff. A big rock would give her trouble."

Her mood turned, and her head tilted to the side. "That's sweet, that you think of all that stuff."

"Thank you," he looked back down at the rings, and after a few moments, she had picked one up, they boxed it, and he had it added to his Visa.

That evening, it took him longer than usual to figure out what to wear. Even after he was dressed, he continued to deliberate, but forced himself to get in the car, coax it to life, and drive to Andy's apartment to pick her up. Stuart was already becoming rumpled, his turtleneck untucked in back and one shoe untied. Andy had a knit wrap over her shoulders, over a black dress, and had gone to a stylist to have her hair done. When Irvin finally had told her what theater they were going to, she'd said, "Well, you should have said that. Telling me it was juggling didn't do very much."

Irvin watched the road carefully that night, the accident in the parking lot still coming to him, knowing his own nerves were on edge. He planned to be as gallant this evening as he could, keep his chatter about time and stars and his usual subjects to a minimum, to completely charm so that once they were back at Andy's and Stuart was in bed, relaxed and perhaps after a glass of wine, he would talk with her about the future, about the comfort in knowing that another person knew where you were. He would present her with the ring then, ask her to marry him, and, he was certain, she would say yes. When the moment overtook him in the crowded theater, and when she did not answer him, he was surprised at how adrift he became, how he felt as though the seat had disconnected beneath him and he were afloat in the blur of the room. He turned to her many times after the proposal, as if locating himself by seeing her, and she would smile or lay her hand on his leg, but it was the times that she hardly noticed, her face awash in the light reflected from the stage, her comfort smooth over the tops of her cheeks, that he knew he hadn't scared her away at least, and that the request had not startled her, had not made her uncomfortable. He could wait, perhaps, for her to come around, see it in the surface of her face.

The morning after the juggling performance, Irvin wakes before the sun is up, sits in his kitchen and smokes as the light leaks over the earth's edge and works into the rooms of his house. He starts to hear the highway, slow to wake on a Saturday, and he remembers after reading the paper that Andy and Stuart are at the park that day, a picnic they had all planned together a few days ago. He is not sure how he will look at her in the daylight, how he will find what she is thinking, now that she is in many ways in orbit around him and he is unable really to locate her.

He decides to go anyway, works through his closet for a sweater he remembers Delia saying he looked good in, shaves twice, brushes his teeth harder than usual, even flosses. He gets his car washed on the way, vacuums the interior, empties the ashtray and sprays it clean inside the car wash bay. Even hoses down the rubber floor mats. He takes the cigarettes out of his pocket, approaches the trash can, shakes his head and returns them to his pocket. He almost lights one, but remembers he has put on cologne, and so pockets them again.

He meets them in the park, the two lounging in the cool sun, breathing plumes of air and preparing to peel oranges. As Irvin strides up, he kneels and takes their hands, removes the oranges. Andy works up onto her knees and, smiling, asks him what he is doing. On the gazebo, across the lawn, a chamber quartet is playing something trilling, a melody that to Irvin sounds like simulated flight, and he then asks Stuart if he wants to learn to juggle, and the boy nods. Irvin shows him the hand movements, reminds him to stare at the top of the arc, to know where his hands are, not to overthrow, to develop a rhythm to help him stay aware of where everything is at every moment. After some time, Stuart is able to suspend the oranges. They fly in tremulous arcs, they fall and he retrieves them for another launch, each new launch unsure, the boy's nervous hands waiting. They still fall to the ground several times, but as they loft into the air, afloat with waves of sound and breath, Irvin's heart flutters at the flight, the magical flurry of bodies, afloat and never still.

## Questions and Activities for Discussion

1. What qualities distinguish your close relationships from casual relationships? Is time the most important factor? When and how does a relationship become intimate? One's life stage and the extant circumstances influence intimacy. Discuss situation, environment, and circumstances.

2. What is relational communication? What types of behavior should/ should not count as communication? What does the study of close relationships entail? How does relationship history influence our current relationships?

3. What do you think happens next for Andy and Irvin? Write the next chapter. Describe how couples handle relational hurts. Why do you think that Andy proposed when he did (i.e., the panic plan, emotions, etc.)?

## For Further Reading and Reference

Cohen, S., Schulz, M. S., Weiss, E., & Waldinger, R. J. (2012). Eye of the beholder: The individual and dyadic contributions of empathic accuracy and perceived empathic effort to relationship satisfaction. *Journal of Family Psychology, 26*(2), 236–245.

Lawrence, J., & Kleinman, B. M. (2006). Intimacy in personal relationships. In A. L. Vangelisiti & D. Perlman (Eds.), *The Cambridge handbook of personal relationships* (pp. 637–653). New York: Cambridge University Press.

Ruppel, E. K., & Curran, M. A. (2012). Relational sacrifices in romantic relationships: Satisfaction and the moderating role of attachment. *Journal Of Social And Personal Relationships, 29*(4), 508-529.

Sillars, A. L., & Vangelisti, A. L. (2006). Communication: Basic properties and their relevance to relationship research. In A. L. Vangelisiti & D. Perlman (Eds.), *The Cambridge handbook of personal relationships* (pp. 331–351). New York: Cambridge University Press.

Tan, R., Overall, N. C., & Taylor, J. L. (2012). Let's talk about us: Attachment, relationship-focused disclosure, and relationship quality. *Personal Relationships, 19*(3), 521–534.

# Case 3

# Life After Death
## Continuing Close Relationships in New and Different Ways

### Tiffani Baldwin

*Keywords:* death and dying, difficult conversations, final conversations, lifespan communication

The sun shone high in the blue sky, wildflowers dotted the rolling hills to the west, wispy clouds drifted above the stretch of two-lane highway that lay ahead of us, and outside the mountain air was sweet and light. Inside the car, however, the air was heavy with my unasked questions. My maternal grandfather and I were driving to the city for a doctor's appointment. Grampa had been diagnosed with a rare neurological disease that would result in the gradual deterioration of his physical and mental abilities and lead, eventually, to his death. I had started taking him to and from his home in the mountains to see a neurologist in the city. I enjoyed this time alone with my Grampa.

My grandfather and I had always been close, and we grew closer as I became an adult. I consider myself very lucky to have known all four of my grandparents well into my adult life. I was 31 years old when my first grandparent, my paternal grandmother, died. The remaining three lived approximately seven more years. Grampa played an active role in my life and was much more than just a grandfather to me. He was a role model, friend, and confidant among other things. I had always been able to talk to him about anything, but I was finding it difficult to initiate a conversation about his illness and ask him all the questions that had been weighing on my heart and mind.

Grampa was a self-described atheist. He did not believe in God

---

*Inside Relationships: A Creative Casebook in Relational Communication*, edited by Sandra L. Faulkner, 48–54. © 2013 Left Coast Press, Inc. All rights reserved.

or any kind of an afterlife. I, on the other hand, do not subscribe to an organized religion but consider myself a spiritual person. While I knew my Grampa's beliefs, I am not sure I had ever discussed mine with him. I do believe that souls continue on after this life, though I do not necessarily believe in Heaven and Hell. Knowing that his death was inevitable—and possibly going to happen sooner rather than later—inspired me to want to talk with him about death and after death.

Death is a taboo topic in Western culture. Many people do not like thinking about it, talking about it or even acknowledging it. We try to shield our children from it, assuming that they must be protected from the darkness and morbidity that is culturally associated with death. Despite its many negative associations, death is a natural part of life; it is the end of life that we all will face someday. Before we confront it personally, most of us will likely experience the death of close and important individuals in our lives, which will dramatically impact ourselves, our lives, and our relationships with others. But how does one talk about death in a culture that teaches avoidance of it?

My family of origin was a little different from traditional American families in that we did talk about the practicality of death on occasion. Grampa was a tax and estate attorney, so the majority of his professional time was spent helping his clients prepare for their eventual demise. He approached death from a logical standpoint and encouraged families to talk about it in realistic terms (finances, medical care, burial arrangements, etc.). He would refer to his own death in matter of fact terms as I was growing up and especially as he continued to age. I never liked being a part of these discussions, but they came with being a member of my family. Though I didn't appreciate talking about the reality of death when I was younger, I am thankful now that my family did.

Still, in the car that day, I was surprised to find myself nervous at the prospect of initiating this difficult conversation about death and afterlife with Grampa. Not only had my family discussed the inevitability of death throughout the years, but also I was studying communication. I reasoned with myself that the combination of these two things should make me feel more comfortable talking about Grampa's death with him: however, despite my internal coaching I felt tongue-tied and ill prepared. There is, after all, a difference between talking about death in practical terms and talking about it in raw emotional terms.

Because of our family history, I knew I could discuss my questions with Grampa. However, none of my communication training or family socialization had taught me *how* to have this conversation with my grandfather. I struggled with how to begin and wondered whether he would want to answer the questions I wanted to ask him. Finally, I took a deep breath and forged forward. "Are you afraid to die?" I asked my grandfather, seemingly out of the blue. This question began a discussion that I will always treasure.

Grampa told me "no," he was not afraid to die. Mostly he hoped he wouldn't end up a burden to his family as a result of the deterioration his condition caused. I asked him if he still believed there was no form of afterlife. He again said "no," he did not believe souls carried on after someone died. He felt that once a person's life was over, that person was simply gone: no soul or energy remained in existence. A small silence ensued. Then, characteristically, after giving my questions some thought, he expanded on his beliefs.

Grampa felt that what we do in this life is important, not because of what it will bring us after this life, but because of what it brings in *this* life. He said that the way a person lives their life and impacts others is how they live on through family and friends after their death. Put another way, he felt aspects of his life would continue after his death through members of the younger generations who were touched in some way by him. When he was finished, I told him a little about my beliefs and asked him to come visit me, or give me signs, if it turns out there was some kind of life after death. He kind of chuckled and said, "Well, sure… if I can."

We both reflected on our discussion as more silence filled the car. I fidgeted in my seat and wondered if he thought my beliefs were strange or if I should say or ask something else. After a short time, he continued on to say that regardless of whether he would be able to visit me or not, I would always remember the things he had taught me and how he would respond to certain events in my life. He said that when good things happened in my life I would know that he was glad for me and was celebrating with me. He said when things weren't so good, he'd be supporting me and encouraging me to "analyze and reassess" the situation to determine ways to make it better.

I smiled through the tears that were now streaming down my face. That was a typical Grampa thing to say. When he saw my tears, he made a sympathetic sound and said that there was no need to cry. He reminded me that he had lived a long and happy life, that we had a close and special relationship, and that it was the natural course of life for him to die. He finished by saying, "But I appreciate the tears. They mean you will miss me!"

Years later, in graduate school, I would learn more about death and dying and how communication plays a role in both. According to the classic work by Elizabeth Kubler-Ross (1981), the dying want to talk about death. They desire honest, open communication. Research has shown that, at the end of their lives, people want to make connections with those closest to them and that all else becomes far less important (Keeley & Yingling, 2007). Social networks tend to shrink as close family and friend relationships become a greater priority for those who are dying. Talking with these loved ones provides the dying individual with a sense of closure, the opportunity to express past resentments, resolve conflicts, and ensure that close others have found the dying one's life meaningful and worthwhile.

Communication scholars studying end of life communication have identified a phenomenon known as final conversations (Keeley, 2007; Keeley & Koenig Kellas, 2005; Keeley & Yingling, 2007). Final conversations are "all interactions, verbal and nonverbal, that a participant had with a loved one that was dying between the point of terminal diagnosis (in cases where this applies) and the moment of death" (Keeley, 2007, p. 227). These conversations may occur hours, days, weeks, months, and in my case, years before the actual death of the loved one. Though Grampa died seven years after that conversation, and we had many other conversations during those seven years, our discussion in the car that day was a significant final conversation for me.

Final conversations can be very beneficial to the survivors. Communicating with dying loved ones about their impending death can make it a little easier to deal with the actual death. This conversation and the many others we were able to have before Grampa died did not diminish my feelings of loss when he finally died; however, they did help me process my emotions in anticipation of his death, and I felt more emotionally prepared for it than I think I would have otherwise.

Eleven months after my grandfather died, his wife, my beloved Gramma Sadie, died. Her death came as quite a shock to my family and me. She had talked about living well beyond my grandfather and having a lot of life left to live after he was gone. However, after caring for my grandfather for many years, she was physically and emotionally spent. My family didn't realize the toll caring for my grandfather had taken on Gramma. In March, we celebrated her birthday by going to one of her favorite restaurants. While there, she paraded around the restaurant waving at people and announcing that she was 88 years old, with a devil-may-care smile shining from her beautiful, wrinkled face.

Six weeks later she was gone. During those six weeks, her health went dramatically downhill, but even when it was apparent that her condition was worsening, I continued to believe she would recover.

There was a lot going on in my life at that time. I was in the fourth year of my doctorate program. I experienced the deaths of both of my grandfathers as well as two close friends. I was also beginning the third trimester of an unexpected and fairly stressful pregnancy. I was emotionally and spiritually drained. Mostly, I was in denial about my grandmother's looming death and didn't want to face the reality that she would likely not live long enough to meet my unborn child. After being close with both sets of my grandparents for my entire life, it was heartbreaking to think that my child would never have the chance to know these wonderful and unique people whom I loved very much and who influenced and inspired me throughout my life.

About a week before her death, Gramma needed hospice care, and the reality of the situation began to settle in. I knew I wanted to have a conversation with her like the one I had with my grandfather. Gramma never talked about her religious or spiritual beliefs, and I was dismayed to realize I had never asked. Were they the same as Grampa's? Did they change as she aged and knew she was going to lose her husband? How did she feel about her own death and the possibility of an afterlife? I didn't know and decided I wanted to find out. However, at that time I had very few emotional reserves from which to draw on in order to have this conversation. She died before I summoned the strength to ask.

I now think about the significance of having the conversation with Grampa and not with Gramma. I now realize much of it had to do with timing and a process known as anticipatory grief (Keeley & Koenig Kellas, 2005). Anticipatory grief occurs when you know a loved one is going to die. In other words, the grieving process does not wait for the actual death to occur. Learning about an impending death begins an emotional process of mourning the anticipated loss. It also presents unique communication opportunities. As I reflect on this now, I realize that I was able to communicate with Grampa about his eventual death because I had more time to prepare emotionally for it. With Gramma, however, by the time I accepted the gravity of her situation, I had merely days to prepare, and in the end it wasn't enough.

Though I did not have the same conversation with my grandmother, it is her presence that I have felt after death more so than my grandfather's. Just short of a year after she died I was about to celebrate my first Mother's Day as a new mom. I found myself really missing Gramma. For at least the last ten years I had spent Mother's Day with Gramma. The prospect of doing something without her felt strange and depressing, even though I had so much to celebrate and be thankful for this year. Just a few days before Mother's Day, I experienced several instances in which I felt her presence. These moments—moments that some might call coincidences and others might call signs—have helped me understand that relationships continue after death (Keeley, 2007; Keeley & Koenig Kellas, 2005).

In my experience, just because a loved one dies does not mean that the relationship with them ends. In fact, it takes on a whole new meaning. Those moments I experienced before my first Mother's Day told me that Gramma was here with me—celebrating and giving thanks for my amazing daughter. I knew in those instances that, like Grampa had indicated in our conversation, she would always be with me. I hear her laughter in my head when something funny happens. I hear her sympathetic voice when things aren't going well.

The same is true for Grampa and the other loved ones I lost in such a short time span. At different moments, I hear or see their reaction— whether it be a facial expression or laughter or words of wisdom—in my head and heart. I instinctively know what they would say in certain situations and am able to share moments in my life with them as a result. I know them in death just as I knew them in life. This does not mean that I do not ache sometimes to see their faces, talk with them, or hug and kiss them. But I know in time the pain will ease and I will continue to settle in to this new type of relationship I am discovering with them. In this way, I am certain that there is life after death.

Also in this way, my daughter will know her great-grandparents and others that came before her. She may not meet them face to face, but she will know them through the stories and memories I share with her. I will tell her that, from the time she was just a few months old, I was able to see in her my Grampa's determination and my Gramma's charm. I will talk with her about death and the importance of end of life communication. I will try to teach her that death is, in fact, an integral aspect of the life cycle that can be hard to deal with. That while our culture regards death and dying as awkward and difficult to talk about, it doesn't have to be that way. Or, at least, that she can forge forward and talk about it anyway. I will do my best to help her learn how to navigate the raw emotions that accompany the death of a loved one. And I will try to instill in her the confidence to talk about this very difficult subject when and how she deems necessary. Above all else, I hope to teach her that death does not mark the end of a relationship. Instead, it marks the continuation of close relationships experienced in new and different ways.

## Questions and Activities for Discussion

1. Have you discussed death and dying with your family members? If so, describe the conversations. If not, why do you think you have not talked about it? Are there any conversations you wish you had been able to have with loved ones that you did not? Does it matter if the death was sudden or expected (e.g., Ellis, C. [1995]. Speaking of dying: An ethnographic short story. *Symbolic Interaction, 18*, 73–81)?

2. Write a script for a conversation about death and dying with a parent and/or caregiver. How would you go about discussing death?

3. What happens to relationships when someone dies? To relational rituals? What implications does the death of a loved one have for the existence of relationships? What ways of remembering a deceased loved one do you have?

## For Further Reading and Reference

Keeley, M. P. (2007). 'Turning toward death together': The functions of messages during final conversations in close relationships. *Journal of Social and Personal Relationships, 24*, 225–253.

Keeley, M. P., & Koenig Kellas, J. (2005). Constructing life and death through final conversation narratives. In L. M. Harter, P. M. Japp, & C. S. Beck (Eds.), *Narratives, health, and healing: Communication theory, research and practice* (pp. 365–390). Mahwah, NJ: Lawrence Erlbaum Associates.

Keeley, M. P., & Yingling, J. M. (2007). *Final conversations: Helping the living and the dying talk to each other.* Acton, MA: VanderWyk & Burnham.

Koenig Kellas, J., & Trees, A. R. (2006). Finding meaning in difficult family experiences: Sense-making and interaction processes during joint family storytelling. *The Journal of Family Communication, 6*, 49–76.

Kubler-Ross, E. (1981). *Living with death and dying.* New York: MacMillan.

# Chapter 2

# Relationship Metaphors and Forms

Chapter 2 contains three essays on what we mean when we use the word "relationship," continuing a discussion from Chapter 1 about definitions and characteristics of close relationships. Kimberly Dark challenges us to define family beyond a nuclear conception of mom, dad, and child, and to instead focus on the meaning of family relationships. Meg Barker asks in a blog whether pop-culture representations of couple-hood, such as Valentine's Day, limit our understanding of relationships. In Twenty-One-Year-Old Virgin, Malorie Palma explains the connection between religious values and upbringing and the pressure to be sexually active in romantic relationships. What becomes obvious when examining pop-culture and academic research on relationships is our copious use of metaphors to explain and understand our connections.

*Metaphors* communicate messages about the kind of relationship that we feel we are "in": *I'm on a roller-coaster ride. Love is blind. I was a love victim. Best friends make the world go around.* They frame our relationship accounts or stories we tell to others (Bochner, Ellis & Tillman-Healy, 1997). Berry's essay in Chapter 3 of this book explores the potential of the stories we tell to (re)write out relational lives. The metaphors present in our stories tell about the state of a relationship through the use of comparisons—*I felt trapped. I was imprisoned,*

*Inside Relationships: A Creative Casebook in Relational Communication,* edited by Sandra L. Faulkner, 55–60. © 2013 Left Coast Press, Inc. All rights reserved.

*chained down. They put me in a cage. I was burning with love. We were stuck in a rut, the same old groove.* In other words, relationship metaphors help us express and guide our feelings about a relationship (and even the way we conduct research). They also constitute a way that we recognize the cultural ideas of good and bad relationships when we talk to one another. What is interesting about this, especially considering Barker's case study below on Valentine's Day (VD), is a research study that showed the odds of breaking up with a romantic partner were five times higher during the two-week period surrounding Valentine's Day (Morse & Neuberg, 2004). It seems that VD can enhance or diminish relational outcomes because we may start looking at the alternatives to our current relationship (*The grass is greener...*). A person may decide that *the relationship is going nowhere* (a path metaphor), and this acts as a catalyst to set relationship outcomes into motion. Holidays like Valentine's Day instigate a set of processes that may be detrimental to romantic relationships. Think of all of the commercials for special gifts that show you care that heighten our expectations. A risky thing. Consider that social exchange theories tell us that we examine the resources we exchange (e.g., time, money, love) in our relationships and compare what we give and what we receive. If the alternatives are more appealing (e.g., another relationship, no relationship) and we feel under-benefited, we may alter what we put into a relationship or even end it (Stafford, 2008). We seek relationships that are rewarding and cost-efficient.

## Relational Scripts

Scripts represent another cognitive schema we use to make sense of our relationships. A script is a guide to action, it represents a coherent sequence of events expected by us in a particular situation and answers the questions: What should we do next? How shall we proceed? For example, we can talk about a greeting script, a restaurant script, a first date script, and a one-night stand script.

Script theory offers a promising framework from which to examine definitions of sex and safer sex and other relationship processes. Sexual scripts are abstractions about sexuality that specify appropriate sexual goals and contexts as well as provide a pattern of behavior and a plan to achieve sexual goals (Simon & Gagnon, 1986, 1987). A scripting perspective allows researchers to examine how socio-cultural contexts influence what people think and do (Gagnon, 1990). Consciously or unconsciously, individuals tend to rely on scripts to tell them how to behave sexually and even what situations are sexual (Simon & Gagnon,

1987). In short, scripts define behaviors that correspond with a culture's expectations about what happens when, where, how, why, and by whom.

Scripts interact at the cultural, interpersonal, and intrapsychic level (Simon & Gagnon, 1986, 1987) and are considered metaphors "for conceptualizing the production of behavior within social life" (Simon & Gagnon, 1986). The cultural-level script refers to instructions for sexual conduct embodied in cultural narratives. Schools, religious leaders, sex educators, and mass media are sources that help create and maintain guidelines and social norms for appropriate sexual conduct. Interpersonal-level scripts reference one's structured patterns of interaction, that is, what sexual behaviors an individual acquires and maintains during sexual interactions. Finally, the intrapsychic-level script speaks to an individual's feelings and fantasies about sexual activity. A person uses these feelings and fantasies to reflect on past behavior and to guide current and future behavior. These levels are not static; rather, they interact with and relate to one another depending on one's culture and life course (Gagnon, 1990). Multiple and conflicting scripts can exist in a given culture. For Latinas, for instance, feminine sexual gender norms require virginity and also male domination; women are placed in a position of choosing which norm to violate (Faulkner & Mansfield, 2002).

## Family Communication about Sex

These experiences echo some research findings that most children think of their parents' communication about sex as problematic, inactive or ineffectual (Rosenthal & Feldman, 1999); that in many households, sexuality is talked about little or not at all (King & Lorusso, 1997); and that the content of communication (if it occurs at all) between mothers and daughters often focuses on the dire consequences of sexual activity and the need to control sexual encounters (Dennis & Wood, 2012; O'Sullivan, Meyer-Bahlburg & Watkins, 2001). You may be asking yourself, where is the talk about pleasure (Fine & McClelland, 2006)? It is (sadly) missing. Fisher (2004) describes sexual communication in families as a "relatively low frequency event with uncertain outcome" (p. 385). In a focus group study with urban African American and Latino families, O'Sullivan and associates (2001) explored mothers' and daughters' communication about sex and found that often in Latino families, sexual discussions were postponed indefinitely; the mothers were waiting until their daughters married or allowing others, such as counselors, teachers, and other family members, to discuss sexual matters. Thus, O'Sullivan and associates (2001) suggest that sex education from sources other than the mother may be more effective given the antagonistic positions that daughters and mothers adopt.

Parents may not be the preferred source of information about sexuality, yet the quality of this communication matters greatly (Rosenthal & Feldman, 1999). Even if parents don't want to talk because of fear (e.g., talk = condoning sexual activity) or lack of skill, the frequency, quality, and topics of sexual and nonsexual communication between parents and children are correlated with lower levels of sexual activity (Driscoll et al., 2001; Fisher, 2004). Some research shows that parental monitoring along with the supervision of dating and the use of family rules and routines can lead teens to delay sexual intercourse and have fewer sexual partners, unless parental control is excessive, overly-intrusive, or coercive (Miller, 2002). In the latter case, parental control has the opposite effect, with high-risk behaviors occurring more frequently.

How we communicate about sex and sexuality may be largely determined by the communication that we were exposed to and participated in growing up. Carey Noland (2010), borrowing Koerner & Fitzpatrick's (2006) family communication patterns theory, highlights different styles of family communication about sex from a conformity orientation, consensual talk, pluralistic conversations, to laissez- faire; the degree of level of directness and the frequency of talk varies. A conversational style is marked by frequent and spontaneous conversations, as Palma describes in her essay in this chapter. The second type of family conversation is conformity orientation. "Families with a high level of conformity orientation stress harmony, avoid conflicts, and have a high level of interdependence of family members" (Noland, 2010, p. 168). Families high in both conversation orientation and conformity orientation enact consensual family communication, in which a tension exists between freedom to talk and conforming to family values: "Parents in consensual families are interested in their children and want to know what they think and have to say about sex, but in the end, they want to make decisions for their children" (Noland, 2010, p. 168). Pluralistic family communication is marked by a high conversation orientation and low conformity orientation, meaning that communication is open, unconstrained, and evaluated based on arguments. Finally, we can talk about the hands-off, laissez-faire communication, where children are on their own when it comes to learning about sex and sexuality. See if you can determine what styles are enacted in the case studies that follow!

# References

Bochner, A. P., Ellis, C., & Tillman-Healy, L. (1997). Relationships as stories. In S. W. Duck (Ed.), *Handbook of personal relationships* (2nd ed., pp. 307–324). Chichester, UK: Wiley.

Dennis, A. C., & Wood, J. T. (2012). "We're not going to have this conversation. But *you get it*": Black mother-daughter communication about sexual relations. *Women's Studies in Communication, 35*(2), 204–233.

Drisoll, A. K., Biggs, M. A., Brindis, C. D., & Yankah, E. (2001). Adolescent Latino reproductive health: A review of the literature. *Hispanic Journal of Behavioral Sciences, 23*, 255–326.

Faulkner, S. L., & Mansfield, P. K. (2002). Reconciling messages: The process of sexual talk for Latinas. *Qualitative Health Research, 12*, 310–328.

Fine, M., & McClelland, S. I. (2006). Sexuality education and desire: Still missing after all these years. *Harvard Educational Review, 76*, 297–338.

Fisher, T. D. (2004). Family foundations of sexuality. In J. H. Harvey, A. Wenzel & S. Sprecher (Eds.), *The handbook of sexuality in close relationships* pp. 385–409. Mahwah, NJ: Lawrence Erlbaum.

Gagnon, J. H. (1990). The explicit and implicit use of the scripting perspective in sex research. In J. Bancroft (Ed.), *Annual review of sex research* (Vol. 1, pp. 1–43). Lake Mills, IA: Stoyles Graphic Services.

King, B. M., & Lorusso, J. (1997). Discussions in the home about sex: Different recollections by parents and children. *Journal of Sex and Marital Therapy, 23*, 52–60.

Koerner, A. F., & Fitzpatrick, M. A. (2006). Family communication patterns theory: A social cognitive approach. In L. A. Baxter & D. O. Braithwaite (Eds.), *Engaging theories in interpersonal communication: Multiple perspectives* (pp. 50–65). Thousand Oaks, CA: Sage.

Miller, B. C. (2002). Family influences on adolescent sexual and contraceptive behavior. *The Journal of Sex Research, 39*(1), 22–26.

Morse, K. A., & Neuberg, S. L. (2004). How do holidays influence relationship processes and outcomes? Examining the instigating and catalytic effects of Valentine's Day. *Personal Relationships, 11*, 509–527.

Noland, C. M. (2010). *Sex talk: The role of communication in intimate relationships*. Santa Barbara, CA: Praeger.

O'Sullivan, L. F., Meyer-Bahlburg, H. F. L., & Watkins, B. X. (2001). Mother-daughter communication about sex among African American and Latino families. *Journal of Adolescent Research, 16*, 269–292.

Rosenthal, D. A., & Feldman, S. S. (1999). The importance of importance: Adolescents' perceptions of parental communication about sexuality. *Journal of Adolescence, 22*, 835–851.

Simon, W., & Gagnon, J. H. (1986). Sexual scripts: Permanence and change. *Archives of Sexual Behavior, 15*, 97–120.

Simon, W., & Gagnon, J. H. (1987). A sexual scripts approach. In J. H. Geer & W. T. O'Donohue (Eds.), *Theories of human sexuality* (pp. 363–383). New York: Plenum.

Stafford, L. (2008). Social exchange theories. In L. A. Baxter & D. O. Braithwaite (Eds.), *Engaging theories in interpersonal communication: Multiple perspectives* (pp. 377–390). Thousand Oaks, CA: Sage.

# Case 4

# Migration Patterns

### Kimberly Dark

*Keywords:* family communication, family roles, queer identities, relationship forms

My son Caleb convinced us to buy the RV. His logic was irresistible. He would sleep on the bed above the cab of the truck, so that I wouldn't have trouble climbing up and I wouldn't fall out in the middle of the night in case I took a sleepwalk. He would learn how to use the giant icky tube that lived inside the back bumper in order to hook up the RV to the dump station. He would wear the latex gloves in the glove box when he hooked it up and turn the switch to let all of the poop fall out. He would also be the one to make sure all of the windows and top-hatches were closed before we took off driving somewhere so that nothing flew away. He would latch all of the cupboards and turn the lock on the refrigerator door to "on," so our mustard didn't squirt all over our living quarters and make a big giant mobile kitchen mess.

Really, this purchase would be one hundred percent comfortable and worry free for me. My precious six-year-old son assured me of this. My only job was to buy the RV. Surely—SURELY—I could do that one, tiny, simple little thing. He said this as he danced around on the sidewalk, still wearing one purple latex glove from his lesson on hooking up the dump hose.

My girlfriend and I were already pretty sure we'd buy it—that's why we took him along on this second look, just to make sure he was into it. I really didn't want ever to touch that dump hose, so it was in my best

*Inside Relationships: A Creative Casebook in Relational Communication,* edited by Sandra L. Faulkner, 61–64. © 2013 Left Coast Press, Inc. All rights reserved.

interest to convince him that I needed convincing. And he was into it. Oh, was he into it.

During the first year of RV ownership we took the quintessential American-family summer vacation: the Grand Canyon, then the Midwest to visit my girlfriend's family. We were gone a month, and then when we returned, I spent two months waiting by the mail for news that my canonization had come through for the miracle of cooking everything over hot coals for a full month. There may have been a stove in that RV, but it was hot as Hades and we had no air conditioner. Every time we'd stop, I'd sling out the charcoal and get the fire going. I had one skillet, and my campfire repertoire included veggie burgers and pancakes. Over and over and over again. After a few months with no news of sainthood, I realized I really did want to make another trip.

During the next two years, we took a number of short trips up the California coast, and one trip down to Mexico. (We also joined a nudist camp where we could store the RV, but that's another story. A whole 'nother couple of stories, really.) The three of us traveled together, and with Caleb's dad, and with our other close family friend who is something of a fourth parent to Caleb. The RV can sleep three comfortably—four if Caleb sleeps with me or his dad—and even five with a sleeping bag in the center aisle-way (we only did that once that I recall).

Sometimes, our family seems exceedingly normal—almost anachronistic really, in our desire for our son to go camping and hiking and learn to work an RV dump station, in our stalwart insistence that he learn to swim, to play a sport, to take music lessons and go roller-skating. He told me recently that we didn't take him to as many athletic events as his friends seem to have attended, but he's definitely seen more theatre and dance performances. If I did anything right, he's watched a little less television than most, too.

But then, to some, because our family is broader than two parents, and the genders vary, we're total freaks. Because we're queer, we're—to be redundant—odd. And not only do the genders vary—so do the gender roles. Once, my son's father came over when our little boy was out in the garage doing woodworking with my girlfriend. As we looked on, he quipped, hand on hip, "I'm glad you're dating someone who can teach our son to be butch." And indeed, our son's now a competent handy man, and a competent dessert maker, thanks to his cake-decorator dad.

Some people worry that a jumbled up family will be confusing to a child—damaging even. Some go so far as to say families like mine will damage our very culture. Everything will be akimbo and our moral compasses will spin wildly, leaving children crying in the streets.

That's just not how it is. I know, because I've parented under these unique conditions. And I think that most families are unique some-how—some just try to hide it. And perhaps that's more damaging to children than simply knowing what's what and who loves them and defining the terms as necessary.

On one weekend RV trip to see the Monarch butterflies resting in Monterey before they flew south to Mexico, my son's father Richard and my girlfriend Katie were both along on the trip with Caleb and me. Caleb was about seven years old. As Richard drove, the three of us sat at the back table—Katie reading her novel, Caleb and I having light conversation. After a thoughtful moment of silence, Caleb looked at me and said, "If you're my mom, and Katie's my step-mom, and Dad's dad—and if Dad's your husband and Katie's your girlfriend—then who is Katie to Dad?"

He wasn't distressed about it, just trying to get all the titles right. I was still trying to sort out the question when Katie calmly looked up from her book and said, "That makes him my step-spouse."

"Oh!" said Caleb, with a look of satisfaction, as though that obvious detail had simply escaped him. And Katie went back to her book. Soon after, we stopped at a gas station—because those RVs really drink it down. I relayed the story to Richard who chuckled and said "makes sense." And then we had a small argument with our son about why we wouldn't buy candy at the mini-mart. He didn't get the M&M'S, but somehow ended up with a lollipop. His dad's a chump that way. We got back in the RV, with me in the driver's seat, and then the three of them started a game of cards.

The Monarch butterflies were beautiful that weekend—lining the trees and becoming a bright orange sunburst as they took flight. We attended a class and went on a hike offered by the natural history museum. Those butterfly migration patterns are amazing—and com-plex. But somehow they figure it all out. And so do we. We figure it out—like it's the most natural thing there is.

## Questions and Activities for Discussion

1. How do you define family? Who does this definition include? What roles do individuals included in your definition play?

2. Draw a family tree or genogram (e.g., www.genopro.com/genogram/) and label the relationships between the components. Provide a narrative account of your genogram that includes:

   a. Interpretation of your genogram: Are gender issues relevant in your family? Explain and provide examples: How has time influenced family members' experiences? For example, if someone had three major life changes in one year, how did this influence him or her? Explain and provide examples. How does the family deal with personal or highly charged information? Explain and provide examples. How have illness, death, disabilities, economic reversals, miscarriages, divorces, etc. influenced others? Explain and provide examples.

   b. The family themes: How have communication patterns repeated within and across generations? What themes are present in your family? That is, who are you? How do you behave?

3. In some cultures friends of the family are called Aunt and Uncle. Can family friends be considered family? Why or why not? What does this broader definition of family imply?

4. Dark states that "most families are unique somehow—some just try to hide it. And perhaps that's more damaging to children than simply knowing what's what and who loves them and defining the terms as necessary." Do you agree with this statement?

## For Further Reading and Reference

Buxton, A. P. (2004). Works in progress: How mixed-orientation couples maintain their marriages after the wives come out. *Journal of Bisexuality*, 58–82.

Haas, S. (2003). Relationship maintenance in same sex couples. In D. J. Canary & M. Dainton (Eds.), *Maintaining relationships through communication* (pp. 209–230). Mahwah, NJ: Lawrence Erlbaum.

Hequembourg, A. (2004). Unscripted motherhood: Lesbian mothers negotiating incompletely institutionalized family relationships. *Journal of Social and Personal Relationships*, 21, 739–762.

Lannutti, P. J. (2005). For better or worse: Exploring the meanings of same-sex marriage within the lesbian, gay, bisexual, and transgendered community. *Journal of Social and Personal Relationships*, 22, 5–18.

# Case 5

# Doing Valentine's Day Differently

### Meg Barker

*Keywords:* LGBTQ relationships, pop culture, relational expectations, relationship rituals, romance, singles

February 13, 2012

From *Rewriting the Rules* Blog
rewritingtherules.wordpress.com/

On Valentine's Day my youngest sister sends cards to seven of her friends, some of whom are single and some in relationships. She's been doing it for years. This simple gesture invites us to ask some profound questions. Why is it that days are set aside to celebrate one particular kind of love, but not others? Along with Valentine's Day we tend to recognize anniversaries of romantic commitments in a way that we don't with other forms of relationship, with precious jewels and metals associated with reaching certain five and ten year points together.

Do such celebrations reflect (and reproduce) a kind of hierarchy of love that is present in our culture? And how might such hierarchies be problematic, both for those who are excluded from them and for those who are included?

The problems of exclusions are often more obvious than those of inclusion. I remember February 14th, as a teenager, when the day only served to exacerbate the pain of unrequited love. Certain songs on the radio still take me back to the cards that I furtively asked a friend to pass on to the object of my affections, only to receive nothing in return. Along with sentimental pop songs and the teen romance books that I wish

*Inside Relationships: A Creative Casebook in Relational Communication*, edited by Sandra L. Faulkner, 65–68.

I'd never discovered, Valentine's Day was part of a tuition into the vital importance of finding 'The One' and the sense of failure and self-doubt that accompanied not being able to do so.

The stigma around singledom only increases with age, such that many of those without partners are faced with a month or so of painful reminders of their not-quite-normal status as they pass gift shops, florists, and adverts for this year's Valentine movie. Single people are not the only exclusions. Valentine's Day usefully reminds us that the kind of romantic love that is assumed is heterosexual. The majority of cards depict images of heterosexual couples, or male and female animals, soft toys, and the like, in the same way that anniversary cards are almost entirely designed to be from a wife/girlfriend to a husband/boyfriend or vice versa. Sitting with a 'same sex' partner in a restaurant on Valentine's night also feels different. Though most are now welcoming, there is a certain edge to the experience, which isn't there at other times. There may well be a similar feeling for others whose relationships aren't considered quite as acceptable: mixed-race couples, couples where one or both don't meet the ideals of conventional attractiveness, those with an age-gap, or people who want to celebrate with multiple partners on a night where every table is set out for two.

Romantic love is intrinsically linked to sexual love, and popular Valentine's gifts include both the sappy (flowers, chocolates, and soft toys) and the sexy (underwear, sex toys, and erotic games). For this reason, other exclusions may include those who are assumed not to be sexual (by virtue of being too young, too old, or disabled, for example), and those who are assumed to be sexual but in fact are not. The person who is asexual and romantic, or the couple whose relationship started sexual but is no longer so, may feel painfully aware of assumptions and expectations around Valentine's night.

Turning to those who are included in Valentine's Day, there are difficulties here as well—although they may not be so obvious. As I mentioned at the start, like anniversaries, Valentine's Day highlights the way we tend to prioritize romantic relationships over all other types. When my sister sends cards to her friends, this is the assumption that she is challenging: why should this one person (a partner) be deemed more important than the others she is close to—people who, in some cases, have been in her life for years?

When we value romantic love so much more highly than friendship there are dangers that we will become isolated in a partnership. There is a sense of privacy around the couple whereby we aren't meant to share what is going on with anyone outside of it. As well as exacerbating the sense of exclusion of our single friends, this can be damaging for those in the couple as they come to rely upon each other for everything, and feel unable to get outside support when they are struggling in the relationship.

Valentine's Day can add to the pressure for those who are going through the kinds of tough periods that all intimate relationships have from time to time. There are expectations and assumptions about how we must feel on Valentine's Day, and the kinds of declarations that we must want to make to each other, which may well not fit where we are currently at. Two common responses to such pressure are to assume that the relationship must be wrong and to bolt from it, or to focus on presenting an outside image, which fits whilst denying (to others and to oneself) that we are struggling, until it has reached a critical point.

Knocking romantic love off its perch as the most important relationship could decrease the pressure upon it. It could also enable some fresh air to circulate, as we are able to spend time separately and to talk about things in the relationship with other people in our lives. This kind of re-evaluation can also expand our understanding of what might be included in romantic love, in friendship, and in the blurry space in between (the friends-with-benefits arrangement, the romantic relationship which has developed into friendship over time, the friendship that has all the intimacy, passion and challenge of a romantic relationship).

I suggest that, rather than ignoring Valentine's Day and trying to get past it, or celebrating it in the conventional way, we might consider doing something different: Send a card to a friend. Watch an unromantic comedy. Celebrate celibacy. Spend the evening alone doing things you enjoy that your partner does not. Take time to recognize all the important relationships in your life. Think about how you might expand love for a partner out to include a friend, a stranger, even an enemy.

## Questions and Activities for Discussion

1. Write a response to this blog post. Do you agree with Barker's assertion that we should consider "doing something different" for Valentine's Day? Why or why not? Reread Barker's last paragraph; is this the solution?

2. Do you send cards or other tokens of affection to friends for Valentine's

Day? If so, why? If no, why not?

3. How does pop culture influence expectations in our relationships (e.g., material vs. immaterial displays of romance)? How do others in our lives influence our expectations? Is Valentine's Day just for heterosexuals? For those in romantic partnerships does giving presents mean one gets a "get out of the dog house free card"? How is Valentine's Day gendered?

## For Further Reading and Reference

Banker, J. E., Kaestle, C. E., & Allen, K. R. (2010). Dating is hard work: A narrative approach to understanding sexual and romantic relationships in young adulthood. *Contemporary Family Therapy: An International Journal, 32*(2), 173–191.

Elia, J. P. (2003). Queering relationships: Toward a paradigmatic shift. *Journal of Homosexuality, 45*, 61–86.

Morse, K. A., & Neuberg, S. L. (2004). How do holidays influence relationship processes and outcomes? Examining the instigating and catalytic effects of Valentine's Day. *Personal Relationships, 11*, 509–527.

Yep, G. (2003). The violence of heteronormativity in communication studies: Notes on injury, healing, and queer world-making. *Journal of Homosexuality, 45*, 11–59.

# Case 6

# Twenty-One-Year-Old Virgin

## Malorie Palma

*Keywords:* family communication, premarital sex, religious values, sexual communication, sexual decisionmaking, virginity

A person's sexual communication can be largely determined by the communication that he or she was exposed to and participated in growing up. Many parents may fear "the talks" about sex, perhaps even the thought of their kid having sex, yet they know that it is something essential to discuss. Families choose to talk about sex in different ways, directly and indirectly, "the talk" versus a series of talks. According to Noland (2010), there are five ways that families go about talking about sex—a conversation orientation, a conformity orientation, consensual talk, pluralistic conversations, and laissez-faire. But I think that some ways are better because an individual's views about sex and his or her ability to communicate about sexuality are strongly affected by these conversations.

"Families that have a high level of conversation orientation communicate with one another freely, frequently, and spontaneously and do not have many time or topic limitations to conversation" (Noland, 2010, p. 167). When I was growing up, my family enacted the conversation orientation: We talked about everything. And as Noland (2010) states, "If parents and children are accustomed to speaking with one another freely and comfortably, then the transition to sex talk is more natural" (p. 168). My whole life, my mom has discussed scenarios about sex with my siblings and me because she felt that open communication

*Inside Relationships: A Creative Casebook in Relational Communication,* edited by Sandra L. Faulkner, 69–73. © 2013 Left Coast Press, Inc. All rights reserved.

would be best. Conversations were frequent and comfortable, making talk about sex easy for everyone. My mom thought we would not lie to her then, especially when I was in high school. She wanted to know where I was, whom I was with, and what I was doing. Of course, in some situations with parents who express such openness, kids may forget that the person they are talking to is *their parent*. Not everything is appropriate to share! I talk to my mom about most things, though I would never tell her minute details about a sexual situation. However, she always made my sister and me feel comfortable enough to talk to her about any sexual situation, because she wanted to ensure that we would be practicing safe sex and keeping our reputations and morals intact. I believe that because of our open communication and being raised in a God-based household, I have chosen to remain a virgin until I get married. *Are you surprised?*

In today's society, with our sexualized media, sexualized clothing, and lax attitudes about sex, it is almost impossible to not communicate in a sexual manner. I can easily recognize how sexual individuals are through their actions, the way they dress, and their overall persona. I am also in tune with my sexual side, but at this point in my life, I am still a virgin. Yes, I have had a variety of boyfriends; some of the relationships were more serious than others, yet I have made a drastic, perhaps unbelievable, decision to remain a virgin. I have surrounded myself with people and been in circumstances that make it seem almost impossible for me to still be virginal. People think it's weird, or cool or whatever else, but to me it's just a decision that I have made based on my life circumstances.

I grew up in a religious household, not a Bible thumping one that would force anything on anyone, but we regularly went to church and talked about God. Once I was old enough to understand what I was learning in church, I began enjoying it, wanting to go to church on my own without my mom forcing me to wake up on Sunday mornings. I grew up Christian, and we learned that it is sinful to have premarital sex. With this in mind, I lived as a normal teenager with influences from the media and my peer group. I never looked down on someone who did have premarital sex, because I am not a judgmental person. However, I kept the idea of premarital sex as sin (for me) in the back of my mind. At the time, religion was a major reason for keeping my virginity intact and not giving in to societal influences.

When I was in high school I had a serious relationship. My boyfriend got on my nerves, so I had a difficult time being fully committed to him. Andy was my first serious boyfriend, thus the topic of sex regularly arose. Though I didn't feel uncomfortable talking about it with him, I knew that I didn't want to have sex with him for many reasons. The first reason was that people say you will be very attached to the first person with whom you have sex. Since I'm such an independent person, I couldn't fathom being that attached to someone. I didn't like the thought of having my emotions dictated by another human being. The second apprehension was my religion and the impact that it had on my life; I knew that I would regret it if I had sex with Andy. And the third reason is the fact that I try so hard to be different than others and at that time everyone was having sex, so I thought *well I am going to be different on yet another occasion*. So even though Andy and I were serious and I had strong feelings for him, I knew it was not the time to have sex with him. We later broke up, and I came to college a virgin.

No one knew when I came to college that I was a virgin. I have always been a sexual person in the way I act and dress, as well as the way I talk, so the people I meet and later became best friends with, questioned my credibility. They didn't know if I was lying or telling the truth, and to them, I was just an attention-seeking stranger. I fell in love with a man my freshmen year, and he completely changed my ideas about men. I thought that he would be the one I would lose my virginity to, but I remained a virgin after a year of no sexual intercourse, thankful that though I was in love with him, I never had sex with him. After that experience, I knew that I was not meant to have sex for a long time.

Now I am twenty-one years old and still a virgin. There is a lot more to the situation than just having my virginity, though. Numerous people know that I am a virgin, which makes me a sort of novelty because though I hang out with people who are sexually active, I have chosen not to be. Also since there are so many people who know, it has turned into a bigger deal than it should be. I still keep my religion in sight and my morals in line, but I know that if I were to have sex, it would be a huge deal. Everyone would talk about it, and it wouldn't be something that I would want to discuss with a lot of people, even though a lot of people would want to discuss it. My friends are afraid that *I am going to die without having sex*, but I'm not concerned because I don't know what I'm missing. There is a sense of wonder that surrounds me with boyfriends I leave, because our connection is not primarily sexual as in their previous relationships. This never fazes me because I know that one day I will find someone that is worth offering that piece of myself to. Being a twenty-one-year-old virgin is unique, especially because I am such a sexual person, and I know a vast majority of my decisions have been based around the way I was raised and the type of communication that occurred in our household.

My mom always made it so easy to talk about everything; therefore, I knew what I needed to know. There was no need for exploration through sexual encounters. I never wanted to rebel or act out because my mom never emphasized sex as a horrible or dirty thing. She did emphasize the fact that sex should be safe, and she preferred for her children to have sex with people that we know and love. But like her religious beliefs, she never forced anything on me. I am glad that I have stood my ground, because I believe this makes me who I am. My actions as an adult are a direct reflection of my family's communication style as well as the ideals by which I was raised.

## Questions and Activities for Discussion

1. What role should parents and parental values take in educating children about sexuality? When should parents and children have conversations about sex? How should parents talk to their children about sex? Are there others who should talk about sex with children (e.g., aunts)? Think about movies that show conversations about sex between parents and children.

2. Are there some things about sex that are not appropriate to discuss with family? Why or why not? Describe the kind of communication about sex you and your family have now and the kind of communication about sex you had growing up.

3. What do you think of Palma's assertion that "I can easily recognize how sexual individuals are through their actions, the way they dress, and their overall persona."? What does it mean to be a sexual person? Can one be sexual without having intercourse with a romantic partner? Why or why not (e.g., does it depend on definitions of sex?)?

## For Further Reading and Reference

Carpenter, L. M. (2001). The ambiguity of "having sex": The subjective experience of virginity loss in the United States. *The Journal of Sex Research, 38,* 127–139.

Fisher, T. D. (2004). Family foundations of sexuality. In J. H. Harvey, A. Wenzel, & S. Sprecher (Eds.), *The handbook of sexuality in close relationships,* pp. 385–409. Mahwah, NJ: Lawrence Erlbaum.

Miller, B. C. (2002). Family influences on adolescent sexual and contraceptive behavior. *The Journal of Sex Research, 39*(1), 22–26.

Noland, C. M. (2010). *Sex talk: The role of communication in intimate relationships.* Santa Barbara, CA: Praeger.

Rosenthal, D. A., & Feldman, S. S. (1999). The importance of importance: Adolescents' perceptions of parental communication about sexuality. *Journal of Adolescence, 22,* 835–851.

Trotter, P. B. (2010). The influence of parental romantic relationships on college students' attitudes about romantic relationships. *College Student Journal, 44*(1), 71–83.

# Chapter 3

# Uncertainty, Information Management, and Disclosure

Chapter 3 details how our expectations, life situations, and uncertainty influence our disclosure decisions in close relationships. Erin Willer uses painting and blogging to understand her feelings of loss and forgiveness surrounding her experiences with infertility and miscarriage. Keith Berry reflects on how mindfulness can facilitate difficult disclosures about sexual orientation and identity, and Kate Magsamen-Conrad presents a fictionalized text message in which a friend expresses concern about her friend's unhealthy partying behavior. What we decide to reveal to or conceal from others has important implications for our close relationships such as development, trust, and solidarity (Altman & Taylor, 1973). *Self-disclosure* in our close relationships can deepen them and contribute to their maintenance, as well as create chaos, discord, and decline. The reasons for disclosure decisions and the concomitant relational outcomes are explored in this chapter's case studies. Researchers have studied reciprocity of disclosure, liking, and sex differences as important components influencing our self-disclosure decisions, yet sex differences in self-disclosure are relatively small (Dindia, 2000). Dindia and Allen's (1992) meta-analysis of sex differences in self-disclosure indicated women disclose more than men, but to whom we disclose matters. The most significant sex differences occurred with female and

---

*Inside Relationships: A Creative Casebook in Relational Communication,* edited by Sandra L. Faulkner, 75–79. © 2013 Left Coast Press, Inc. All rights reserved.

female partners disclosing more compared to female and male partners and male and male partners. What this means is that it is difficult to predict self-disclosure based on sex alone.

Self-disclosure is verbal communication that reveals something private about the self—such as thoughts, feelings, and experiences—to others: Are you worried about a friend's partner choice? Do you disclose a previous STI (sexually transmitted disease) to a potential sexual partner? Are you "catching feelings" for a friend? Have you ever smoked pot? Disclosure is a multi-dimensional construct that involves relationship expectations, trust, intimacy, expected and actual outcomes of disclosure decisions, breadth and depth, valence, frequency, duration, and timing (Altman & Taylor, 1973; Greene & Faulkner, 2002; Wheeless, 1978). We can view self-disclosure as an intrapersonal-interpersonal dialectic where the intrapersonal element focuses on individuals' cognitive and behavioral processes, such as thoughts about disclosure and actual disclosure, and the interpersonal element highlights relationship processes (Dindia, 1994). Motivation, cost-benefit ratios, gender, culture, and context also influence our decisions to share private information (Petronio, 2002).

Culture is an important part of the disclosure process, as you will see in the following case studies, because it highlights important reasons we disclose or do not disclose private information (Chen, 2002; Hastings, 2000). Disclosure of sexual information to romantic partners in a study on Latinas' sexual talk in relationships revealed that women were motivated to disclose if they felt comfortable with a friend or partner and expected or received a positive response to talk (Faulkner & Mansfield, 2002; Faulkner, 2003). Women want to be seen as moral and are motivated to keep relationships positive. They often feel trapped between a dialectic of cultural discourses of romantic relationships as being sexual and cultural expectations for virginity (Baxter, 2004). Thus, identity management processes are especially salient for some individuals because of membership in stigmatized groups (e.g., lesbian, gay, bisexual, transgender, queer), cultural expectations, and relationship motivations (Hecht & Faulkner, 2000). Some identities (e.g., sexual identity, religious affiliation) are not easily ascribable and typically become known through a disclosure process that allows or denies others access to this private information (Faulkner & Hecht, 2006). For example, the extent to which LGBTQ Jewish Americans conceal or reveal their identities, find supportive communities, experience pressure to leave their LGBTQ and/or Jewish communities, and how they experience themselves and their relationships varies according to factors such as self-definition and regard, social support, how they want others to regard them, and how they feel their actions represent themselves (Faulkner & Hecht, 2011; Shneer & Aviv, 2002).

## Communication Privacy Management

One theory that is useful for framing disclosure decisions is Communication Privacy Management (Petronio, 2002) because of the emphasis on the co-owned nature of private information. CPM addresses how we balance the need to make public disclosures with the need for privacy. In our close relationships, we expect others to disclose. However, disclosure to others involves risk; therefore, we regulate disclosure of private information to protect ourselves. Disclosure of private information, for instance sexual orientation, concern about a friend's behavior, or anger, involves individual and collective boundaries. Individuals believe that they possess exclusive ownership rights to their private information, so in order to manage the disclosure and receipt of personal information, an individual raises a "metaphoric boundary" that serves as a form of protection and a way to decrease the possibility of losing face. We have multiple goals for revealing and concealing in addition to our experiences of multiple consequences for these decisions (Caughlin & Vangelisti, 2009). We may be interested in maintaining the relationship, positive identities, or social networks, for instance. It is important to disclose positive and negative information to others, to tell our secrets in order to obtain needed support, but if the person we disclose to is judgmental, indiscreet, and/or reacts poorly, there can be poor consequences for our health and relationships (Kelly & Macready, 2009).

Boundaries regulate the flow of private information between oneself and others. Individuals use boundaries and draw them tightly when they want protection and to decrease the possibility of losing face. When boundaries are permeable, others are allowed access. Balancing levels of permeability and control allows a person to manage the degree of openness achieved with others. Individuals achieve this balance through rules that regulate access to private information. Rules help individuals determine to whom they will reveal information, how much to reveal, and when, where, and under what circumstances to not reveal by regulating the level of boundary access and boundary protection. Relational uncertainty also contributes to rules we make about disclosure, though it inhibits our ability to communicate directly with a relational partner and interpret messages effectively (Knobloch & Satterlee, 2009). If we do not know how someone will react, we may tell nothing by avoiding or only tell part of something by being ambiguous. For example, one may have a rule that all information is to be shared with the family but no personal information is shared outside the family. This rule specifies that the family, not individuals, owns private information, and this represents a highly restrictive, nonpermeable boundary to those outside this group.

Once information is revealed, it places recipients in the position of co-owning the disclosure. CPM supposes the formation of disclosure rules, some based on gendered and cultured suppositions. We can see the boundary management process in Keith Berry's personal narrative when he chooses mindfulness surrounding sexual identity information after poor past reactions. If a friend tells her mother a secret you asked her not to, this represents a transgression of a collective boundary in your friendship and turbulence in disclosure rules. You assumed she would not tell anyone, and she may feel that the need for family members to know information trumps friendship.

## References

Altman, I., & Taylor, D. A. (1973). *Social penetration: The development of interpersonal relationships.* New York: Holt, Rinehart, & Wilson.

Baxter, L. A. (2004). Relationships as dialogues. *Personal Relationships, 11,* 1–22.

Caughlin, J. P., & Vangelisit, A. L. (2009). Why people conceal or reveal secrets: A multiple goals theory perspective. In T. D. Afifi & W. A. Afifi (Eds.), *Uncertainty, information management, and disclosure: Decisions, theories and applications* (pp. 279–299). New York: Routledge.

Chen, L. (2002). Communication in intercultural relationships. In W. B. Gudykunst & B. Mody (Eds.), *Handbook of international and intercultural communication* (2nd ed., pp. 241–257). Thousand Oaks, CA: Sage.

Dindia, K. (1994). The intrapersonal-interpersonal dialectical process of self-disclosure, In S. Duck (Ed.), *Understanding relationship processes IV: The dynamics of relationships* (pp. 27–57). Newbury Park, CA: Sage.

Dindia, K. (2000). Sex differences in self-disclosure, reciprocity of self-disclosure, and self-disclosure and liking: Three meta-analyses reviewed. In S. Petronio (Ed.), *Balancing the secrets of private disclosures* (pp. 21–35). Mahwah, NJ: Lawrence Erlbaum.

Dindia, K., & Allen, M. (1992). Sex-differences in self-disclosure: A meta-analysis. *Psychological Bulletin, 112,* 106–124.

Faulkner, S. L. (2003). Good girl or flirt girl: Latinas' definitions and meanings of sex and sexual relationships. *Hispanic Journal of Behavioral Sciences, 25,* 174–200.

Faulkner, S. L., & Hecht, M. L. (2006). Tides in the ocean: A layered approach to culture and communication. In B. B. Whaley & W. Samter (Eds.), *Explaining communication: Contemporary theories and exemplars* (pp. 383–402). Mahwah, NJ: Lawrence Erlbaum.

Faulkner, S. L. & Hecht, M. L. (2011). The negotiation of closetable identities: A narrative analysis of LGBTQ Jewish identity. *Journal of Social and Personal Relationships, 28*(6), 829–847.

Faulkner, S. L., & Mansfield, P. K. (2002). Reconciling messages: The process of sexual talk for Latinas. *Qualitative Health Research, 12,* 310–328.

Greene, K., & Faulkner, S. L. (2002). Expected versus actual responses to disclosure in relationships of HIV-positive African-American adolescent females. *Communication Studies, 53,* 297–331.

Hastings, S. (2000). Asian Indian "self-suppression" and self-disclosure: Enactment and adaptation of cultural identity. *Journal of Language and Social Psychology, 19,* 85–109.

Hecht, M. L., & Faulkner, S. L. (2000). Sometimes Jewish, sometimes not: The closeting of Jewish American identity. *Communication Studies, 51,* 372–387.

Kelly, A., & Macready, D. (2009). Why disclosing to a confidant can be so good (or bad) for us. In T. D. Afifi & W. A. Afifi (Eds.), *Uncertainty, information management, and disclosure: decisions, theories and applications* (pp. 384–401). New York: Routledge.

Knobloch, L. K., & Satterlee, K. L. (2009). Relational uncertainty: Theory and application. In T. D. Afifi & W. A. Afifi (Eds.), *Uncertainty, information management, and disclosure: Decisions, theories and applications* (pp. 106–127). New York: Routledge.

Petronio, S. (2002). *Boundaries of privacy: Dialectics of disclosure.* New York: SUNY Press.

Shneer, D., & Aviv, C. (Eds.) (2002). *Queer Jews.* New York: Routledge.

Wheeless, L. R. (1978). A follow-up study of the relationships among trust, disclosure, and interpersonal solidarity. *Human Communication Research, 4,* 143–157.

# Case 7

# BIRTHing ARTiculations

### Erin K. Willer

*Keywords:* art therapy, fertility, forgiveness, therapeutic writing

## In the Mourning There Will Be Life

Tuesday, April 24, 2012
From: http://birthingarticulations.blogspot.com/
*BIRTHing ARTiculations: Paintings of Infertility, Loss, and Motherhood*

This painting is one of the most meaningful for me that I have done to date. I drew it after our second miscarriage. In total across all of our in-vitro treatments, we have had 15 embryos, none of which has survived. The most likely culprits are my eggs. The rest of my body functions fine when it is pregnant; my husband has been tested and is in great shape. At the time I drew this, I wanted to capture my grief over losing my baby, but also my grief over realizing that 0/15 basically equals a loss of my fertility.

I was frustrated with the drawing because my husband said the robin looked like a baby bird. I didn't want it to look like a baby bird. I wanted it to look like a mother who came home to discover that her 15 baby eggs were shattered! I let the painting sit for months. I couldn't bring myself to work on it. Plus, it's a lot bigger than most of the paintings I've done, which made it feel more intimidating.

During the time when this painting sat, we began to look into egg donation as an option for having a baby. We decided that this will be our new path, and we will embark on an egg donor cycle this summer. Over

*Inside Relationships: A Creative Casebook in Relational Communication,* edited by Sandra L. Faulkner, 80–85. © 2013 Left Coast Press, Inc. All rights reserved.

the last few months, in addition to working on becoming a more mentally healthy person in general, I have worked hard to mend my heart and head after all of the losses we have suffered. In order to begin to prepare myself for our upcoming journey, I began at my psychologist's suggestion to do some artwork that would help put me in a positive space. Given none of my artwork to date had been very positive, this seemed so foreign to me. But I really wanted to start to do some more positively-framed pieces (in addition to my dark ones :)). Despite wanting to do this, I still had the mother robin masquerading as the baby bird with the smashed eggs lurking on my easel. I felt like I had to finish the painting before I could make a transition to a new kind of art.

So a couple of weeks ago it dawned on me. The robin is both grieving mother and baby bird. She represents both my heartache over my 15 embryos that will never be and the new possibilities that potentially will emerge from my shattered eggs. In this way, the painting represents where I have been and all that awaits me. Once I realized this, I finished the painting pretty quickly, understanding that in the mourning there will be life.

## Giving the Eggstraordinary Part II

Wednesday, June 13, 2012

This IVF cycle has proved to be full of times of celebration, drama, and unease. Things moved along beautifully for the first couple of weeks. Our egg donor made it through the follicle stimulation with no trouble, and it felt so good to be able to breathe easily at every update on her progress. My body also has been holding up its end of the deal, building up a nice thick uterine lining. I also finally figured out what else to give the donor in addition to the painting I did for her. One of the reasons why we picked her, in addition to her medical history, proven success in previous cycles, age, etc., was because her favorite book growing up was *To Kill a Mockingbird*. This is also my favorite book, and so I took this as a sign that she is the one. So I got her a 50th anniversary edition copy of the book and another one that includes interviews of people who talk about how the book has impacted their lives. I also found the perfect card and thought of the perfect things to write. As I mentioned in my previous post, this gift meant so much to me, and I was so relieved that I was at peace with it. I indeed had found THE gift. Or so I thought.

As seems to always happen at some point during IVF treatment, my hope and optimism came to a crashing halt. I had an appointment to check on my uterine lining. Although it continued to look good, the ultrasound technician found a hydrosalpinx (fluid pocket) in the remaining piece of my right fallopian tube (I had it removed in 2009). This was a Saturday; we waited all day to hear from the doctor who was on call about what this might mean. After a day of overwhelming anxiety, she called and said that my doctor wanted to look at it himself, and that worst case scenario, I would need to have the remaining piece of tube removed or blocked before moving forward with IVF. If the fluid from the hydrosalpinx makes it into the uterus, it can impact embryo implantation. This would mean having to freeze the embryos and me starting all over again with a new cycle. Of course this happened on a Saturday, and so we had a long wait until Monday when we were scheduled to meet with my doctor.

In the meantime, the following day was egg retrieval day. My husband went in to give his sample (in the navy room as he likes to call it ;)) and despite the news of the previous day, we were feeling excited that this was the day the embryos would begin their journey. Our hopefulness was bitch slapped yet again. We got a call from one of the embryologists that they were only able to get six eggs, four of which were mature. Now, this may seem like a good number, and it is if you are a typical infertility patient. However, for a donor this is a horrible number. During our donor's last cycle with another couple she had 18 mature eggs! She admitted that she had taken her trigger shot (the one that tells the follicles to release the eggs) almost three hours early the night before. The timing needs to be perfect so that by retrieval time, the eggs are ready to be "harvested." Since she took the shot too early, she ovulated out most of the eggs by the time they went in to retrieve them. We were speechless. The ridiculousness of it all seemed so unfathomable.

After making it through yet another intense day, Monday came and we had our appointment with our doctor. We prepared ourselves for the worst. Surprisingly, he determined that the hydrosalpinx is in such a place that there is not a threat of it making it to my uterus. We were clear for transfer on Friday. In the meantime, we prayed that we would have embryos left to transfer. With so few we were unsure if the transfer would happen despite the good news on Monday. Thankfully, we ended up with two perfect embryos and transferred those. The other two did not make it, so we have none to freeze. We are in the two-week wait and will find out if we are pregnant next week.

Ok, now to the point of this post. Geesh. Last week was a really hard time for me because of what happened with the donor. We took such care to choose her, each of us ranking numerous donors on our own and then coming together to discuss our top choices. I put so much care into choosing the perfect gift for her. Despite this, she let us down. She took away the chance for future siblings who share a genetic connection with one another, even if they don't share one with me. She took away the beautiful story I intended to tell my children about what an amazing person she is to have given them life. I fumed. I wanted to ask for the painting I made for her back. After a couple of days though, I decided that I could not keep up such anger, such bitterness and regret. So I decided to give her one last gift: I chose to forgive her. For the sake of my health and the babies that are hopefully rocking it out inside me, I let go. Like me, okay, really all of us, she is a good person who made a mistake. If there is one thing that I have learned over the last year, it is that I am not perfect and that I don't need to be. As I learn to be gentler on myself, I learn to do the same for others. I was lying in bed thinking all of this through last week, and as soon as I came to this decision, a palpable feeling washed over me. I felt a sense of relief. I felt like a mother. What an even more beautiful story to tell our children than the one I had originally planned— another invaluable gift she is giving to all of us.

## Questions and Activities for Discussion

1. Have you ever kept a journal (e.g., blog, art journal) about a difficult situation in your life? If so, what did the journal help you do? If not, imagine what such a journal would help you do? What does Willer's art blog help her articulate?

2. Make a collage (e.g., painting, magazine, on-line) of a difficult situation in a close relationship (e.g., a fight, an unexpected disclosure). Write an artist statement in which you discuss what the collage is about, how it represents the difficult situation, and how creating the collage helped you articulate the situation.

3. Part of Willer's blog is about forgiveness. What situations in our close relationships merit an apology and forgiveness? Picking an argument? Dating someone a friend finds attractive? Describe such a situation and how you would apologize (or accept an apology).

## For Further Reading and Reference

Bute, J. J. (2009). "Nobody thinks twice about asking": Women with a fertility problem and requests for information. *Health Communication, 24*(8), 752–763.

Scher, S. J., & Darley, J. M. (1997). How effective are the things people say to apologize? Effects of the realization of the apology speech act. *Journal of Psycholinguistic Research, 26,* 127–140.

Silva, S., & Machado, H. (2011). Heterosexual couples' uses and meanings of ovarian stimulation: Relatedness, embodiment and emotions. *Health: An Interdisciplinary Journal For The Social Study Of Health, Illness & Medicine, 15*(6), 620–632.

Steuber, K. R., & Solomon, D. H. (2012). Relational uncertainty, partner interference, and privacy boundary turbulence: Explaining spousal discrepancies in infertility disclosures. *Journal of Social & Personal Relationships, 29*(1), 3–27.

# Case 8

# Storying Mindfulness, (Re)imagining Burn

Keith Berry

*Keywords:* coming out, LGBT, mindfulness, relational stories, self-help

*We all have a story we must repeat until we get it right, a story whose conveniences must be corrected and whose simplifications must be seen through before we are done with it, or it with us.* (Yoshino, 2007, p. 50)

*There's nothing more advanced than relating with others. There's nothing more advanced than communication—compassionate communication.... This means allowing ourselves to feel what we feel and not pushing it away. It means accepting every aspect of ourselves, even the parts we don't like.* (Chödrön, 2002, pp. 101–102)[1]

I am sitting and visiting with friends at the beach. The day brings sunshine and scorching heat. Light winds tease us and hint at the possibility of cooling and relief. My attention is drawn to a young boy and girl playing nearby. They're trying to build a sand castle and have been working tirelessly most of the day. They're committed, which shows by their persistence in rebuilding the castle each time the waves crash it over and by sunburned and reddened bodies. "Come take another break," yells their father. "It's bad out there. Protect yourself!" Reluctantly the kids return to the shade of their family's umbrella. Having stepped outside their play, they feel their burn and seek relief. Like they are dancing on hot coals, the kids jump and yell repeatedly,

*Inside Relationships: A Creative Casebook in Relational Communication,* edited by Sandra L. Faulkner, 86–96. © 2013 Left Coast Press, Inc. All rights reserved.

"Arggggggggh, it burns!" Wanting instant relief, they rub pieces of ice from the cooler up and down their bright red arms, hands and feet. After only moments of attention, they exhale, "Ah...all better!" Giggles replace their panic, as the ice chills and tickles the surface of their skin. Quickly their attention returns to the shore, where they soon return to do more building and, likely, more burning.

I begin with this image of kids attempting to soothe themselves, believing it can prompt deeper reflection on how many people generally seek relief within the difficult situations comprising our lives. I hope to provoke a curious and creative exploration on how experiences of hardship shape the stories of our lives and the complex ways we relate to and use those stories. Dwelling at the heart of interactions and relationships is the need/opportunity to (re)imagine our and others' burn. Stories, good or bad, are central to this work, the importance reflected in everyday communication: "What's *his story*, anyway," someone asks a friend, whom a coworker is mistreating. "This is the story I'm living," one best friend says to another. "My life is a never-ending drama!" Persons pursue stories, often to clarify, and sometimes to be certain about, what those stories mean and the role they play in our lives. Yet, the pursuit of insight about stories of struggle can be tricky, and often the ways we pursue insight and growth amplify the very struggles persons are working to overcome. Stories diversely shape lives in ways that are, at once, exhilarating and arduous, rewarding and worrisome.

My story aims to compassionately explore what it might look like and mean to relate more mindfully, and to be more mindful persons, even as life sometimes makes this relating and being painful. I use narrative fragments from a number of relational contexts in my lived experience to show—to creative and reflexively "story"—how mindfulness can be marred by mindlessness, and sometimes or often in complicated ways. My aim is to show tensions between the two practices, and how mindfulness can offer an instructive way to cool the burn that can accompany persons' stories living with life's difficulties.

◀

It is 1995 and I am working in music radio as a disc jockey. Being in between full-time jobs at the time, I am driving between Chicago, where I live, and Peoria, Illinois, where I work part time at Mix 93.3. The weekly trek provides ample windshield time, prompting lots of time for thinking, and, in turn, frustration about where I am, and where I want to be, in my life.

The radio profession at this time is all about landing on-air positions in key timeslots, such as mornings, midday, afternoons, or evenings. "How many (audition) tapes you got out?" a friend asks me, concerned about my search. I respond, "I've got a few. Maybe a few more going out tomorrow. I'm still on it." The nature of the hunt is draining, as it requires applicants to be regularly searching for the next perfect "gig," creating the "tightest demo," and submitting an application package that grabs attention and demonstrates personalities at our best. This means guessing what radio programmers want in and out of me—that is, which "me" will be presented and how. "I just don't think I'm what they want," I confess to a friend. "They want someone different. I can try to tweak my demo to make it work. We'll see."

⬅

I identify as an agnostic Buddhist. Appealing to me are the ways Buddhism as a life philosophy offers open and non-judgmental learning about relating to ourselves and others in our ever-complex worlds. Its teachings instruct people to embrace the impermanence of life (i.e., change is constant, nothing's permanent) and the universality of suffering or dissatisfaction in/with our lives. Of particular interest is how people work to alleviate the dissatisfaction. Central to Buddhist teachings are the ways breathing is and should be a centering place for persons amid good and bad times, an anchor always there, even when we're not thinking about it. Also central is the dedication to living mindfully.

Mindlessness and mindfulness dwell as twin impulses present in communication and communicators. Each is not possible without the other.

"Mindfulness" is the simple but challenging practice and process of becoming more present with/for others and ourselves, noticing as much as we possibly can in experience from one moment to the next, and working to interact more compassionately (see Chödrön, 2002, 2010). It entails peacefully aspiring to explore our "attachments," or the ways people cling—sometimes feverously and often outside our awareness—to others, experiences, ideas, feelings, objects, etc., and to the stories we tell ourselves. Mindfulness means relating through loving kindness, which includes working to befriend ourselves. As friends, we try to live as openly as possible, prioritizing care and peace; in this sense, we aim to minimize criticism and harm, toward ourselves and others. Mindfulness entails sharing the gift of "presence" (Hanh, 2001), "being here" directly, without deception, gently, and playfully as we relate to/with others, ourselves and experiences "as they are."

"Mindlessness" involves relating to/in life simplistically (see Langer, 1989). It entails using narrow-minded and categorical thinking/feeling. Judgment, stereotypes, and cultural scripts comprise mindlessness. Persons interact through overly strict rules and automatic or habitual behaviors. Doing so often closes persons to possibilities for living and learning, and can create any number of problems (e.g., lack of awareness, cold and distant relationships with others and ourselves).

Mindfulness instructs people to be introspective, to recognize and affirm our ways of living and the inherent interconnectedness of people. It invites us to learn from moments of mindlessness, and to do so in ways that stress acceptance and wellbeing. As I convey the stories in the remainder of the chapter, I sporadically use *italics* to recognize and share the insights that come to me through my attempts to reflect and write mindfully.

*You practice opening the heart, eyes, ears and other senses in any given moment. The pull of familiar and safe things and habits, the possibility of getting attached to them, and, yet, the competing goal not to be attached to anything—the combination of responses appears in waves. You notice yourself noticing the competing and recognize how difficult trying to focus can be.*

*You're known to blast the volume on your television. The quiet and still space that immediately follows turning off the television grabs your attention in calming ways. As intimidating as mediation sounds, you are reminded there's something to stillness.*

*You sometimes catch yourself holding your breath, naturally. Amused and intrigued you think about why this is so, about the other things onto which you might still be holding, and about how experiences and relating might be different, airier and lighter even, with more breath.*

Windshield time is also spent ruminating about not yet having "come out" as a gay man. These thoughts are persistent, sometimes racing, and rarely satisfying.

"It's time to finally be yourself."

"Do it, but you cannot tell your grandparents."

"Coming out will show that I am proud of who I am."

"Inch your way out; you're 'bi' and not gay."

"It's about time," I judge harshly and project critique on others. "At least you don't do drag."

"I'm a 'masculine' gay man, 'normal' and 'sane.'"

"I am 'straight acting.'"

These thoughts link coming out with strategic and evaluative work that is tiring, sometimes exhausting. I plan who will know first—"Kathleen, my sister, we're close and she's the safest." "Mom next, as she'll probably get it more." "My friend Robert next, because he's my best friend. I don't want him to be hurt if others, say less close friends, hear the news before him."

Planning like this also requires a rigorous practice of self-restraint and self-control. Loving allies stress, "Remember, sweetie, coming out is a process, not an event. Don't go too fast." I vacillate between moments of wanting no one and everyone to know. "What business is it of others?" clashes with "Why wouldn't I share who I am…if there's nothing 'wrong' with it." For something like being myself, which I want to feel as "natural" and comfortable, my coming out process often feels fabricated and forced.

Through these preoccupations I am submerged within relating that entices and compels movement *toward* something. I await and plan for the next radio gig. The worries illustrate "in-between" moments in which I focus on where I am going, who I will be, or who I was, rather than where and who I am—and the beauty and importance of that—in any one given moment. They comprise rumination of the sort that Buddhists tend to refer to as "monkey brain" or "monkey mind." They steer my attention to specific and often limiting ways of interacting and being. Searching for a better experience, and perhaps a newer and improved "me," they are shards of past mindless burn.

⊟

*You believe in living in the "now." Yet, stories typically involves the past in some way. You wonder about the relationships persons have with stories, and how storytelling might inadvertently encourage holding on. You've been there quite a few times.*

*"There is no one else to be than who we are right now." You believe this teaching in theory; yet recognize how challenging it is to "do" interactions*

*and relationships in such a way. You no longer feel the same anger with others, known and unknown, who have tried to convince you otherwise. You fear how homophobia entices LGBT—especially young LGBT—to believe that who they are, and those whom they love, as is, are not enough.*

*You hear endeared others persistently tell big stories to others, stories about experiences in which you were involved. Those stories are told in ways that involve great embellishment or outright lying. Remembering we are all connected, all one, the storytelling concerns you. You wonder about their relationship to burn, and where those stories take them.*

◄]

I have a tricky relationship with "positive thinking." I was reared to focus on and emphasize the positive, and thankfully so. This emphasis often has carried me through hardship, and still today, my first impulse tends to be positive. Still, relating like this has not necessarily been free of complications.

"This, too, shall pass."

"As you think it, so shall you be."

"You gather more bees with honey."

"Happy thoughts!"

"If you can conceive it, you can achieve it."

"Accentuate the positive."

"Keep your eyes on the finish line."

"Begin with the end in mind."

Like an Olympic athlete whose training for the gold is accompanied by dedicated focus and visualization, I lived my training within realms of positivity—indeed, a deceptively endearing relational partner—passionately and strictly. The messages were rigid. With no or less room for alternate focuses and realities, or other meanings and interpretations, I lived positivity in ways that often were harsh and less complex.

◄]

*Mindfulness entails working to live gently and softly, and to do less harm to ourselves and others. You reflect on the rather intense ways you were fooled by positivity, and perhaps, how you fooled yourself.*

*You think of the ways mindfulness challenges persons to stay with suffering, to not run and hide, as our ways of relating to those experiences perhaps serve as the most profound teacher of who we are and how we relate to ourselves and others. You smile and continue reflecting.*

⊡

I first came to mindfulness, or perhaps it came to me, through self-help programs. Before coming out, I became a huge fan of Leo Buscaglia, the late professor of education and famous self-help guru. I was enamored with the ways Buscaglia and other public figures like him at the time made mindfulness seem. Or perhaps it was more how *I* took to their teachings. They were people whom I did not know, but with whom I held a powerful relationship. Indeed, I was hooked, drawn to what I believed effective mindfulness to be, much like a mosquito is drawn to a glowing and humming bug light.

Knowing dark experiences and thoughts, I was drawn to the *lightness* exuded from their enthusiasm. Their teachings emphasized the positive, and in airy and good-feeling ways. Having known feelings of not being included as I saw others being in the past, I swam in the promise of *acceptance*. If only I lived positively, I would feel included and better. I identified with and quickly took to a mission of *kindness*, for life had provided me my fair share of the opposite. Sunken by the prospect that if I didn't do something, if I didn't change in some specific way, I might end up unhappy, persuasive messages encouraging *joy* felt automatically attractive. I was titillated by the prospect of bliss, and dedicated myself to living in ways that would set aside hints of despair. A need for *love*, for *self-love*, carried me and guided it all. My relationship with self-help discourse was emotional and personal. I was "in it to win it."

Yet, relating to the positive in this way helped create an unplanned outcome: a de-emphasis on the importance of engaging and learning about the negative, about engaging human suffering. There's a way in which such relating charmed me into only studying difficulties and hardship superficially, presuming that "the negative" would prevent me from living positively. Talking about negative stuff would make me a negative person. In this sense, although I felt I was living "mindfully," actually I lived in ways that were selectively mindful, or perhaps, a cherry-picked mindfulness.

⊡

*You remember learning about how persons instinctively put on "armor" to create security and protection when facing difficulties. You laugh to yourself, thinking how good you used to be "armoring up."*

*You think about how, like in my story of the children on the beach, at those earlier times in your life, you were not ready to deal with the fear tied up with these challenging situations. Perhaps dissatisfaction meant danger. Perhaps you befriended yourself in the best ways you knew how, through self-protection, even as it sometimes closed you to the learning that could happen from taking more risks.*

*You think about how "ice-cube therapy" might have been soothing temporarily, but ultimately, better ways of befriending yourself, more open ways, awaited you.*

Time and practice have helped me reshape and expand the ways I relate to the uncertainty and burn of hardship. Of course, difficult issues like homophobia in US culture had no plans of going away on their own. In fact, the ways in which I engaged these burns only increased when left unattended. Yet, in many ways, I stumbled into a greater comfort level. I laughed, cried, yelled, dwelled, and festered through many moments that, as time passed, I began looking at and living through differently. I began to notice myself being more "okay" with each moment, a feeling of "okayness" which I was interested in building. Still, inseparable from this evolution were other changes that occurred that provided a perspective through which I could be more mindful, and more properly so.

The self I brought into relationships changed quite dramatically since my days in radio. I was out, happy and proud, and no longer had the fears of the closet with which to contend. "I'm so glad those days are behind me," I would often say to friends and family. "It was a different culture we faced then, more hate, less acceptance. No positive role models." Discrimination and marginalization were especially strong in the late '90s, when I came out, which made contending with homophobia and heteronormativity tough. Indeed, still today, amid some positive change concerning LGBT civil rights, much work remains uncompleted. Nevertheless, no longer having a secret to hold, I could be myself more easily. The burn, and my relationship to it, lessened and shifted.

Relationships maintained through this process challenged me to expand my comfort levels with the negative, encouraging me to see value in exploring different ways to bravely *value* and *use* the burn. They helped teach me to think differently about what burn was, what it meant, and how it could be used for something better and invaluable. In this sense, storytelling assisted me in seeing more clearly the mindfulness lessons instructing people to use our relationship to suffering as the best teacher we have.

Yet, living this story in these newer ways also came with risks. I still had developed very familiar and trusted ways of grasping difficult interactions and uncertainties. Contemplating taking on research projects about highly personal issues, I sometimes would share with friends, "I don't want to hurt in my writing the people I still care about." "I know I'm ready, but am I *really ready*?" I was ready enough. I adopted a spirit of experimentation through my writing, trusting that writing reflexively would offer a viable pathway for exploring relational difficulties and complexities, for beginning to understand what I had not yet learned how to understand, the ways in which I had not yet learned how to learn.

Reflexive writing became an open space in which to play with ideas, experiences, relationships and hurt, to make sense more mindfully of the stuff through which I was working. In this sense, reflexivity has enabled invaluable opportunities for working in novel ways, and for performing myself differently (see Berry, 2013). Indeed, experimenting through story enabled direct, yet more gentle and open, ways to reconcile burn and understand myself and others anew. Although always still connected to others, it has enabled a different type of turning inward, so as to more fully and comfortably understand the happenings and complexities and joys and pains of living outwardly.

*You "end" this story feeling as though you have a fuller understanding of burn, the protective ways of relating to/with burn, and the complex ways in which this burn has impacted you. You're happy for only feeling acceptance—not self-regret—for past difficulties. However, should regret arise, you have grown to be more open to gently recognizing the feelings and considering what it might teach you. You have learned to "let go" more frequently and, usually, more compassionately.*

*Your mind races and wanders far less than it did in the past. When it does veer from the present moment, you notice that shift more readily, and judge it less. You notice the calmness that comes with this awareness. In these moments, you are being more mindful than mindless. You are cultivating mindfulness itself.*

*You remain convinced we all have a story, a story made up of many stories that matter to others and ourselves. They are stories intertwined with the relationships in our lives, stories with which we must contend. Yet, you see mostly harm in believing there is any good reason to "correct" our stories or get them "right." Still, because interactions, relationships and identities are processes that we negotiate with others and ourselves, you know the demands for correction will continue.*

*You are tempted to write in ways that make for a big and powerful conclusion to this chapter, to get this story "right." Like all stories, because this one is always and already in progress, you end by simply noting the temptation. You hope this story benefits others and yourself in ways that resonate with what it means to all our respective days at the beach.*

## Questions and Activities for Discussion

1. Berry writes that "persons pursue stories, often to clarify, and sometimes to be certain about, what those stories mean and the role they play in our lives. Yet, the pursuit of insight about stories of struggle can be tricky, and often the ways we pursue insight and growth amplify the very struggles persons are working to overcome." What are some stories you are pursuing? Consider the stories and italicize (i.e., write/think) the ways you are being mindful and mindless.

2. In what ways does Berry work to mindfully (re)imagine connections and issues between mindfulness, mindlessness, and communication? When is it important to be mindful in our relationships? Is it ever okay to be mindless? How does the particular relationship influence this?

3. Berry talks in some ways about how expected response and relational expectations about disclosures are part of mindfulness. How does the role of uncertainty and self-disclosure work in a relational context?

## Note

1. I want to thank my colleague and friend Chris Patti for his returning me to this passage, for our dialogue on the project, and for his own mindful work on compassionate communication (see, for example, Patti, 2012).

## For Further Reading and Reference

Berry, K. (2013). Spinning autoethnographic reflexivity, cultural critique and negotiating selves. In S. Holman Jones, T. E. Adams, & C. Ellis (Eds.), *The handbook of autoethnography* (pp. 209–227). Walnut Grove, CA: Left Coast Press, Inc.

Chödrön, P. (2002). *When things fall apart: Heart advice for difficult times.* Boston: Shambhala.

Chödrön, P. (2010). *The wisdom of no escape and the path of loving-kindness.* Boston: Shambhala.

Hanh, T. N. (2001). *Anger: Wisdom for cooling the flames.* New York: Berkeley.

Langer, E. J. (1989). *Mindfulness.* Reading, MA: Perseus Books.

Patti, C. J. (2012). Split shadows: Myths of a lost father and son. *Qualitative Inquiry, 18,* 153–161.

Yoshino, K. (2007). *Covering: The hidden assault on our civil rights.* New York: Random

# Case 9

# "Are You Calling Me a Slut?"
## Sharing Personal Information
## in Close Relationships

Kate Magsamen-Conrad

*Keywords:* disclosure outcomes, relationship expectations,
self-disclosure

Relationships are communication. They are how we learn about each
other. They are how we share our fears, joys, and sorrows. Communication is also what constitutes our relationships. Sometimes it is easy
to share our personal information with others, whereas at other times
it seems more complicated. We may have a variety of reasons why we
will or will not share certain information with certain individuals.

## Hannah's Story

Kaitlyn and I have been friends for seven years. We are very close. We
have the kind of relationship that I know will last. I can picture her in
my wedding someday. I went to take this survey for one of my classes,
and they asked me to tell them about something I hadn't shared with a
friend. It's about Kaitlyn. Well, it's about my feelings about something
Kaitlyn is doing. I've talked with some of our friends about this, and
we all feel the same way. But I was pretty scared about trying to tell
*Kaitlyn* what I think about this—trying to figure out how to put it into
words. And I was afraid that she wouldn't want to be friends with me
anymore if I told her. I was *certain* that it would not go well, at least initially. I knew it would hurt her feelings. I thought it would cause some
drama in our group of friends. But I'm scared and I think she's going
to get hurt so I felt I needed to tell her. And I'd been thinking about

*Inside Relationships: A Creative Casebook in Relational Communication*, edited by
Sandra L. Faulkner, 97–101. © 2013 Left Coast Press, Inc. All rights reserved.

it since that survey a few weeks ago. So I decided to text her about it. Here's what happened:

**12:35 a.m.**

Me: Heyy

K:   What's up, girl?

Me: U studying?

K:   no!

Me: Theres something ive been wanting to talk to you about…

K:   k?

Me: I don't want you to be mad at me though

K:   hannah just tell me

Me: forget about it, your going to get upset

K:   we have been friends forever…just tell me!

K:   I promise I wont be mad. You know you can tell me anything

**12:45 a.m.**

Me: Im kinda scared about how you act at parties

K:   what do you mean

**12:50 a.m.**

Me: like I think sometimes you can get a little out of hand. Sometimes I feel like you drink too much to try to forget your problems

Me: and im scared your gonna get hurt sometime

Me: like that guys are gonna take advantage of you

Me: I love you and don't want to see you get hurt

Me: please don't be mad at me

**1:05 a.m.**

Me: Kaitlyn?

Me: i knew I should of listened to Clarissa and not even brought this up

**1:10 a.m.**

K:   Well you basically just called me a slut

Me: no I didn't Kaitlyn…I said im concerned for your safety. This isn't an attack on you and im not trying to make you feel like we are all ganging up on you. I just want to make sure that you are being safe when we go out

K:   I don't understand

Me: don't take this the wrong way because I certainly don't think you are a slut but I just think that sometimes guys might get the wrong impression because you try to "get with them" so much

K: k

K: like when?

Me: Like last night when we went to Mu Theta's party...you slammed the rest of your beer, took a shot, grabbed another beer and then said "my goal is to go home with Dave tonight"

K: I don't remember that ever happening

Me: I didn't think you would and that's why I wanted to bring it up to you, girl

K: was I really THAT bad?

Me: kinda....

K: I am really sorry.....

K: I didn't think I was ever that bad

Me: Its okay, girl. We made sure you were safe and got home but we all jus want to make sure that you can take care of yourself. You know what I mean?

**1:30 a.m.**

Me: Do you think we could maybe try to work on this? I would be willing to help you with it....maybe we could all do it together? Kind of like a pact to each other to make sure we are all taking care of ourselves and each other?

K: I would really like that...I have been tryng to cover up my problems by drinking and I know its not healthy

Me: I am totally willing to try to help you with this, girl. That's what friends are for, riight?

K: I am really glad you told me about this. Its nice to know that some people really do care about my health and safety

Me: I hope youd do the same thing for me if you were worried about me

Me: I love you

K: I love you too, girl

As you can see, it went a lot better than I expected. True, I didn't discuss *everything* that was bothering me about the situation. But I feel like it could have gone a lot worse. And I'm even more certain that we will be friends forever.

## Questions and Activities for Discussion

1. What makes information personal, private, or secret? What kinds of things (e.g., the information, the relationship, whose perspective) do people think about when they are considering sharing personal or private information with others? How do the potential response and expected outcome play a role? Does the manner in which one discloses information matter (e.g., text message, Instant Message)?

2. Think about a secret or private piece of information (e.g., coming out, worry about a partner's behavior) that you have not shared with a friend, family member or romantic partner. Would you plan the inter-action? How would time and past responses play a role in the disclo-sure? Write a script for the disclosure.

3. How did the disclosure between Hannah and Kaitlyn affect their rela-tionship? How do you think the interaction might have been different if the information had been about Hannah instead of about Hannah's fear about Kaitlyn's actions? What other reactions could Kaitlyn have had? How would that have affected the interaction and ultimately their relationship?

## For Further Reading and Reference

Afifi, T., & Afifi, W. (2009). (Eds.). *Uncertainty, information management, and disclosure: Decisions, theories and applications.* New York: Routledge.

Dindia, K. (2002). Self-disclosure research: Knowledge through meta-analysis. In M. Allen, R. Preiss, B. Gayle, & N. Burrell (Eds.), *Interpersonal communica-tion research: Advances through meta-analysis* (pp. 169–185). Mahwah, NJ: Lawrence Erlbaum.

Friedman, A. L., & Bloodgood, B. (2010). 'Something we'd rather not talk about': Findings from CDC exploratory research on sexually transmitted disease communication with girls and women. *Journal of Women's Health, 19*(10), 1823–1831.

Greene, K., Derlega, V. J., & Mathews, A. (2006). Self-disclosure in personal rela-tionships. In A. L. Vangelisti & D. Perlman (Eds.), *The Cambridge handbook of personal relationships* (pp. 409–427). Cambridge, UK: Cambridge University Press.

Greene, K., Magsamen-Conrad, K., Venetis, M. K., Checton, M. G., Bagdasarov, Z., & Banerjee, S. C. (2012). Assessing health diagnosis disclosure decisions in relationships: Testing the disclosure decision-making model. *Health Commu-nication, 27*, 356–368.

Miller-Ott, A. E., Kelly, L., Duran, R. L. (2012). The effects of cell phone usage rules on satisfaction in romantic relationships. *Communication Quarterly,* *60*(1), 17–34.

Petronio, S. (2002). *Boundaries of privacy: Dialectics of disclosure.* Albany: State University of New York Press.

Venetis, M. K., Greene, K., Magsamen-Conrad, K., Banerjee, S. C., Checton, M. G., & Bagdasarov, Z. (2012). "You can't tell anyone but..." Exploring the use of privacy rules and boundary management. *Communication Monographs, 79,* 344–365.

# Chapter 4

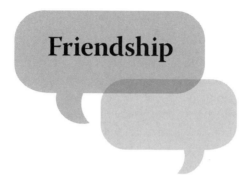

# Friendship

Chapter 4 explores what we mean by friendship, how we develop and maintain friendships, and the role they play in our relational lives. In a photo-essay, Lindsey Boyd represents interviews with friends about how situation, environment and personal dispositions influenced the formation of their romantic relationships and friendships. Galbus's meditation on the lack of scripts for the ending of friendships asks us to consider what friends mean in the context of our lives, and the Martha's Vineyard Communication Association gives us a story of how a group of friends and colleagues contend with illness in their friendship circle. All of these cases present the role of friendship in our lives as multi-faceted; what do you consider to be the most important characteristics of a friend? Should a friend be loyal, trustworthy, similar, supportive, fun? Students usually list these as the most important qualities when I ask them what being a friend means. I add *voluntary* to the list of friendship characteristics, especially when compared with other relationships, such as family and work. We make a conscious choice to be friends with someone, though definitions of friend differ depending on the level of intimacy, from best friends to casual friends (Hays, 1985), and by activity, whether we engage in doing (instrumental goals) or being (social support) more often. Rawlins (2009) tells us that friendship offers "compelling ideals and concrete

*Inside Relationships: A Creative Casebook in Relational Communication*, edited by Sandra L. Faulkner, 103–106. © 2013 Left Coast Press, Inc. All rights reserved.

practices for grappling ethically with the challenges of contemporary life" (p. 11). This suggests friendship serves an important function in our relational lives, from personal enhancement and task fulfillment to social and material support.

## Relational Dialectics Theory

Relational Dialectics Theory (RDT) can help us frame our experiences of friendship (and other close relationships) because of a focus on central and marginalized discourses in relational life and how meaning is constructed from the interplay of competing discourses (Baxter & Braithwaite, 2008). *Discourse* references cultural and personal talk about relationships, such as what we say to one another and what we see in movies and magazines. Unlike many relational theories, the focus is on discourse rather than the individual as the unit of analysis; we ask what does cultural and personal talk about relationships tell us? Our task is "to understand how the interplay of discourses constructs meaning" (Baxter, 2011, p. 13), how relationships are constructed through talk and the communication practices of the involved parties. The idea is that the discourse present in our relationships and in our larger cultural worlds can create tension when different messages exist. "Power resides in the systems of meaning—the discourses—through which social reality as we know it is constructed" (Baxter, 2011, p. 124). Getting to define social reality is power. That is, we experience tension between the meaning of the past and present in our relationships, our interactions with others, including larger cultural messages we talk about, in addition to what we think others will say and how they will respond to us. For example, what happens if a friend moves away? Are you still friends? How often and how do you talk? There are some ideas in popular culture that friendship is fragile (Wiseman, 1986). Public breakups of friendships, such as being unfriended on Facebook can be painful (Bevan, Pfyl & Barclay, 2012). However, Becker et al. (2009) found that geographic distance may change a close relationship into a more distant one, but individuals are able to maintain their friendships. These researchers suggest we consider a friendship to be more flexible than fragile; that is we alter our friendships through changes in commitment and maintenance behaviors to accommodate our needs inside and outside our relationships.

In another example, Faulkner and her colleagues (2011) studied sexual and relational health messages in media targeted toward women who have sex with women (WSW) to find that competing discourses must be negotiated in order to make the sexual lives and sexual health of WSW intelligible. The emphasis on knowing one's own body, exploring one's desire and pleasure, being conscious of identities and the role of social networks, and especially talking to partners about sexual pleasure and desire contrasted with discourse of WSW's sexual shame, invisibility, and silence. Through the use of individual and coupled women's stories in sexuality education texts and magazines, media texts contended with the competition between discourses by giving voice to marginalized discourses. That is, the voicing of marginal discourses of relational identities and behaviors is set against dominant ideas of static notions of identity and conceptualizations of WSW's sexuality to ultimately transform WSW's sexuality and provide new meaning, a discursive transformation.

In regard to friendship in particular, Rawlins, (2009) focuses a dialectic perspective on examining the tensions of being friends. For instance, the dialectic of *private and public* shows us the voluntary nature of friendship and the concomitant challenges. Because friendship complements, competes with, and/or replaces other personal relationships we have, there is a tension between how we integrate it into our personal and social worlds. Do you hang out with your friends or a romantic partner or your mom if you have a day off from work? Other tensions in friendships include ideas of the self as *independent and dependent*, one is an individual and a part of a social group, and between the *ideal and real*. We experience tension between cultural ideas of friendship and how these ideas play out in our everyday enactment of being friends. No one can live up to the ideal standards, though we use these ideals to judge our friendships. We experience tensions between *expressiveness and protectiveness*, between wanting to be open and needing to be discreet. Do you tell your friend you hate her new partner? Do you tell your friend you know his boyfriend is cheating on him?

## Ethical Practices of Friendship

All of the cases in this chapter reflect and embody ideals of friendship and what Rawlins (2009) would label ethical practices. I reiterate the voluntary nature of friendship to suggest the behavior that helps maintains friendship entails mutual concern, trust, honesty, equality, learning about the other; in other words, friendship is a "conscientiously interested" relationship (Rawlins, 2009). When we are happy with our friends, we often enhance our positive evaluations of them (Morry, Reich & Kito, 2010). Friendship can lead one to participate in larger political discourse as Rawlins (2009) argues, "Conscientious interest in others cultivated through personal friendships and friendship networks can provide an ethical pull toward broader political activity" (p. 184). Imagine if the friend circle described in Shepler and Duggan's case study began a support group for others affected by cancer. Imagine if they determined such cancers are often due to environmental causes and began a group who targeted policy makers, specifically engaging others to change environmental law. This would illustrate engagement with the dialectic of *acceptance and judgment* (who we are and who we should become) as well as *affection and instrumentality* (caring for and using friendship). We determine what differences matter and play up our similarities. We balance needs for support from our friends with caring for them.

## References

Baxter, L. (2011). *Voicing relationships: A dialogic perspective.* Thousand Oaks, CA: Sage.

Baxter, L. A., & Braithwaite, D. O. (Eds.). (2008). *Engaging theories in interpersonal communication: Multiple perspectives.* Thousand Oaks, CA: Sage.

Bevan, J. L., Pfyl, J., & Barclay, B. (2012). Negative emotional and cognitive consequences to being unfriended on Facebook: An exploratory study. *Computers in Human Behavior, 28,* 1458–1464.

Becker, J. A. H., Johnson, A. J., Craig, E. A., Gilchrist, E. S., Haigh, M. M., & Lane, L. T. (2009). Friendships are flexible, not fragile: Turning points in geographically-close and long-distance friendships. *Journal of Social & Personal Relationships, 26*(4), 347–369.

Faulkner, S. L., Davis, A. M., Hicks, M. V., & Lannutti, P. J. (2011, November). A Content Analysis of Sexual and Relational Health Messages for Women Who Have Sex with Women. Paper presented at the annual meeting of the National Communication Association, New Orleans, Louisiana.

Hays, R. B. (1985). A longitudinal study of friendship development. *Journal of Personality and Social Psychology, 48,* 909–924.

Morry, M. M., Reich, T., & Kito, M. (2010). How do I see you relative to myself? Relationship quality as a predictor of self- and partner-enhancement within cross-sex friendships, dating relationships, and marriages. *Journal of Social Psychology, 150*(4), 369–392.

Rawlins, W. (2009). *The compass of friendship: Narratives, identities, and dialogues.* Thousand Oaks, CA: Sage.

Wiseman, J. P. (1986). Friendship: Bonds and binds in a voluntary relationship. *Journal of Social and Personal Relationships, 3,* 191–211.

# Case 10

# Our Choice without a Choice
## Similarities in Friendships and Romantic Relationships

### Lindsey T. Boyd

*Keywords:* attraction, expectations, face-work, friendships, romantic relationships

## My Photo Project: Tying It Together

The photo-essay that follows is a project on college friendships and romantic relationships that I completed for a relational communication course. My task was to interview university students (two men and two women) about friendships and romantic relationships they had initiated after starting college. I interviewed my friends, because I thought they would be the ones that would feel the most comfortable talking with me. I also thought they would be completely honest in their answers.

The two women whom I interviewed were my roommates for three years and my friends since my first semester in college. I watched their romantic relationships and friendships throughout the years, so it was interesting to get their perspective on what worked or didn't work. As a relational outsider, it is a lot easier to be critical about the way things function. You aren't emotionally committed to your friend's significant other, so it is easy to think of getting rid of him or her! As I interviewed the women, I realized that they had both met their boyfriends in a bar and had similar problems in their relationships. I knew that they valued a lot of the same things in their friendships, because they had been good friends with each other and me for four years.

*Inside Relationships: A Creative Casebook in Relational Communication,* edited by Sandra L. Faulkner, 107–115. © 2013 Left Coast Press, Inc. All rights reserved.

The two men I interviewed I also had known since my freshman year of college. The two men met freshman year, joined the same fraternity, and have been friends ever since. I knew that both of them would feel comfortable talking to me about their relationships because they had both come to me previously for relationship advice. They both met their girlfriends at their fraternity's weekend party. They had a lot of the same reasons for being in their romantic relationships, but they had different reasons for leaving the relationships. They used fraternity parties as a way to get to know women and initiated relationships with the women who continued to show up at the weekend parties. If the women were around often and if they continued to come around, it was easy for the men to fall into a relationship.

I decided to make a visual representation of the relationships I talked about with my interviewees. In my relational communication course, we often discussed the concept of "face." I think that when we choose a relationship and commit to a relationship, it is because of the face that we represent and the face we feel fits our life style. I blacked or whited out the faces of the interviewees and their significant others. The white faces represent the women and their relationships. The black faces represent the men and their relationships. On the relational partner's face, I used words to describe where the relationship started and the characteristics that attracted him or her to that relationship. On the interviewees' faces, I put the challenges with the relationship and why the relationships didn't work.

## Romantic Relationships

### The Make Up to Break Up Relationship

When I interviewed Bree about her one-year romantic relationship, she was upset. As her close friend, I knew it would be difficult for her to talk about, but I found out a lot about the relationship I didn't know. They met in a bar one night through mutual friends and really hit it off from the beginning. She had had one serious relationship in her life before meeting him, but he seemed to be the kind of guy she had always pictured herself with. He was a great time. They enjoyed going to the bars together. She loved that he loved her friends. He understood when she had a bad day. He knew how to make her laugh, even on her worst days. She found him attractive, which kept her interested. They had mutual friends, which brought them together in the first place.

However, there were a lot of issues that tore them apart. He cheated multiple different times. He would leave her if he wasn't feeling comfortable in the relationship, but then he would show back up when he decided he felt comfortable again. When she wanted to know where he was, he would not tell her, even if he was with his mother. Every time they broke up, Bree felt like she wasn't good enough for him. Every time he would cheat, she wanted to know why he couldn't just be satisfied with her. She found him to be too emotional at times, but he found her to be too emotional all the time.

The relationship was convenient because they had the mutual friends, and they had common interests that kept them together. She felt that because he lived across the street from her, it kept their relationship going for as long as it lasted. Eventually, she left the relationship physically, but she said that emotionally she is still committed to him. The "make up to break up" couple is something many of us have witnessed. It is common, especially in college relationships. Bree thinks that Drew still might be the one, and she is holding out for him to change and for him to commit.

## The On Again, Off Again

Michelle met Dave one night at a bar and that has been the basis for their relationship. When they don't really have anything else to do, they go to the bar together. She loved that he was caring and that he would show up just to say "hi." She explained that she could really see a future with him because he was her first long relationship. They had been together for a year, but had broken up several times. He got along well with her family, for the most part, and he really worked to help his family out as much as he could because they had problems. Michelle respected him for that because she would do the same for her family. She felt like they were both goofy and generally had a great time together.

There were a lot of issues in the relationship that kept pulling them apart, though. He lied all of the time and not about things that were normal things to lie about. He would lie on Facebook about trips he was taking when he was actually staying with her. He moved in to her house without paying for rent, groceries, or bills. He used her truck a few times without asking and drove it all the way to Michigan for things with his family. He continued to talk to another woman he had dated before and told Michelle he missed the other woman while he and Michelle were together. He worked during the summer, and he would leave for four months without a trace. Then he would show back up in to her life like nothing had ever happened.

## The Should Have, Could Have

Eric met his girlfriend at a fraternity party. She was his first serious relationship. A lot of the reason that they got along was because of their proximity; they were always together, so it was easy to make a relationship happen. They had many mutual friends, so they continued to run in to each other. They had a lot of fun together at parties with friends. It was easy for them to make plans because they usually ended up in the same place anyway. He found her to be funny and attractive. He felt like she cared about him more than anyone had ever cared about him; she was loyal to him in that he never had to worry about her cheating on him. They had little fights like any other couple, but it wasn't anything too outrageous.

The distance that they were apart over the summer is what ended their relationship. They were only talking a few times a week; the internet wasn't maintaining their relationship in the way he would have liked. In order to sort out what he felt about her, he started dating someone new without telling her. When they got back to school, they had a hard time because she found out about the other woman. Eventually, he broke things off with her, but he claimed he didn't really know why they never got back together. They never had *the conversation* about breaking up; they both just accepted that it was over. He still misses her, but he can't talk to her about it.

### The Love To Hate

Josh met his girlfriend at a fraternity party that she went to every weekend, and they began to talk. They had a lot of mutual friends, so a relationship developed easily. Her humor and outgoing demeanor were attractive. He brought her home multiple times, and his family really liked her. She talked on the phone to his sister once a week. He described her as "a little crazy," but the drama in the relationship made things more exciting for him. He said he never really knew what would happen and that was a good thing. They didn't fall into a routine.

After a year, she started talking to him about getting married and quitting school. She kept bringing up having kids and starting a family with him. He freaked out and started to back away from the relationship. The more he backed away, the more phone calls his sister got about him, the more phone calls his friends got about him, and the more she showed up at his house unannounced. He found out that she already had one kid, and that she didn't even live on campus. She started to seem a little too crazy, though the drama was what excited him about her in the first place.

# Friendships

In order represent the friendships my interviewees discussed, I took a picture of the friends together, marked out their faces, and put the characteristics they wanted in their friendships on the other person's face. Many of the friendships began because of proximity and continued because of either location or convenience and similar social habits.

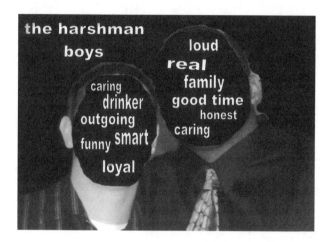

### Eric and Josh—The Harshman Boys

Eric and his friends, including Josh, met in the dorm (Harshman) where they all lived on the same floor. Many of them joined the same fraternity, making it easy to maintain a friendship. He described his friends as funny, loyal, smart, outgoing, caring, and drinkers. A lot of what they do together involves throwing parties. He said that you couldn't expect to be friends with someone if you don't have the same interests. His interests include going out, partying, and having a good time.

Josh had a lot of friends because of the fraternity that he joined. He also lived in Harshman and met a lot of the same people as Eric. Josh and Eric joined the same fraternity, and their friendship grew. When Josh described his friends, he used the words loud, real, family, good time, honest, and caring. They went to the same parties every weekend and spent a large amount of time together. He thought his friends at college were similar to his friends from home, making it easy for them to get along. Josh considered that drinking on the weekends brought them closer together, and he felt like they had a lot of the same interests.

### Michelle and Bree—The Slob Squad

Michelle explained that she wanted a friend that was a lot like her. All of her college friends were in the same sorority, and they all left the sorority together and have lived together for the last three years. She looks for friends that are outgoing, fun, trustworthy, real, caring and honest. She considered her friends to be like family and said that these friendships were different than in high school because of the college experience. She felt like they all grew up together.

Bree had the same friends as Michelle. They all lived in the same sorority house, apartment, or off campus house. Bree described her friends as honest, caring, funny, hungry, partiers, and laid back. The women spent all of their time together and reminded Bree of a lot of her friends from home. She considered her friends from home to be her best friends, so it was nice to find friends at college who were similar. She said it made the transition to college and the friendships easier.

## The Environment Is Most Important

I enjoyed doing this project because it gave me an opportunity to look at the relationships around me. I was able to connect with two sets of friends in a way that I didn't think was possible. I knew that they were close, but I didn't realize that I could tell the story of their relationships regardless of the person's perspective I was taking. They all shared similar stories of looking for individuals with similar traits. The most important thing that I learned is that many of our relationships are initiated because of convenience. They involve people that have the same interests in close proximity. When I look at my own relationships, I realize that I never really ran into a random person and created a relationship. I feel like a lot of these things are predetermined.

## Questions and Activities for Discussion

1. Boyd contends that as an outsider to the relationships she was describing, it was easier to imagine them dissolving. What role does distance have in reflecting on relationship satisfaction and functioning? How did her role as friend to her interviewees allow her to see and not see? She wrote that "I think that when we choose a relationship and commit to a relationship, it is because of the face that we represent and the face we feel fits our life style."

2. What was the biggest predictor of relationship initiation- environment, situation or personal characteristics? Would this pattern hold for other individual's relationships? Why or why not? Discuss the role that environment, life stage and personal characteristics play in our friendships and romantic relationships.

3. Engage in a similar assignment. Interview a friend about a friendship he or she has and ask the following: 1) what characteristics they desire in a friend; 2) what caused them to initiate a friendship; and 3) was the environment, life stage or personal characteristics most important? Summarize and discuss the meaning of your interview.

## For Further Reading and Reference

Becker, J. A. H., Johnson, A. J., Craig, E. A., Gilchrist, E. S., Haigh, M. M., & Lane, L. T. (2009). Friendships are flexible, not fragile: Turning points in geographically-close and long-distance friendships. *Journal of Social & Personal Relationships, 26*(4), 347–369.

Rawlins, W. (2009). *The compass of friendship: Narratives, identities, and dialogues.* Thousand Oaks, CA: Sage.

Preciado, P. S., Tom A. B, Burk, W. J., Stattin, H., & Kerr, M. (2012). Does proximity matter? Distance dependence of adolescent friendships. *Social Networks, 34*(1), 18–31.

Zurbriggen, E., Ramsey, L., Jaworski, B. (2011). Self- and partner-objectification in romantic relationships: Associations with media consumption and relationship satisfaction. *Sex Roles, 64*(7/8), 449–462.

# Case 11

# Goodbye Friend

### Julia A. Galbus

*Keywords:* dissolution, meditation, relationship rituals, scripts

When I was in the second grade, Michelle was my best friend. I don't remember much about her except that she was beautiful, and newly diagnosed with diabetes. I watched her learn to give herself shots. We spent time together every day, and when we argued, one of our mothers would send us over to the other's house to apologize, with an offering in hand: a stick of Doublemint gum, a strawberry, a daisy. I was being trained to be a friend and remained one until she moved away a year or two later. In high school, I had a friend whose family life was difficult: a stepmother, a dead mother, two reckless brothers, and an alcoholic father. When her boyfriend drowned, I skipped school to sit with her. We took refuge in the basement choir room, a safe place where all feelings were given voice. We sat quietly together. I received a detention for my absence. That was fair and worth the punishment.

I have always had good friends. They have been reliable, engaging, intelligent people who cared about my welfare and who welcomed me into their lives. The strongest ones currently are women with whom I have some history. We met through work or school or the gym. We have enough in common to attend a play or exchange a piece of writing or cook or knit or work out together. Our families overlap, so we celebrate birthdays, holidays, milestones. I neither know nor expect that we will always be friends, but something substantial would have

*Inside Relationships: A Creative Casebook in Relational Communication*, edited by Sandra L. Faulkner, 116–122. © 2013 Left Coast Press, Inc. All rights reserved.

to come between us for the friendship to dissolve. We are loyal, and we appreciate each other. When I think of them, I feel gratitude, support, encouragement. I do my best to offer the same. We know the rhythms of each other's schedules, and we support growth and choices that alter our paths. We adapt to each other.

But behind and beneath my friends' glorious and profound affection lurk the memories of relationships that sputtered out like fireworks, a big bang followed by silence. I do not get to know why the other person made the choice he or she did to sever the relationship, abruptly and deliberately. I may not want to know. A boyfriend once backed out of my driveway on foot, as if he were afraid to turn his back to me, and in his eyes I saw a brutal fear I had never witnessed. His gaze revealed an illness he had mentioned in passing, but it was new to see it unveil itself. Intellectual knowledge pales in the wake of such an experience. We never spoke again. One man left an empty syringe on the kitchen table, an unspoken goodbye and an unambiguous signal. Another one let third-hand gossip determine her departure. She said that someone else said that I said...and that was that. The ending crashes, explodes, or bursts a bubble of sufficiency. Once I learned that a friend had gathered damning evidence from all the people she was close to, just in case she needed it for blackmail. She was a power broker, someone who never trusted because she couldn't be trusted. Another woman had a stash of empty single-serving wine bottles hidden in her glove box, a sign that she had been mired deeply in her own unwillingness to grow beyond where she was that day. When that relationship ended, I let go. She said the words, and I acquiesced. It was time. I changed the locks to my house.

I have lost friends. Sometimes I let others drift away, or I drift myself, or our lives change so much that there isn't enough energy to continue. I have people with whom I used to run, or volunteer, but without that activity, there was no glue. The relationship dissolved. Other friendships never launch because the timing is out of sync. It is normal for ties to wax and wane, to fade with altered circumstance. The endings intrigue me. In stories, I want the conclusion to be both surprising and appropriate. In daily life, I appreciate the formulaic but honestly vague "maybe we can do something sometime." A few endings have been blunt and true. Right after college, one man walked away because he was afraid he had grown emotionally closer to me than to his wife, although we had no romantic attraction. He didn't want to create friction, nor the appearance of a problem. Fair enough: relationships have hierarchies and some outrank others. At least I knew.

With lovers we make formal breaks. We say, I don't want to see you anymore, meaning it somewhat literally: I wish I would not have to see you ever again. Or we thoughtlessly and dishonestly demote the relationship to "mere" friendship, although our friends are often held in higher esteem than some of our former partners. With lovers, the breakups are memorable, monumental, sometimes devastating. We receive blunt force from someone else's choice to sever a tie. Maybe there had been warning signs. Maybe the root cause was more serious than we might have understood at the time. In my experience, it is shocking regardless of whether the break comes from a romantic partner or a friend. And yet, we have cultural norms for handling the romantic disaster, but not for the parting of friends.

I like logic. I appreciate the clean breaks, the artificial "if x then y," where the consequent is known. I think I might have made a good lawyer, being fundamentally adversarial, although the profession would not have suited me otherwise. I like rules to a game, boundaries, guidelines. They suit my sense of fair play. They also implicitly recognize that other people can get hurt, and rules can soften the blow. Sometimes, an unhappy ending is "not personal," but merely a decision made in a way that doesn't please me. It makes sense, then, that implicit contracts inhabit most friendships. Each of us has expectations and preferences. As a friend, I am expected to understand and accommodate the fact that one person can't abide the sound of food being chewed. A roommate can't sleep if there is a dirty dish in the sink. Another one needs a nightlight. A friend develops a code for those situations where she has an obligation for which she'd like company, but doesn't want to impose, so you have clear room to refuse without prejudice. The preferences are instructions for use: this is how I work, and if you want to be my friend, these are my interests, warnings, desires and the behaviors I avoid. We lay out the rules over time, as needed. We might start with simple things, like a preference for Thai food over Korean. Gradually, the deeper issues become apparent. Like water tables, they seep up through the ground, rising after a hard rain. Often they are revealed over time in the same way an old house reveals its structural quirks. The third stair squeaks, as does the second place you step in the master bedroom closet. There are water stains where the roof once leaked. The bathroom tile is original. We excavate. Things crop up. Sometimes what rises is untenable.

One of my contractual desires is a sense of privacy that borders on secrecy. I suspect it stems from my brothers' childhood habit of breaking things I cared about. At the age of ten I decided that if they didn't know which objects mattered, they could not destroy them. Whatever the source of my habitual discretion, there is nothing about me that I want to broadcast to everyone I know. I don't want to be accessible all the time. I turn off my cell phone without anxiety; it doesn't get a place at the table. Too much indiscriminate openness undermines my sense of what defines relationship. If we are the stories we tell, then selecting the story, the variation and the level of detail, is part of the process of creating a relationship. Nobody needs all my stories, nor do I need all of his or hers. I respect the fact that people have personal histories, secrets. Often past events are best unmentioned, not only because they have passed but also because reviving them can be painful. Healing means moving forward, and being open to the moment at hand, not constantly ruminating over old plots. It also means concealing the identity of those who have caused me harm. I have moved on.

At the same time, my professional life has changed my guidelines about what gets told at work. Early in my career, a mentor advised me that power structures affect information and interpretation. He suggested that I tell people as much as I legally could about any professional situation that came up. It avoided some of the worry and wonder, the fiction that we sometimes create to fill the unexpected void. Telling can preserve the peace. Telling can dissolve paranoia, or at least redirect it. Privacy may best be balanced by deliberate openness.

I value the commitments I make. Once I befriend someone, I consider it a promise to support that person's goals, to spend time together, and to be honest, direct and gentle if something comes up that needs to be discussed. I offer my grounded attention. I won't flit off into a stream of advice or comparison. Friends meet the needs of mind and heart. My mind likes logic, clarity, an order to things. My heart likes knowing where it is welcome.

When I work with college freshmen, the traditional sort who tend to be between seventeen and nineteen years old, they usually cling to their recent friendships, believing and hoping their friends will never change, that they will always "be there." This is true, also, for their boyfriends and girlfriends who are in another town. Often, what we really want is to be able to change ourselves, while wishing the other's loyalty and familiarity would stay "the same." The truth is, we are changing. We should be changing, because the opposite is stagnation. Our most fundamental human job is to grow, to evolve and screw up and correct and learn. We should want the same for our friends, even our former friends, even those who left tinder and ashes in their wake.

I understand the desire for permanence, the wish that a magical day would not end, a desire to cling to what is sweet. I have let go of permanence the best I could because I had no choice. Abrupt endings have been forced upon me. I had to feel my way through them, to survive without making good sense of someone's thunderstorm through my life. Endings are difficult, and sometimes predictable. Even when we recognize a familiar rhythm and sense that the energy is dissipating, that our buddy's unique habits grate rather than charm, it is hard. I know I'm done when I'm no longer willing to argue.

I wish that significant friendships had better endings. I wish the end could be formal, and kinder. I wish we had a cultural ritual for announcing an ending when it was appropriate. We do say goodbye when friends move away, but that is not the same. Often, I have suffered more from not knowing than from the pain of information, even if it is inaccurate. I would prefer to learn a painful truth about myself, and move on. There are dozens of situations about which we cannot have answers. Some of them are preventable.

Maybe we don't end things because we are cowards. I was friends with a couple who lived together for five years. The boyfriend began to see someone else, but kept it secret. He planned to leave his girlfriend a note at the house when she was working, hoping to escape without explicit conversation. He wanted what would be easiest for him. He expected her to tell her teenaged children that he had left. When she found him packing, and he admitted his plan, and left slightly more quickly, she was blindsided. Another friend was less lucky. Her girlfriend left but took everything, the furniture and the television, the dishes and the books. Theft from strangers is easier to comprehend than theft from roommates, housemates, soulmates. Still, the capacity of those close to us to inflict deep wounds astounds me every time. We are beyond the territory of apologetic offerings for a minor offense.

Many people are broken, and doing the best they can. They operate from injury so deep that they are unaware that old wounds rule their days. They have to locate and feel their fractures before they can seek healing. When we witness friends in that state, we hope that someday they might decide to open. In the meantime, their injured self is rugged, insular and sharp. We should only befriend with caution.

I don't have answers about how to end friendships. I know what I want lately: to be honest, to be kind, to do the least harm. I want to remember that ultimately each person's life task is to pursue what makes his or her soul sing. If that means I'm left out of the chorus, it has to be okay. Somewhere in a deep, still place, I also realize I was part of each dynamic. I played some role. I made choices to stay, to participate, to look the other way, to be silent.

Friendships end. People go away, or fall apart, or say goodbye, or sneak out. Everything is impermanent. Everyone suffers. But we may also grow. When I consider the loss and grief from former friends, I also remember the ones who remain. One couple took over my kitchen and cooked for our families the day before I got married. Another comes over to cook with me in my new kitchen, and shares the produce from her garden. I have people to call when things fall apart. That is the gift that makes the weight of impermanent friends bearable.

## Questions and Activities for Discussion

1. Galbus mentions that there is no script for breaking off friendships. "And yet, we have cultural norms for handling the romantic disaster, but not for the parting of friends." What does this tell you about forming friendships? About the end of friendships? Write a script from your own life about how friendships begin and end. Would the existence of the script make things easier (the knowing rather than the not knowing)?

2. Write a meditation about lost friendships using Galbus's piece as inspiration. In your writing, discuss the importance of your friendships, how the friendships ended, why you think that may be, and your feelings about the loss.

3. What does it mean to be friends? Do friendships serve different purposes in our lives than romantic relationships? How? Are rules explicit or implicit contracts as Galbus suggests? What happens when a friend breaks the rules?

## For Further Reading and Reference

Diggs, R. C., & Clark, K. D. (2002). *It's a struggle but worth It*: Identifying and managing identities in an interracial friendship. *Communication Quarterly*, *50*, 368–390.

Galupo, M. P. (2007). Women's close friendships across sexual orientation: A comparative analysis of lesbian-heterosexual and bisexual-heterosexual women's friendships. *Sex Roles, 56*(7/8), 473–482.

Galupo, M. P. (2009). Cross-category friendship patterns: Comparison of heterosexual and sexual minority adults. *Journal of Social & Personal Relationships, 26*(6/7), 811–831.

Hall, J. A., Larson, K. A., & Watts, A. (2011). Satisfying friendship maintenance expectations: The role of friendship standards and biological sex. *Human Communication Research, 37*(4), 529–552.

# Case 12

# Friendships and Social Support in Coping with Illness Diagnosis

## The Story of Sherry and the Martha's Vineyard Communication Association

Sherry Shepler and Ashley Duggan

*Keywords:* coping, friendship development, privacy management, social support

### The Evolution of a Friendship Network

We call ourselves the Martha's Vineyard Communication Association... MVCA[1] for short. The MVCA has evolved over years of dinners, shared experiences, and professional conferences. Most of us have been teaching communication in Boston-area colleges for 30 years. Ten years ago, Sara invited Bonnie, Anne, Roberta and Rita for an overnight visit to her summer cottage on Martha's Vineyard. Since we initially knew each other professionally, we joked about this being an "official" mini-conference. Our established "conference" tradition is to arrive on the mid-morning ferry, eat lunch, go to the beach, and shower for drinks and appetizers on the deck. Then we eat dinner out or eat Sara's grilled chicken. We always have morning bagels at Espresso Love.

The annual "mini-conference" expanded over the first few years to two nights and to include a few more favorite friends. When Sherry joined, we upped the ante for hospitality. Sherry is a great cook and expert pastry chef, creating eight-layer cakes that could be featured in a baking magazine. We met Nancy through the Eastern Communication Association. When Nancy joined MVCA, she added even more laughter and wine. Ashley, our youngest and newest member of the MVCA, describes the group as her favorite quasi-professional "organization," or the group that loves food and wine most.

*Inside Relationships: A Creative Casebook in Relational Communication*, edited by Sandra L. Faulkner, 123–132. © 2013 Left Coast Press, Inc. All rights reserved.

We celebrate new grandbabies, grieve the loss of loved ones, honor one another's accomplishments, and mark milestones, all over lots of wine, good food, and laughter. We are connected by our love of the communication field, our love of teaching and research, and now after so many years as a collective, our shared history of friendship and support.

In mid-June, the MVCA completed our annual "conference" at Sara's Martha's Vineyard summer home. Someone did the math and calculated this was our tenth anniversary, but since we hadn't made appropriate anniversary preparations, we called it our ninth year and decided to celebrate with large fanfare for our "milestone anniversary" next summer. Sherry is usually quieter (perhaps more appropriately, not as LOUD as some of us), but seemed especially reserved on this outing. She made reference to challenges at work, but she also wondered aloud whether it could be something else.

## Get the MRI

Soon after, Sherry had a meeting with her department chair, who expressed concerns about Sherry's language usage. As evidence, she had printed a series of email messages Sherry had written over the last few months and suggested that Sherry see a doctor as soon as possible. To the doctor, Sherry confirmed that she too had noticed language difficulty, particularly finding herself mid-sentence not having words to capture her thoughts.

Sherry was grateful for the Saturday afternoon MRI appointment. She thought she and her husband Mike would drop in, get the MRI, grab a bite downtown, and head back home to catch the Red Sox. The first sign things would not go as planned was when the MRI tech told Sherry that the doctor wanted to see her... TODAY... on Saturday afternoon, and escorted Sherry and Mike down a long hallway, where they were isolated from other patients and staff. That was the moment Sherry knew something was really wrong.

The doctor seemed so young. "I don't want to alarm you, but we saw *something* on the MRI, requiring additional tests." An ambulance took Sherry to the Beth Israel Deaconess Emergency Room, and the 45-minute wait felt interminable. Mike tried to keep the mood light and harkened back to the young doctor's advice, "There's no need to go all gloom and doom." Holding onto those words, they waited.

The long emergency room visit began with Sherry, a nurse, and an intern. Then Mike, neurosurgery and neurology residents joined.

Sherry received a chest x-ray. She was sure she should have eaten; she was not supposed to be here; she felt fine. She worried about her dog, it was well past dinnertime, dark, and they had left no light on for him. It wasn't until the chief of the emergency room came in to talk about the diagnosis that Sherry knew. There was a pretty large tumor growing in her brain, and it was most likely malignant.

Mike remembers the nurse who took Sherry's blood pressure consoling Sherry when Mike moved away to get a full view of the x-ray. They all held hands and cried—the nurse, Mike, Sherry. Then Sherry and Mike were left alone. Sherry could not get a fix on reality. It had no real substance. She felt the same; she just had a language problem.

The mundane helps one cope. Sherry needed to go to the bathroom. Mike had a terrible allergy and went though boxes of hospital tissues. It was after 10 p.m. They were hungry. Sherry was admitted to the hospital and moved into her room. Mike got water and crackers from the vending machine. This was their first intimate view of the hurry-and-wait hospital game. Another MRI was scheduled for the following morning. Because of the depth and size of the brain tumor, surgery was not an option. An attempt to remove the tumor could cause irreparable harm to speech, memory, and personality. The neurology and oncology teams recommended a biopsy of the brain.

## Will You Call Everyone for Me?

One of the first people Sherry called was Anne.

Anne had her ringer turned off but noticed mid-morning that Sherry called. No message. She had missed a call from Sherry at home, but again, no message. At 10 p.m., a few minutes into mindless television, the phone rang.

"Hey, Sherry!" Anne answered the call, "I saw you called a couple of times today, but no message. What's going on?" Her friend of over two decades had a mass in her brain. She did not want to leave a message. Sherry explained that the mystery of the language struggle had been solved. The mass was located in the speech center of her brain. She was in the hospital and had been there for a few days. "Where?" "What?" "How?" Anne tried to make sense of what Sherry was saying.

"I can't think of what to say," Anne responded, "I need to process this."

"I know it's a lot to take in," Sherry said patiently, "you don't have to say anything now."

"A lot to take in?" Ann thought, " A LOT TO TAKE IN? You've got a brain tumor, but you're worried about me?" But she didn't say it aloud. The cruel irony of a professor—a communication professor—with a tumor in the part of her brain that controlled speech was not lost on Anne, even at that point.

"Will you call everyone for me?" Sherry asked. By everyone, Anne knew she meant the circle of friends. The women who had just spent three days on Martha's Vineyard a few short weeks ago for our annual end of the school year retreat. Women who had gathered with spouses and partners to celebrate Sherry's tenure in March. Women who had gathered for the Breast Cancer Walk when Rita was diagnosed. Women who had celebrated a son's bar mitzvah and a daughter's first child. Women who were there on opening night for Roberta's play and drank toasts at Bonnie's retirement party.

## Processing and Disclosure

"I have bad news, Sherry is in the hospital and the emergency room doctor has given her the diagnosis of a brain tumor, inoperable, and she needs to have a biopsy." Anne's voice told a serious story. The information seemed too much to grasp at one time, but it sank in fast, and we all waited for more information. Room number and visiting hours; doctors were saying be prepared for the tumor to be malignant.

When one or more of us went to visit Sherry, we found ourselves staying for hours. Doctors came and went. We wondered whether we were invading Sherry's privacy and kept offering to step out when another doctor came in for another check or to let Sherry know about the next set of tests. Each time we began to leave, Sherry told us to stay. It seemed to strengthen Sherry to have people around her, even during private times.

Each time one of us visited, we started a phone chain to keep others in the loop. We were not sure who knew what; we shared information over texts, over email, over the phone. We were reminded of the ways cell phones can enmesh difficult health information with everyday life. One evening after visiting Sherry, Rita and Bonnie headed for Charley's for dinner and wine, and to send everyone any information via text messages and phone conversations from the table, the entryway, and even the parking lot.

On some level, we wondered how Sherry could go through this. On another level, we had enough experiences that we could relate. It brought Roberta back to a night in the hospital more than 40 years ago, where she sat alone in a strange hospital bed, feeling terrified. Roberta knew that the nights are the worst. Instead of future plans, one dwells not on the future but on how long the future, and the kind of future it will be. But mostly, it's the loneliness of living the night alone, with only your thoughts to keep you company. In the morning, when the visitors started arriving, the sense of normalcy is regained. We were determined to fill the daylight space, both in the hospital and at home.

We had all been through Rita's breast cancer five years earlier and already we knew we were great for each other in a crisis, but we also knew that we all handle these situations in different ways. Roberta retreats and tries not to think about it, and Anne bursts into tears immediately.

## From Caregiver to Recipient of Support: A Sherry-Worthy Day

Nancy was not the first to tease Sherry—Had she queried the hospital staff about sharing the kitchen so she could bake cakes for her visitors? We knew she would have to learn to accept friends visiting with a myriad of treats, and to accept the support she was receiving, rather than thinking of ways to make her friends feel comfortable.

The day before the biopsy, an MVCA contingent squeezed into "Sherry's lounge," since we took over the solarium when we overflowed her room. We have an MVCA term, "Sherry worthy," something Ashley came up with it when we planning Sherry's tenure party. It means that dessert lives up to Sherry's fabulous pastry chef standards. Since it was the day before her biopsy, nearly the whole group was there to listen, cry a little and laugh a lot, and give her a day that was "Sherry worthy."

But first, we had to get to the hospital. And the adventures involved in arriving at this destination were truly worthy of extended MVCA commentary. In sum, Roberta, the consummate city girl, knew exactly where to go and got there with Bonnie. Rita, with no sense of direction and no GPS, did not have an easy time but eventually arrived. Nancy, with a GPS in hand but with East/West Campus confusion, finally arrived after a series of "where am I" calls.

For lunch Roberta and Bonnie brought an array of Whole Foods sandwiches, salads and fruit. Rita brought a "Sherry worthy" chocolate ganache cake with mocha frosting, and an entire box of cookies for Roberta—who "does not eat cake" (Roberta's famous words). Nancy arrived with three liters of Diet Coke to support the MVCA addiction. Within minutes of our arrival, we shared big hugs, lunch, and extended commentaries.

It almost felt like an ordinary MVCA gathering. The table is where we gather and solve the problems of the world, as well as some of our own. That day was no exception, from all outward appearances. But there was a quietness, a tautness that was unusual. We spent the first hour avoiding the conversation that we knew had to happen, so we had extended commentaries about the ring tones on Rita's cell phone (a separate tone for each MVCA member), navigating in the city, the lack of hospital gown styles. One question broke the ice, and then a barrage followed. We are all professors and we thrive on information...but we are friends, and we wanted to respect Sherry's boundaries.

Sometimes teaching communication interferes with spontaneity—you tend to over think a situation. To everyone's relief, Sherry shared a chronological explanation of how she came to be in the hospital with a brain tumor, less than the two weeks after we had all been together on the Vineyard. Then there were questions related to treatment. Radiation is a one-time process, so Sherry needed to decide whether to do it then or wait until the situation worsened. Rita shared what she learned from her own cancer treatment and suggested things Sherry might want to discuss with the doctors... whether she could fly after the biopsy, the side effects of the steroids.

Doctors and nurses drifted in and out, with medical orders, pills, blood pressure gauges, as well as explanations—explanations about the biopsy process and what to expect the next day. Colleagues from Sherry's university stopped by, adding to the array of bakery products. Underlying the lighter conversations, there were hints of deep-seated fears. Would we all grow old together? Will this be as painful as my neighbor's biopsy? Do the doctors agree on the course of treatment?

Sherry remained remarkably calm, somewhat relieved to know the "something" that was wrong. And we all played our part, sharing stories, joking, asking questions, and of course, passing around the desserts. There is an acceptance that comes with this group of women, we love and support each other amidst our quirks, weaknesses, strengths, and gifts. Today it's Sherry's turn to be the center of our attention, something she never seeks, but with grace and good humor, she accepts, with our love and support. In turn, we are humbled to be invited to share this journey with her.

## Good Humor over a Bad Haircut

After almost a week in the hospital, Sherry had the biopsy. Anne, who has the longest relationship with Sherry, stopped by on her way home from the Cape and found Mike in the cafeteria. This was the first time Anne had seen Mike since getting the news, and she immediately became teary-eyed as she and Mike talked through the week's details. Ashley joined them later. Mike kept checking his cell phone for messages—the surgical center promised to call when Sherry's surgery was completed. Still no word. Anne stayed until about 4 p.m. and promised to visit Sherry again in two days.

Ashley asked Mike if he wanted to take a walk, to explore the neighborhood. Beth Israel is located in the Longwood area of Boston. To one direction is a densely packed area of world-class hospital networks. To the other direction is a densely populated neighborhood of researchers, clinicians, students, and families. As they walked, they heard relentless car horns. It was hard to tell whether it was possible to hear the cell phone, so Mike held it in his hand and made sure the vibration was also turned on. Back to the hospital an hour later, Mike's phone still did not show a missed call. Stopping by the family waiting area, they were informed that Sherry was in recovery, and would be ready to go to her room in 30 minutes.

Sherry was in good spirits. Her color looked good; she was cheerful and chatty. Then Sherry had the first glimpse of herself after the biopsy when she saw in the mirror where her hair had been shaved. Iodine used to prep her scalp before the procedure now left stains the color of red clay along the roots of the hair that remained. A dark blue line marked the center of the shaved area where a bit of blood still dripped from the incision line. ARGGHHH!! "I don't think my stylist can fix this haircut."

Sherry shared her experiences with the procedure; the worst part was "getting the halo screwed in." Rather than heavenly adornment, the halo stabilizes the patient's head during the operation. Four shots were administered to Sherry's head to help numb the pain, but Sherry still found the procedure painful. Once the halo was in place, the neurosurgeon stabilized the halo by pushing posts from the eardrums outside the head, increasing the pain. "The surgeon told me I would soon feel like Darth Vader, with a mask set on top of the halo to give guide marks. The mask didn't hurt, and the next memory was the anesthesia, and recovery room, sans halo."

## Friendship amidst the Multitude of Professional Teams

When Sherry left the hospital, Roberta was most consistent in visiting her at home, before her appointment with the "teams" of professionals who would decide her course of treatment. Roberta was concerned that Sherry would be apprehensive about the appointment that would determine her life for the next few months. Roberta believed that the daylight hours, at least, should be filled with narratives of a positive future. Roberta and Sherry chatted easily and talked about school, the options available for work during the fall semester while she is in treatment, her upcoming trip to Wisconsin to see her family.

Ten days after the biopsy Sherry received definitive results. On Monday morning, Sherry had an appointment with the neurosurgeon. We kept our cell phones nearby. On Monday afternoon, Anne was the bearer of the news: Sherry had a "stage two" cancerous tumor. It felt strange to be happy about the news because a stage two cancer is still cancer with serious ramifications for treatment and health issues. However, we all were scared that the tumor would be worse, and Sherry also seemed to be prepared for worse news. The best news of the day was that the doctor spoke about the ramifications of the treatment "five, ten and fifteen years down the road."

Now that we knew we had years with Sherry, we needed a "treatment with Sherry" routine. The doctor said they are going at it with everything they've got, chemo, radiation—all the weapons in their arsenal—five days a week for six weeks starting August first.

The last bit of information concerned possible side effects during her treatment. If we are doing "treatment with Sherry" then we needed to know what to expect. The doctors listed some significant positive and negative side effects. A positive effect is that Sherry's word retrieval, speech, and writing difficulties should improve significantly, particularly with steroid treatments. To facilitate a more rapid recovery, the once-a-day steroid dosage was doubled to twice a day. Negative steroid side effects to monitor included soreness in her mouth and "roid rage." Additional side effects from the radiation include fatigue and hair loss, while the side effects from the chemotherapy will be mild. Radiation treatment poses potential additional long-term side effects including the worsening of speech after treatment, and memory loss.

The medical team encouraged Sherry to focus on living as normally as possible. Sherry should expect to regain lost language skills, and plan on eventually being able to return to work. The medical team left out being able to return to the MVCA's annual meeting, the tenth year celebration that we expect to be a celebration of friendship, love, and longevity.

## A New Normal, a Return to the Vineyard, and Next Steps

Many of the MVCA who were in town took an extra "mini-conference" to the Vineyard before Sherry left for Wisconsin and before she began treatment. We wonder how much interaction Sherry wants and when our concern crosses privacy boundaries.

Sitting on Sara's deck with ice cream and wine, conversation returned to Sherry's dilemma. She planned to receive both chemo and radiation. Sherry's chromosomes number 1 and 19 indicate receptivity to chemo, and she can take the pill form. Sherry received a call from her oncologist indicating that she might be able to do chemo alone, saving the radiation for later if she needed it. However, another call followed, where the doctor referred to a "frisky" stage 2, and strongly suggested radiation. Sherry seemed a bit overwhelmed by yet one more decision, especially since she thought everything had been finalized regarding treatment. She called her cousin Tim, a pathologist, for his advice. Tim reassured Sherry that he would check the literature and get her the information necessary to help her with the decision. Sherry's verbal skills seemed improved with the steroids.

After the Vineyard, Sherry went to Wisconsin to see her family, to connect with them face-to-face; her parents will soon arrive for a month-long visit. As she starts treatment, Sherry depends on the strong networks she has: her family, the MVCA, her colleagues, and friends. Sara has invited Sherry to come back to the Vineyard with her parents, surely a respite from the treatment. The rest of the MVCA will host a dinner to meet. We will go to doctors' appointments when needed and arrange ongoing gatherings around treatment. We were sure to remind Sherry to request a chemotherapy drug that does not adversely interact with wine.

### Questions and Activities for Discussion

1. What does it mean to support a friend? How does social support work for the MVCA? How does a group of friends work out roles? What does his or her group of friends say about a person?

2. How do rituals play a role in the friendships described here? Describe rituals in which your friendship group engages. How do the rituals help maintain your friendships? In what other ways do you maintain friendships?

3. How do illness and other life events influence our friendships? Have you had relationship challenges in your friendships? Describe the challenges and how you and your friends dealt with them.

## Note

1. MVCA is the Martha Vineyard's Communication Association consisting of: Sherry Shepler, Saint Anselm College; Ashley Duggan, Boston College; Roberta Kosberg, Curry College; Rita Rosenthal, Boston College; Nancy Willets, Cape Cod Community College; Anne Mattina, Stonehill College; Bonnie Jefferson,Boston College; Sara Weintraub, Regis College; and this story also includes Sherry's spouse, Mike Meadows, Fisher College.

## For Further Reading and Reference

Duggan, A. P. (2006). Understanding interpersonal communication processes across health contexts: Advances in the last decade and challenges for the next decade. *Journal of Health Communication, 11*(1), 93–108.

Allen, L. F., Babin, E. A., & McEwan, B. (2012). Emotional investment: An exploration of young adult friends' emotional experience and expression using an investment model framework. *Journal of Social and Personal Relationships, 29*(2), 206–227.

Morry, M. M., Reich, T., & Kito, M. (2010). How do I see you relative to myself? Relationship quality as a predictor of self- and partner-enhancement within cross-sex friendships, dating relationships, and marriages. *Journal of Social Psychology, 150*(4), 369–392.

Moremen, R. D. (2008). The downside of friendship: Sources of strain in older women's friendships. *Journal of Women & Aging, 20*(1/2), 169–187.

Petronio, S., Sargent, J., Andea, L., Reganis, P., Cichocki, D. (2004). Family and friends as healthcare advocates: Dilemmas of confidentiality and privacy. *Journal of Social and Personal Relationships, 21*(1), 33–52.

Segrin, C., Burke, T. J., & Dunivan, M. (2012). Loneliness and poor health within families. *Journal of Social and Personal Relationships, 29*(5), 597–611.

Wright, K. B., & Patterson, B. R. (2006). Socioemotional selectivity theory and the macrodynamics of friendship: The role of friendship style and communication in friendship across the lifespan. *Communication Research Reports, 23*(3), 163–170.

# Chapter 5

# Family

Chapter 5 explores family communication through cases that query how family dynamics contribute to and hinder relational health. Ellen Leslie and Frances Spaulding ask questions about how a religious response could help the challenge of physical and emotional abuse in religious households. Using a diary format, Marne Austin presents a mother-daughter story of anorexia and why family communication is part of the healing process. Sandra Faulkner's personal narrative about an intended ambivalent pregnancy addresses dialectics of work-life issues, certainty and uncertainty, and family decision-making. The cases in this chapter use *accidental ethnography* as a technique to write about family, what Chris Poulus (2008) suggested as a method to story our lives and bring forward what may be lost in our unconscious—eating disorders, stigmatized identities, suicide, abuse, and other difficult topics. This entails writing about dreams, clues, memories, and reflections from the unconscious, from seemingly "accidental signs and impulses that surge up and, from time to time, really grip us, take hold of us, call us out and throw us down, sweep us away, and carry us to places we may not have even imagined" (Poulus, 2008, p. 47). The goal of this kind of writing is to reveal and make conscious secrets that harm families and communities.

*Inside Relationships: A Creative Casebook in Relational Communication,* edited by Sandra L. Faulkner, 133–136. © 2013 Left Coast Press, Inc. All rights reserved.

Accidental ethnography means writing and rewriting family secrets that haunt us and break into our day-to-day relating (anyway). "Telling the story, despite anxiety, is the path to healing. And, anyways, storytelling is far more potent, far more fascinating, far more engaging than secret-keeping" (Poulus, 2008, p. 187). If we write about hurtful secrets, if we reveal harmful patterns of interaction, then we may be able to tell better stories and offer more possibilities. Communication privacy management theory (see Chapter 3 for a full discussion) suggests that the revelation or concealment of family secrets depends on our motivation for disclosing, as well as what family disclosure rules are in place. For example, you may need to disclose abuse to a new relational partner, though the family rule is silence about personal family business to outsiders. You may want to talk about your same-sex partner with your parents, and they may avoid discussing her because of discomfort. The difference between personal motivation and the need to disclose family secrets and violate family disclosure rules creates turbulence. Topic avoidance can lead to dissatisfaction. In a study on lesbian parents, research showed that parents had to deal with outsiders' questions about the validity and morality of their families (Breshears, 2011). The parents had to reassure their children that talking about sexual orientation was appropriate despite reprimands that family identity was a taboo topic. Thus, the storying of relational (and family) life is important, as the authors in this book explicitly and implicitly argue. Discourse within families may be especially important in non-traditional families (Galvin, 2006). Once you understand family patterns, then you can see if you repeat any of them and can understand how family helps resist or adapt to outside forces and crises that arise (Koerner & Fitzpatrick, 2008).

When is it appropriate to use accidental ethnography? The ethical implications of revealing and deciding to conceal secrets may be addressed if we talk through definitions of family and the function family serves in our lives. It may be obvious (I hope) that there is no ideal family, so I begin with the fact that families are social constructions (Wood, 2002). The definition of family can refer to families of procreation and origin, including nuclear and extended family residing in one household, who have established biological or socio-legal legitimacy because of shared genetics, marriage or adoption. We can also consider family to be interdependent individuals who work to fulfill psychosocial tasks that help with mutual need fulfillment, nurturance and development. This leads me to ask the following questions: What is immediate family? Do these definitions include interracial families? LGBT families? Divorced and blended families? Families without children? Family is a network of people who live together over long periods of time bound by ties of marriage, blood, or commitment, legal *or* otherwise (Galvin, Brommel, & Bylund, 2004). There can be families of choice (Wood, 2002). We create family in communication; communication takes place inside families, creates and sustains them. Family is transactional. Thus, it may be best to consider family as a group of intimates who generate a sense of home and group identity, experience strong ties of loyalty and emotion, and share a sense of history and a future (Wood, 2002).

## Relational Messages within Families

Relationships are enacted and formed through the relational members' communication processes and, in turn, the nature of the relationship is influenced by ongoing communication between the members. Relational messages influence our self-concepts; talking to others in our families about our feelings about them can increase or decrease self-worth (Dailey, 2010). Affection exchange theory (AET) offers an explanation for why we communicate affection to one another and with what consequences (Floyd, 2006). Floyd suggests that we are born with the need and capacity for affection and that affection serves viability and procreative needs. These needs are unconsciously enacted in our close biologically rooted relationships. Behaviors that show intense positive regard for the other are usually read as such by the other. For instance, hugging your daughter is a sign of love and is unconsciously a motivation to pass on genetic material. The theory proposes that those of us who grew up in affectionate households tend to be affectionate as adults. We can enact affection through the use of *confirming messages* that make one value the self more, directly acknowledge the other, offer supportive feedback, clarifying responses, and express positive feedback better than *disconfirming messages* that make one devalue the self (Dailey, 2006). For example, Austin in her case study describes confirming messages from her mother as helping in her disordered eating. Consider what it means to use confirming messages and why this is important as you read the following case studies.

# References

Breshears, D. (2011). Understanding communication between lesbian parents and their children regarding outside discourse about family identity. *Journal of GLBT Family Studies, 7*(3), 264–284.

Dailey, R. M. (2006). Confirmation in parent-adolescent relationships and adolescent openness: Toward extending confirmation theory. *Communication Monographs, 73*, 434–458.

Dailey, R. M. (2010). Testing components of confirmation: How acceptance and challenge from mothers, fathers, and siblings are related to adolescent self-concept. *Communication Monographs, 77*(4), 592–617.

Floyd, K. (2006). *Communicating affection: Interpersonal behavior and social context.* Cambridge, UK: Cambridge University Press.

Galvin, K. M. (2006). Diversity's impact on defining the family: Discourse dependence and identity. In L. H. Turner & R. West (Eds.), *The family communication sourcebook* (pp. 3–20). Thousand Oaks, CA: Sage.

Galvin, K. M., Brummel, B. J., & Bylund, C. L. (2004). *Family communication: Cohesion and change* (6th ed). New York: Pearson.

Koerner, A. F., & Fitzpatrick, M. A. (2008). Family communication patterns theory: A social cognitive approach. In L. A. Baxter & D. O. Braithwaite (Eds.), *Engaging theories in interpersonal communication: Multiple perspectives* (pp. 50–65). Thousand Oaks, CA: Sage.

Poulus, C. N. (2008). *Accidental ethnography: An inquiry into family secrecy.* Walnut Creek, CA: Left Coast Press, Inc.

Wilmot, W. (2003). The relational perspective. In K. M. Galvin & P. J. Cooper (Eds.), *Making connections: Readings in relational communication* (3rd ed., pp. 11–19). Los Angeles: Roxbury.

Wood, J. T. (2002). In J. Stewart (Ed.), *Bridges not walls: A book about interpersonal communication* (8th ed., pp. 289–298). New York: McGraw Hill.

# Case 13

# Is God like My Father?
## Exploring Abusive Family Relationships through Sibling Narratives

### Ellen Leslie and Frances Spaulding

*Keywords:* family systems, marriage, religion, sibling relationships, verbal abuse

This story represents our personal journey as both victims and scholars. As researchers, we are only beginning to understand and heal from the verbal and emotional abuse we experienced both as children in a "Christian"[1] home and from the lack of response and acknowledgment of our abuse by our religious community. By sharing and writing our narratives, we have experienced a sense of understanding about the complexities of what makes a family dysfunctional and a parent abusive, and how faith can be both a place that provides healing yet also be a place that allows domestic abuse to continue.

Verbal abuse, particularly the emotional manipulation and control we grew up with, is something that has not been widely examined by researchers. Yet this form of abuse—the verbal and emotional damage that manipulative behavior can cause—often has long-lasting side effects and implications for the victims.

We hope our narratives draw attention to domestic abuse in Christian culture—a place where abuse is too often overlooked and undefined. Specifically, we want to use story as a means to understand how discourses of power within Christian culture are constructed through the manipulation of Biblical language in order to justify abuse. Often such language is employed out of context in order to establish a power relationship within intimate relationships—resulting in a pattern of verbal,

---

*Inside Relationships: A Creative Casebook in Relational Communication,* edited by Sandra L. Faulkner, 137–150. © 2013 Left Coast Press, Inc. All rights reserved.

emotional, and sometimes physical abuse. This is not to condemn Christianity as inherently abusive, but only to draw attention to the potential for abuse and suggest some ways of addressing this type of abuse within Christian culture. How should the Christian community respond to family abuse? As our narratives demonstrate, the situation is multifaceted. Denominational doctrines, family secrecy, and social pressures all factor into if and when domestic abuse is revealed to a church family. Since we are both the researchers and the victims, we have intentionally changed the names of people in the story and fictionalized minor story elements such as where we grew up and our names to protect our privacy and the privacy of our family.[2] Additionally, because this study is deeply rooted in our religious tradition, which has both enabled abuse in our family and at the same time has helped us cope with the continuing affects of abuse, we have included some personal spiritual moments in the narratives to illustrate the dialectic tension of faith as both liberating and oppressing.

## Frances Caught in the Middle

*If we are to become healthy, functioning human beings we must face our darker selves. And in facing—and to a large extent—accepting, even embracing, that darkness—that Mr. Hyde who lives within each of us Jekylls—we can come to peace and wholeness.* (Poulos, 2008, p. 129)

Dad is driving us into church Sunday morning. Mom is in the passenger seat, and I'm sitting behind her in the back. I'm home from college for a holiday break. Every time I come back I know things haven't changed. I hope things will be calm, but they never are. Sundays have always been, and remain, the worst day of the week. Like every other Sunday, my parents are fighting.

"I'm damn tired of you trying to push me out of the house on Sunday morning. All you do is nag, nag, nag," Dad grumbles.

"Well, you know I have to be to church early to set up for Sunday School. You've been up since five a.m. and we never leave until nine. I don't understand why you can't get yourself ready and be out the door at a decent time. You're doing this to spite me," Mom responds.

"Oh, forgive me for getting up at five this morning so I can have some time to myself. I forgot the world is supposed to revolve around you." Dad twirls a finger in the air as he talks. I'm afraid he's going to forget he's driving and take both hands off the wheel.

The car rides always disintegrates into a heated discussion on Sunday mornings, and Dad always takes an opposing view to mom. I hate it when they do this. Dad is mocking Mom, provoking her, and when she gets mad, turning it around on her and playing the victim or superior being.

"You never listen or care about what's important to me!" Mom shouts.

"I don't listen because all you do is bitch and complain and make me feel bad," Dad yells back.

By this point I'm frustrated and angry. I've been working at a shelter for abused women and I can't stand another minute of Dad calling Mom names and saying everything is always her fault. I hate seeing this. I help abused women all week, yet I can't help my own mother. I just want this to stop for her sake, for mine, and for my sister's.

I blurt out, "That's an abuser's excuse, saying that 'It's not my fault but Mom's.'"

Dad starts defending himself, "I told her not to..."

"Abusers say that, too," I shoot back.

"Well, she is responsible..."

"That's another excuse," I snap. I can see Dad calculating his next move as he tenses up slightly, clenching the steering wheel.

"You think I am abusive?"

I start to freak out. Maybe it wasn't a good idea to say that. What will happen now? I suddenly realize I need to be *a lot* more cautious with my words. I'm worried Dad will remember what just happened and make Mom pay for it later. My effort to make things better for my mom might have just made things worse.

"What do you mean I'm abusive? What excuses do *abusers* make?"

I can tell he is trying to catch me in my words. He wants to find something he can point at Mom and say she does this sort of thing, not him.

"According to the book I am reading, abusers blame other people, conditions, or past events for their actions, events such as a bad childhood, mental illness, or saying the other person pushed them too far," I reply.

"So you got this idea from a book?"

"Yes." If he believes I got this idea from a book instead of thinking I got it from Mom, then maybe she won't be in as much trouble. However, the truth is that I've always felt Dad is abusive.

"How do *abusers* act?"

I decide to answer in a way which points to him instead of Mom. "Some people act like the victim and others act like they are trying to help the person they are controlling and manipulating." Every time Dad says *"abuser,"* it feels like a slap in the face. He stresses the syllables in the word, making me feel dirty for calling him that. He's reminding me I've gone too far, and every time I answer, I try not to say that word again in the vain hope that he will forget what we are talking about and change the subject.

"Well, what are the different kinds of abuses?"

Mom, frustrated, intercedes. "Stop asking these questions. We know what you are trying to do."

"What am I trying to do? Can't I show an interest in what she's learning?" he responds, trying to sound sincere.

"You aren't showing an interest; you're trying to trap her so you can shift the attention to me."

Dad answers in a sad, disappointed tone, "I can't believe you would think so low of me."

The car stops. We're at church and the conversation ends because we have to walk in with smiles on our faces and pretend nothing is wrong.

*Dear Heavenly Father, I know you love me unconditionally, but it is difficult to understand you or feel close to you when I do not know how a loving father cares for his children with no strings attached. I know you never seek to hurt those who are close to you. Please, give me wisdom and discernment in difficult situations and the strength to deal with who I have become because of my family's choices. Thank you for accepting me in my brokenness, never expecting perfection.*

## Ellen Deals with the Aftermath

I've been tense all day. I'm trying to cope. I've taken my Xanax. I've done my relaxation exercises on the way to church, but I can't get rid of this nagging sense that today is a bad day. I feel this way most Sundays. Last year my husband told me I always pick fights with him right before we leave for church. I didn't understand why I could feel fine all week, but every Sunday, about ten minutes before we leave for our three minute car ride to church, I begin to panic and look for reasons to get angry. I didn't connect the dots until I realized that Sunday has always been the day my parents fought. It's the one day a week Dad came home, and he used the day to either ignore every request Mom made or to subtly pick out flaws in her. It always led to a major fight.

My phone rings.

"Hello?" Paul, my husband, says as he picks up the phone. "Ellen, it's your mom."

I grab the upstairs extension. "Hi, Mom."

"Ellen, do you think your dad is abusive?" Mom whispers into the phone.

*Oh my God, what has brought on this conversation? Calm down, deep breaths, I tell myself.*

"Honestly, yes I do. He's verbally abusive to you and sometimes to Frances. I stay on his good side by being the peacemaker."

There is complete silence on the other end of the line. I can hear Mom choking up.

"I always thought we gave you guys a stable home."

"Mom, there is a big difference between two people staying married because they feel they have no other choice, and two people being married because they're committed and love each other. What brought on this question?" I really have no idea what is going on. Why now, after over twenty years, is this conversation happening *today*?

"Frances told your dad he was abusive today on the way into church. We were fighting, and she got upset with how he was treating me and jumped in to help."

"Oh, why did she have to get in the middle of it? It's best just to walk away."

"I know. Now he wants the name of the book she's reading, and he's going to read it and point out how I'm really the abusive one in the relationship."

"Does he realize the book Frances is referring to is written about men abusing their wives, not the other way around? I've read the book. I don't know how he can twist the meaning of the book so much, but then again, it's Dad."

Mom is silent. I hate it when she gets like this. She's given up. I've been pushing her for three years to consider how unhealthy her marriage is and how it's totally broken her self-esteem. She won't listen. She feels trapped, and if she leaves Dad she's afraid she'll go to hell. I can't convince her that the God I know wouldn't possibly expect her to stay in a relationship based on abuse.

Mom has been quiet for a couple of moments now. "Mom, you have to read this book. I know you're going to get upset reading it because you will see Dad in it. However, you cannot allow him to read a book on spousal abuse and twist it to use against you. You are the victim, not him."

"I can't leave him. If I try to he will utterly destroy me. He's said as much to me in the past." Mom's voice is breaking, and she's crying.

"Mom, I know this is difficult for you. It's difficult for me. However, we have to address this situation at some point. I'm dealing with it. I can cope, but this has affected me and I don't want it to continue to affect you, too."

"I didn't know..." Mom whispers, her voice fading. I hate doing this to her. I hate adding to her grief, but we have lived a life of deception for so long that I no longer want to hide it. I want to fight it.

It's now been four months since that conversation, and my mother has yet to read that book. The cycle continues. There is no end, no peace.

*Oh Lord, give me the strength to continue to deal with the ups and downs of my family. Thank you that you are not like my father. You don't judge me. You love me unconditionally. Without my faith, I think I would have given up a long time ago.*

It could be easy to read my family's narrative and assume my father is just an absentee dad, maybe a bit selfish, but not abusive. Yet abuse comes in many forms. It comes in the form of religious manipulation and emotional manipulation; it comes in the form of violence or neglect. It is easier to spot bruises than internal wounds. What we have dealt with for over twenty years is buried deep inside us. For Ellen, the effects manifest themselves through generalized anxiety disorder; for Frances, in the continual struggle to let go of hate and to form some sort of relationship with her father. No one believes us, and buried within us is an intense pain that no one understands.

## Frances's Childhood Memories
### Dad Forces Me To Take Music Lessons

*Most abusive men do not rely entirely on outright verbal abuse, threats, or physical intimidation. They find that they can gain more power by using subtler tactics of manipulation that are much harder to name or identify.* (Bancroft, 2004, p. 28)

I'm a smart aleck young teen who doesn't want to go to her voice lesson. So I challenge my father's authority.

"I'm not going," I say, looking him straight in the eyes, crossing my arms in defiance. I have told him all week I didn't want to go, but he wouldn't listen. I stand at the end of the hallway facing my dad with my hands on my hips. "I will *not* go."

"You will go," Dad says. "It's your choice—you can go with me nicely, or I'll make you go."

I glare at him. "I would like to see you try."

Without further reaction Dad calmly takes my left arm and twists it behind my back. I feel painful pressure where my shoulder and arm meet. He guides me down the hallway, down the stairs, out the door, and into the car. The whole time he calmly says over and over, "Don't resist, or I will break your arm. Don't think I won't do it."

Dad and I are the only ones at home when this happens. I feel humiliated, helpless, alone, and betrayed. I try so hard not to cry during the short drive to my lesson, but I can't help it. I feel violated. The entire lesson I keep repeating in my head "Don't cry, don't cry, don't let him see you cry." When we get home from the lesson, I throw myself on my bed and sob.

Any musical instrument I ever show the slightest interest in, Dad arranges for lessons. Then he pressures me, sometimes to the point of blackmail, to continue after I have decided I don't want to. Awhile after the incident with voice lessons, I take violin lessons that I soon decide to quit. I wait until the last minute to tell Dad I am not going to my lesson, and this time when I tell him, I lock myself in the bathroom so he can't get me.

"What am I going to tell the teacher?" Dad yells through the bathroom door.

I don't respond.

"Damn it, you need to open the shitty door!"

Mom is also there, yelling for me to open the door. She pounds on the door over and over again, hollering for me to open it. I know the bathroom is the perfect hideaway. The hinges are on my side of the door. I have a sink and toilet, and if I'd thought to bring in food, I could have lasted for days.

Dad finally gives up because it is time for my lesson. Cussing under his breath, he leaves.

After he leaves, I unlock the door and tell Mom why I locked myself in the bathroom.

"Mom, I know you're probably mad at me. I had a reason why I did it." I probably wouldn't have told her about Dad physically forcing me to go to voice lessons if I hadn't thought he would try to force me also to go to violin lessons. I still don't tell Mom that as he forced me to the car he had continually threatened to break my arm if I didn't go.

I didn't get in trouble for what I did, but Mom never talked to me about what I told her. Mom just stared at me, stunned. I think she was scared after I told her about Dad forcing me out of the house. She said she would talk to him. I sometimes wonder if the incident did happen, if Dad really threatened to physically harm me and forced me out of the house. I know I'm the only one who remembers it. I will not let myself forget what I know is true.

## Alone with My Parents

*The abuser stomps on the victim verbally and emotionally until she feels like a nonperson. He thus elevates himself in his own eyes to a powerful conqueror who has won control of his own castle.* (Branson & Silva, 2007, p. 19)

My sister Ellen is at college, and it's only my dad, my mom, and myself in the house now. They're having one of their normal fights, but it has disintegrated to my dad degrading my mom with name-calling such as "bitch" and telling her, "You aren't good for *fucking* anything, you can't get a *decent* job, and make any kind of *shitty* contribution, or treat me with the *proper respect* I *shitting* deserve." He's throwing around his regular plethora of random profanity. I can feel my mom's distress. Her face crumples in pain as I see my dad pointing his finger at her. She's in the kitchen, gripping the back of a kitchen chair for support. She isn't even able to finish any of her statements she's crying so hard, and Dad isn't really giving her any chance to speak. All she is able to do is stutter her first few words before a new stream of tears and sobs erupts. I remember Ellen telling me not to get involved in their fights, that I will just make it worse, but it hurts me to see my mom like this. "Be quiet!" I yell at Dad over and over again until he finally stops his verbal attack on Mom and can hear what I have to say. I think that if he puts me in my mom's position, he might stop because he always seems to treat my sister and me differently than he does my mom—not always better, but differently.

I ask him, "Dad, if I were married, would you want my husband to treat me the way you're treating Mom now?"

My dad looks at me and says almost calmly and expressionlessly, "If you were acting the way your mom is, you'd deserve it."

I'm speechless. I stand there, unable to react. I turn and leave the room, weeping as quietly as I can. When Dad finally goes to the basement, I leave my room to find Mom so I can give her a hug. It will be only a little comfort, but it's all I can do.

# Ellen's Childhood Memories
## Dad Gets Angry and Goes Too Far

I've buried this memory in the deep recesses of my mind because the actual details are too painful for me to dwell on. I want to think my family is "normal" and not admit that my father has sometimes bordered on physical abuse of my mother. He has a Jekyll and Hyde personality, and I don't like what I see when he takes off the friendly mask that he wears in public.

I'm about twelve. My sister and I escape to the basement to avoid hearing Dad yell at Mom. I hate these moments. Suddenly, I hear feet on the stairs, and my mom appears in the basement doorway, running away from Dad. Dad is right behind her. He runs around her to block her coming into our room. I'm scared. I've never seen Dad like this. His body is tense; his face is contorted into an angry sneer.

"Let me leave!" Mom yells.

"No, you aren't going anywhere," Dad calmly tells her. How can he be so calm when he looks so angry? Suddenly he grabs Mom's arm and begins twisting it. She falls to the floor.

"You're hurting me," she whimpers.

"Dad! Stop it! Stop it!" I yell, running to pull him away from Mom. It's as if Dad emerges from a fog. He lets go and walks away. Mom wipes her eyes and goes back upstairs.

It's at that moment I become afraid of my father. I vow to never again interfere. I don't want to bring out this scary, insane side of him. This isn't the father I know. Yet this side does exist. I want to forget this memory, and I do. For over ten years I haven't thought about this incident. It is too painful; too frightening. Why do I need to remember this memory? Remembering implies that I need to deal with this, and I don't want to deal with it.

# Can You Understand My Pain? Faith and Domestic Abuse

Within the church there is pressure for abusive men to be seen as operating outside the bounds of accepted Christian culture. From our experience, we see the issue of abuse not as a critique of Christianity, but a critique of pastors, lay leaders and church members across the country who cannot see the abuse happening within their own congregations. There have been more investigations into why domestic abuse is not addressed in the church, and the research illustrates the lack of counselor training for pastors and the push towards reconciliation in marriage (Groth, 2003).

However, we want to make clear that domestic abuse is not restricted to Christian culture; it is important that we realize the power of religious manipulation to keep people in abusive relationships. Abusers and victims can use various religious lenses to justify their reasons (Battaglia, 2001). The church must begin to recognize and condemn the use of Biblical references to justify abuse. Male-headship in the home does not give a man the right to abuse his wife. Yet to both the abuser and the abused, Biblical interpretation plays a crucial role in how the relationship is perceived. Many Christian women who experience intimate partner abuse feel it is their duty as a Christian wife to sacrifice and forgive their spouse. The children in these relationships often feel, as we did, that they must respect the father and not say anything about what is truly going on inside the home (Wang et al., 2009). Both of us continue to experience rejection and resistance as we share our family's story with friends at our churches. Frances is much more open about the family dynamics than Ellen. Yet when it comes to sharing our story with our Christian friends, we both feel incredible resistance from people listening to and accepting our family narrative. They think we are lying.

## Ellen Tries to Teach a Christian Marriage Class

Why did I want to teach a Sunday school class about marriage? I had the great idea that my husband Paul and I would co-teach a class on what Christian marriage should be like. We attend a church in the Wesleyan tradition with a strong egalitarian history and a theology that promotes complete gender equality. The class started off as a simple idea. Paul and I would teach the history and Wesleyan theology of gender equality for a month, and then two other couples would teach about balancing marriage and children. Simple plan, easy to implement—yeah right. We've been under attack all month. It all began when we suggested equality and partnership in marriage was a theologically sound alternative to male headship and female submission.

The first week I shared a bit of my family's story. I don't share a lot about my family background because I want to protect my privacy and my parents' privacy. However, I felt I needed to speak up.

"I grew up in a home with a father who would take the concept of male headship and use scripture to manipulate my family. If a marriage puts the will of one spouse over the other, then you're creating a situation where abuse could occur."

I caused quite a stir because the next time I was at church one of the men in our class approached me about my beliefs on gender equality. For some reason, opponents of gender equality always approach me and not Paul. I guess they think that, as the "weaker sex" I will cave from their strong, manly advice. They don't know who they're up against.

"I'm sorry you had a bad experience with male headship growing up, but that doesn't make the system wrong. It's the way God ordained marriage to operate," this man explains.

"I know you and your wife," I respond. "You guys don't practice this. Your wife is independent, and your teenage daughter is one of the most sassy, self-reliant girls I know. You're telling me that you actually enforce *your* will on your wife, even if she is opposed to it?"

He stands there for a minute and finally answers, "Yeah, I'm the husband; I have final say."

How has this behavior become so rhetorically entrenched in evangelical society? One of the couples teaching the parenting and marriage section quit before their unit started. They felt uncomfortable with our position on gender equality. They quit via e-mail. The wife allowed her husband to send us a lengthy e-mail about how theologically off-base we were.

The husband said in the e-mail:

> We believe that God conveys most his message openly. When Ephesians 5:22 says that "the husband is the head of the wife as Christ is the head of the church," we feel that is what it means...A wife that submits to her husband as unto the Lord—even if the husband is in the wrong—is obeying God and winning His favor.... I Peter 2:19-21 talks specifically about slavery, but we believe the principal is the same here: 'For it is commendable if a man bears up under the pain of unjust suffering because he is conscious of God. But how is it to your credit if you receive a beating for doing wrong and endure it? But if you suffer for doing good and you endure it, this is commendable before God.

I couldn't read the e-mail when it came. I let Paul respond because I felt so hurt that, once again, my story was being brushed aside as an "anomaly."

How can he say that God will punish the abuser in heaven and the wife who withstands the abuse will be rewarded? Can one win "God's favor" by allowing abuse to continue? How is that Biblical? I have a very difficult time lining up my vision of a loving God and a caring Savior with a God who allows my father to abuse my family just because he's been "ordained" head of the home. Why can't people listen and understand the slippery slope male headship leads to? This is why I have remained quiet for so long about my family. No one listens. There is no space for dialogue or room for any theological view that opposes male headship. We must have room for this conversation if change is ever going to occur.

## Ignoring Abuse in Christian Homes

Domestic abuse is often ignored in evangelical culture. As Steven Tracy illustrates in his essay, "Calling the Evangelical Church to Truth—Domestic Violence and the Gospel" (2011), the idea that domestic abuse can occur in a Christian homes threatens our idealized view of marriage. The role of the Christian husband as the decision maker, the provider, and the leader has become so naturalized in evangelical society that there is no longer room for differing theological views on gender roles.

As we reflected on our childhood memories and experiences, both of us came to see that many of the behavioral and emotional issues we dealt with as children were directly tied to the dysfunctional family environment we survived. Yet young sisters are not known for being sympathetic to one another and these emotional and behavioral issues often drew us apart instead of together. Collaborating on these narratives has been a healing process, drawing us closer as siblings. Through studying our own family, we have learned that there are no easy solutions when it comes to dealing with the complex matrix of family abuse, religion, and parenting. Within evangelical culture there is a strong tendency to deny domestic abuse and its ties to religious ideology. The manipulation of religious language and religious ideology is central to allowing abuse to be ignored in churches and Christian families. At the most basic level Christian theology is about liberation and personal empowerment through faith, yet the rhetoric of male dominance has become so entrenched as "normal" behavior in many Christian homes, especially conservative Christian homes, that the effects and underlying social consequences of domestic abuse cannot be dealt with until the rhetoric begins to change. Christian women often feel they are not free to leave abusive relationships not so much because the Bible forbids it (it does not) but because their entire world is tied to a discourse community that supports inequality.

Scholarship, such as our narratives, prepares us as members of our own faith communities to speak of truth and healing to the complex nexus of religion and abuse. Only when we are silent do those who wish to control us win. As we quickly realized while conducting this research, our "story" is truly not ours alone. In our universities, communities, and classrooms there are others who have similar stories, and it is only through increased scholarship and attention to these issues—in research, the classroom, and community—that domestic abuse can begin to be effectively addressed.

## Questions and Activities for Discussion

1. How do the memories of the two sisters differ? How do they converge? What does the interweaving of their perspectives tell you about abuse as a family system?

2. Is there a difference between physical and emotional abuse? Does it matter? How does abuse influence our relationships with our families? With others outside the family system?

3. The authors write that scholarship and writing about abuse are ways to begin healing and also demonstrate that abuse is a common story. How is this so? How can religious beliefs be part of the solution?

## Notes

1 Our stories are only a case study about how one form of religious discourse can produce violence. We understand that the term "Christian" has multiple definitions and our experiences cannot be generalized to all Christian homes or theology. We have grown up in the evangelical tradition where the relationship between community, theology and evangelical Christian popular culture greatly influences how gender roles are perceived and allows male leadership to be considered the normal model for Christian families. Therefore, the study is not attempting to generalize this experience to other faith traditions, but to draw attention to the fact that when male dominance is considered "normal" behavior then domestic abuse is often ignored because the line between what is acceptable and unacceptable behavior from the family's leader has been blurred to the point of theological confusion. People are too afraid to address the issue.

2 In addition to considering privacy issues and changing our names and basic story elements, as researchers we have attempted to take a relational ethics

approach to this study (Ellis, 2007). As Poulos (2008) notes, "A relational ethics is an ethics that raises more questions than it answers, that calls the researcher, at every turn, to search, to question, to confront self, other, and secret directly, dynamically, with heart, with care" (63). By fictionalizing our names and our family we attempt to protect not only our mother, who has been a victim of the verbal abuse of our father, but also our father, who is also a victim in many ways. Our father grew up in a dysfunctional home without role models. While his actions are not excusable, patterns of abuse often appear cyclical (Branson & Silva, 2007). So our father, who was abused as a child, grew up to abuse his own wife and children without fully recognizing his behavior.

# For Further Reading and Reference

Bancroft, L. (2005). *When dad hurts mom: Helping your children heal the wounds of witnessing abuse.* New York: Berkley Books.

Battaglia, L. (2001). Conservative protestant ideology and wife abuse: Reflections on discrepancy between theory and data. *Journal of Religion & Abuse, 2*(4), 31–45.

Branson, B., & Silva, P. (2007). *Violence among us: Ministry to families in crisis.* Valley Forge, PA: Judson Press.

Ellis, C. (2007). Telling secrets, revealing lives: Relational ethics in research with intimate others. *Qualitative Inquiry, 13*(1), 3–29.

Groth, B. (2003). Job is a woman: Pastoral care to victims of domestic abuse. *American Journal of Pastoral Counseling, 6*(4), 23–41.

Haakan, J., Fussell, H. & Mankowski, E. (2007). Bringing the church to its knees: Evangelical Christianity, feminism, and domestic violence discourse. *Psychotherapy and Politics International, 5*(2), 103–115.

Poulos, C. (2008). *Accidental ethnography: An inquiry into family secrecy.* Walnut Creek, CA: Left Coast Press, Inc..

Tracy, S. (2011). Calling the evangelical church to truth—Domestic violence and the gospel. In N. Nason-Clark, C. Clark-Kroeger, & B. Fisher (Eds.), *Responding to abuse in Christian homes: A challenge to churches and their leaders* (pp. 28–46). Eugene, OR: WIPF & Stock.

Wang, M.C., Levitt, H., Horne, S., & Klesges, L. (2009). Christian women in IPV relationships: An exploratory study of religious factors. *Journal of Psychology and Christianity, 28*(3), 224–235.

# Case 14

# Diary of Anorexia

## Marne Austin

*Keywords:* disordered eating, family communication, peer influence, relational secrets, self-esteem

## October 2, 2010

When I was eleven, I was hospitalized for half of my sixth grade year for anorexia. This isn't the secret. Many people know this, and I share it willingly if in some conversation it seems appropriate. I present it as something that happened a long time ago. When I talk about it with friends, colleagues, family, whomever, because I locate it in my past, I speak about my eating disorder in a displaced "long ago" or clinical sense. I think I've tried to convince myself that that constitutes *really* talking about it, that it's a good thing and will aid in others' and my own understandings of the disease, but that's absolutely untrue. It's like going through the motions and saying "oh yes, I advocate openness" but then running stealthily into a dark cave to partake in guilty indulgence in the secret—much like the behaviors "former" eating disordered people continue to enact. See, I did it again—displacement, clinical—no, we hav—damn! *I* have to let the secret out, even if the only one it is a secret to is me.

The secret is this: I am still battling the disease, this eating disorder, and there's never a moment that it doesn't exist for me. Although someone can look at me and think there's no way she's battling an eating disorder (because I think a lot of people expect to see either extreme emaciation or extreme obesity—neither of which describes me), it's an

*Inside Relationships: A Creative Casebook in Relational Communication,* edited by Sandra L. Faulkner, 151–160. © 2013 Left Coast Press, Inc. All rights reserved.

ever-present, completely counterproductive, claws-gripping-at-my-soul phantom lurking in the (at times not so) dark corners of my mind that I can't say is an entity separate from me... as much as I wish it were.

I think people without the experience of eating disorders, either their own or intimate others', don't understand that just because we're out of the hospitals and we aren't seeking active treatment (besides perhaps some less-than-broadcasted counseling), that the disease is gone, or at least that "the worst is over." We function, we go about our business, we work, we have relationships, we laugh, we smile (and absolutely genuinely)—but I'm...::take a two minute pause to look off into nothingness::...I can't with any confidence say that the worst is over. Although I've been able to go about my life, accomplish some pretty cool things, and have had amazing experiences, the eating disorder has always been there. *ALWAYS.* I can't remember a day, wait, barely even a *moment,* in over fourteen years where there was not an undercurrent of eating disorder. Even in the happiest of moments:

**Black Belt Graduation** (rockin' the stage with enormous unanticipated applause from the audience)

- o "Man, I look good 'cause I'm 120 pounds.'" ← eating one meal a day

**New Relationship** (being with the one person to this point in my life I can say I would be happy to spend every day with—I'm even comfortable during sex)

- o "I've got to stay thin otherwise this won't be good for either of us." ← starving

**Bachelor's Graduation**

- o "I'm 119 pounds and wear a size 8. People like me because I'm functioning well in school. I feel good about myself being thin and working out." ← I'm starving myself, have days where I binge, followed by days of nonstop exercise and not eating

**Master's Graduation**

- o I'm the biggest I've ever been. It's basically been two years straight of binging because I'm so miserable at New Mexico. I feel worthless. My work is shit, and it's even worse because I can't even control my fucking weight." ← binging seriously for years straight

**Girls' Pajama Party with My Closest/Most Valuable Gal Pals**

○ "When will this be over so I can ransack the cupboard's and refrigerator's contents without anyone seeing this horrible side of me?" ← Seemingly healthy weight and always positive attitude

How many awesome experiences have I missed because of this secret? I bail on friends, back out on plans, and mask *it* with the excuses: "I'm sick." "I have some stomach issues today." "An emergency has come up...." Or, how many times have I not been present in the moment because I'm thinking about my weight or the next time I can pig out? How many relationships have I not been able to maintain because I keep this a secret, and my flakiness as a friend or girlfriend comes off as a personal disgruntlement with them, or they think I'm not the person I say I am? It's really all of the issues in my head. It's so hypocritical because I'm always telling others, *you know, we have to take advantage of all these opportunities, we have to live life!* I firmly believe this; I want to be able to do—no, I want to be able to let myself do— this...always. I find that I speak so often in terms of who I want to be, hoping that that will, through time and constant verbal reinforcement, come to actually be. And I think to a certain extent it works... but I wonder, too, if in...no—I know in doing so there are times when it merely masks what exists and in doing so only prolongs and reinforces this deep dark secret. Like Poulus (2008) said,

> The problem with secret memories is that, no matter how much you try to ignore or bury them, they won't stay put. They show up in the strangest of places, at the oddest of times. Triggered by seemingly random events in our everyday world. (p. 38)

Only I'm not sure that it just "shows up" in this case—unless we say that in "showing up," it becomes more apparent than during every other moment when it exists in the background, the shadowed corner, glaring. And I think the most dangerous part of it for me is that it becomes naturalized. I'm so used to it and the behaviors that I started because of its presence that I do now without thinking.

And so this is where I know it's really not a secret. One of the funniest things about those of us with eating disorders is that we like to think we have everyone convinced that we're "normal." Which, I know, we're not. People notice that I don't eat when there are snacks, that I bring food to potlucks yet don't partake, that I host get-togethers at my house and serve food but don't eat it. They know I have to eat; I mean, how else does she have the weight that she does? And I'm not ultra skinny by any means, in fact I'm overweight—but I try not to think about that and try to reframe it as "dude, I can run frickin' thirteen miles, no problem. I'm "healthy"—so I don't think the worry is there for them about me not eating. Or, there's kind of the other end, where people see that I don't eat and say, "Wow, you have such great self-discipline," as if it's a good thing. I can't fault them at all—this whole thing is not a critique of my peers, rather of myself. But I hear that phrase often and I mean, perhaps others not in my position would take that as a compliment, and I know it's intended to be one, but it's so laden with darkness that my thought is "if you only knew." It's a stab, a reminder that there is something wrong with me...it's not self-discipline because what it means is that at some point, whether tonight or a few nights from now or weeks from now, all that "discipline" will go to hell and it will be a fury of thoughtless, ravaging, can't-even-taste-the-damn-food-but-can't-scarf-it-down-fast-enough mastication that can put... that I *allow* to put me down for sometimes over a week!

So I know people notice. I know people notice my (not) eating behaviors. I know people notice that I take leave from life for days. I know people notice I bail with lame excuses. But my secret is very much alive, I think, in ways that people outside of me, and even me inside my head, aren't aware of in terms of its depth and the grasp it has on my being. Though, as always, I am hopeful looking over what I've written so far; I don't think I've ever presented the secret quite in this way. Perhaps Poulus (2008) is right in that although families "work hard to control impressions others have of them" (p. 39), perhaps by writing about my secret in this way, by verbalizing MY story, I can work towards healing. I can divulge this secret to help my family and friends help me. I can cry and just get it out...and who knows...perhaps even help someone else?

## Setting the Stage
### October 2, 1985–Mom's Journal

Today is Marne's birthday—almost. She's 7 months old. It's hard to believe our "little" baby is this old already. She weighs in at 17 lbs. 4 oz. and over 27 inches tall....

She's a beautiful little girl. We certainly are lucky to have this wonderful child. I only hope and pray we raise her right. Guess I'll have to define "right" soon.

She's now lying in her crib. After all my usual ploys to get her back to sleep—I've given up. Told her I really love her (to soothe my guilt for leaving her) and laid her in her bed. Wound up her mobile and light. Each minute of quiet is promising, but a periodic sneeze, cough, or gurgle lets me know she's still in complete control of her environment. Which coincidentally includes her parents.

## October 3, 1985—Mom's Journal

Jim and Marne picked me up for lunch today. I just love it when I get in the car, she looks deeply into my eyes for a few seconds then slowly grins in recognition of her mom. Sometimes she looks at me so intently, it's like she's trying to peer into my brain to find out what's in there. I try to open my eyes widely and my mind to let her in to discover whatever she may.

## October 9, 1985—Mom's Journal

Called Jim at home. He was in the process of feeding Marne. After explaining in great detail and apparent frustration what a mess Marne was making, he declared he wasn't feeding her anymore. "She can just wait until you come home." On several occasions in the past, she has refused to eat for him, but when I came home she sat right up and ate hungrily. The secret is to starve her first... should I tell him...

## My Reflection

All of my memories of my family are positive ones. I have never had a moment where I doubted my parents' and brother's love for me. I have always known and genuinely felt that no matter what is going on in my personal and professional life, home is a place I can go, where my parents' unconditional love never falls into the background for even an instant.

When I was four years old, we moved from the Mainland United States to Hawaii. In Hawaii, I quickly learned that I was different from many of my peers. I was tall. I was "haole." My last name sounded different. I did not have straight black hair (I had blonde hair until about second grade). When asked what ethnicity I was, I couldn't say "Japanese," "Chinese," "Philipino," and I hated the answer "You're American" that was given to me by my parents. When I started school, I gradually began gaining weight. In the fourth grade, I was much taller than most of my classmates and weighed about twice as much. I always felt out of place in school, I was ridiculed for my weight, and I was tired of it. I realized I couldn't be Asian (even though I went so far as to go to Japanese school every day for several years after school to learn Japanese—a language the majority of my Japanese peers didn't even speak). I couldn't be shorter. I couldn't have a last name like Suzuki or Lee, but I could "learn" to be skinny like them. Then perhaps I would fit in, they wouldn't make fun of me, and I would be accepted or even sought out by my peers.

Even though at school and amongst my peers I was dissatisfied with who I was, my home life was always a place of unconditional acceptance, enjoyment, love, and laughter. I knew my parents loved me just because I was me. I didn't have to do anything extraordinary to gain their acceptance—though of course they were always proud of all of my accomplishments. At home, I knew who I was in that I was my family. There was never a more positive force and place than my family and home. This is also why it became so painful when I was a sick, because the one place that was "safe" for me, the place that was always happy, became a place of tears and pain—all caused by me and my anorexia.

## A Dark Event in a Lighted Place
### May 25, 1996—Mom's Journal

Sometimes it's quite painful to fight, argue, cajole, rationalize—all we can think of—to try to nudge Marne back to the sweet, silly kid she used to be. In July of 1995 she decided that she was too fat. I agreed with her, so she started on a journey that hasn't been very fun for us. At first the weight loss was quite exciting—a tremendous example of strength and will power for such a young girl—everyone was awed at her dedication. The physical transformation was breathtaking—from a double-chinned kid who could only wear adult x-large shirts to a beautiful, sculptured young lady who now wears a kid's size. Yes, the physical transformation was indeed noteworthy—but it took its toll on the psychological persona of our beautiful daughter.

We are very concerned about our darling girl and wonder if we should put her into counseling. She understands the concerns and consequences of her not eating properly. However, she is so driven to not become fat again—there's a horrendous battle going on within her—our question is who will win the battle.

### November 22, 2010—Interview

Marne: So how would you say that the relationship changed, like for you, how do you feel that you approached me differently and how did we interact that was different during that time leading up to it and the actual diagnosis and hospitalization. How did the relationship change?

Mom: I can remember one incident. And maybe this, it is an episode. You know? It's not peanut butter across the entire relationship. But there was one time when I was cooking something and trying to be very sensitive to your needs and I was cooking it and you wouldn't eat it. And it was something like steamed broccoli And I said, "Why won't you eat it? Don't you trust me?" and you said, "No." :::poof Aaaahhh (sound of arrow going through heart)::: you know? So it was one incident, but I think in some respects it may have flavored a little bit of how you felt about me more so than I felt about you. You know so in terms of our relationship, it was a struggle; it was the disease that was the struggle. Not your dad and I's love for you in any capacity. So did it change our relationship? Sure, anytime, but it wasn't us as people; it was the disease or an addiction of some kind.

## November 2010—
## Recalling a Turning Point in My Hospitalization

"Your mother is the cause of all your problems."

Interesting. Let me think...

I was told everyday that I was loved...

We were always smiling, laughing...

*Cause of all my problems...*

My parents spoiled me rotten...

Called the mainland when they couldn't find Fraggle Rock dolls in the islands.

I was enrolled in every afterschool program I was interested in:

> Japanese school
> Gifted and Talented
> Junior Police Officers
> Girl Scouts
> Soccer
> Basketball
> Swimming

T-ball
Arts
Hawaii Youth Symphony Orchestra
Summer school....

*Cause of all my problems, cause of all my problems...*

When my best friend Patti moved to New Jersey, I proposed that I get all A's or lose ten pounds and as a reward, I could go visit her.

I got all A's = parents put me on a flight to New Jersey to fly alone across the Pacific and Mainland US alone to visit her (which they would have done anyway even if I hadn't proposed a deal)...

*Cause of all my problems...*

I was always picked up from school or daycare with a hug and a smile...

*Cause of all my problems...*

I went to bed every night knowing that my family loved me, that I loved them, and there was never anything I could do that would make my parents dislike or not love me...

*Cause of all my problems.*

That's it! There's only one answer as to why this professional, this psychiatrist assigned to my case, would unveil to me (and conveniently NOT my mom) that my mother was the cause of all my problems: she gave birth to me!

Wow, thank you so much for that clarity. I mean, wow, how wrong was I: going around life thinking my family loved me, that my mother had my best interests at heart. I mean really, thank God you nipped the problem at the bud, Dr. Richson! Now, I can move on and actually recover from my disease because I now know the source of my problems: my mother!

Even at eleven years old, living in a dark, ominous, lonely world of anorexia, I knew that this was the biggest shit piece of information that I had ever been handed, no, *bestoowwweedd.* Oh benevolent, omniscient shrink, thanks for completely invalidating any ounce of credibility I blindly gave you upon my admission. Obviously, you completely missed the fact that even though I inhabit this lonely, depression-filled, evil world of an eating disorder, I am not truly alone because it is due to my mom's (and dad's) unconditional love for me that I am here in the hospital. Though I am alone in my head and I don't even understand the condition in which I have found myself, I know I'm not alone and so long as I'm with my parents and they are on my team (and always will be, thank you very much!), I am not alone—I am safe because they will do absolutely everything in their power to help their baby girl!

It was at this moment during my hospitalization that I was shoved into an acute awareness of how much love my mom had for me. The day my parents admitted me to a mental hospital (all stigma attached) was easily the most difficult, heart-tearing day in their lives. This declaration by a professional that my mom was the sole cause of my eating disorder created an incredible dissonance. No doctor was ever going to tell me that she had any malign, insufficient love or view of me. She was MY mom.

## November 22, 2010—Interview

Mom: So you know, years ago there was a bumper sticker that said "Shit happens"? *Life* happens to people, and how you deal with it, how you come out of it, some people come out better, some people don't, you know? I see people who come out of families who are just totally dysfunctional, come out very good. There are some people who come out of what I consider relatively functional families and, come out good, have struggles, but some of them just go to the dark side. Some of it is just part of our test, part of our growth. Yep, I gave you birth, sue me. I gave life to you ::laugh:: meaning I can't deal with it, you're going to have to. You know that Dad and I will walk by your side till the day we all drop dead in this life and pick up in the next life. We will never abandon you. A lot of the things that we don't understand, but it's obvious now with the things you're doing, you don't understand them either. So it's a journey that we're all on together.

## Questions and Activities for Discussion

1. Like Poulus (2008) says, "The problem with secret memories is that, no matter how much you try to ignore or bury them, they won't stay put. They show up in the strangest of places, at the oddest of times.

Triggered by seemingly random events in our everyday world" (p. 38). Are there other family/relational secrets that have the potential to create unhealthy coping behaviors? Have you ever known anyone with a blind spot/unwillingness to address unhealthy behavior? If so, did you do anything about it? Should you do anything about it?

2. What can be done to help those with disordered eating? What does Austin's story point out as important for us as a society and us as relational partners to focus on? What is the connection between self-esteem/personal identity, peer influence, and close relationships?

3. Austin wrote about cognitive dissonance between professional advice and family support. Is disordered eating a social problem (e.g., pro-anorexia web sites, the fashion industry), a communication problem, a problem with a family system? How does social support make a difference? What advice would you give someone in a position like Austin's?

4. How could blogging help (e.g., http://thefatgirlblog.com) and hinder what Austin is advocating?

## For Further Reading and Reference

Anderson, M. (1995). Mother-daughter connection: The healing force in the treatment of eating disorders. *Journal of Feminist Family Therapy, 6*(4), 3–19.

Kraus, W. (2006). The narrative negotiation of identity and belonging. *Narrative Inquiry, 16*(1), 103–111.

Poulus, C. N. (2008). *Accidental ethnography: An inquiry into family secrecy.* Walnut Creek, CA: Left Coast Press, Inc.

Punyanunt-Carter, N. M. (2008). Father-daughter relationships: Examining family communication patterns and interpersonal communication satisfaction. *Communication Research Reports, 25*(1), 23–33.

# Case 15

# That Baby Will Cost You
## An Intended Ambivalent Pregnancy

Sandra L. Faulkner

*Keywords:* ambivalence, children, medicalization, personal narrative, pregnancy, relational dialectics theory, work-family issues

*When people tell stories about their relationships, they often dress up events as simpler, more linear, and perhaps even more logical than the way in which they are actually experienced, and so too, perhaps do researchers.* (Duck, 2011, p. 14)

## Cost: Eighteen Academic Articles

It is visible. The fashionable princess seam top strewn with red and yellow poppies doesn't cover enough. I must talk about being knocked up every time I shake someone's hand or lean in for a hug. "Babies cost an article a year." Mitch tells me this when we sit down behind the book display table wedged into one end of the Qualitative Inquiry Conference registration room. His press's books just unpacked from boxes are stacked high enough to offer some privacy. The typical conference smell of freshly inked paper and stale coffee dispels some anxiety about whether my manuscript on poetry as research method, which he will publish, is good enough.

"Yeah, I'm pregnant." I pat my stylish fetus mound with the expected gesture. His flat statement about the cost of what I have named the Faulkner Fetus (to the horror or amusement of a few) pops my bravado. Others are just now noticing the six-and-a-half-month lump, which I have carried to her first academic conference. I grip a fully caffeinated latte from the student union and wonder if he thinks anything of my beverage choice? I did say no to an extra shot of espresso. And this is only cup two, the last of my self-imposed daily allotment.

This thought and all of the questions I have been asking myself about my pregnancy, and those I have been imagining others will ask me, annoy me. The truth is I have never fully wanted to be pregnant or have children. Not in that 100 percent way I thought pregnant women should feel. Would feel. In fact, I had attended a few childfree by choice support group meetings at my university the previous year. Though, the truth is also this: I felt like a childfree fraud sitting in a circle with the other attendees who enacted an absolute certainty. I confessed disinterest in children because of the environmental impact, gendered expectations, love for solitude and work. However, immediately after getting married I had spent four solo months teaching in Madrid, manufacturing a mental picture of a child. A child built with the most attractive features of Josh and myself, of course. *"Just missing mi esposa,"* I reasoned as I traveled with students and other professors while Josh remained in Syracuse to care for the house and our pet rat. I can't remember if I ever told Josh about the only two childfree meetings I had attended before getting pregnant the following month. We did at least talk about children before we decided to get married. I told him, "I'm ambivalent."

"I'm ambivalent, too," he said.

I have abhorred every second, minute, and hour of being pregnant. My imaginings of the annoyances I would experience are being born out in precise detail like some kind of bas-relief. And now, in one of the arenas where I have learned to feel competent, my book publisher affirms this antipathy with an explicit cost analysis. *"This kid will not cost me articles!"* I think as I watch conference attendees browse the current and classic releases of everything research method. Then, as is usual lately, conflicting thoughts ruin my concentration. I ask myself whether I really do care, or only feel I *should* care as I feel Baby Girl kick my ribcage with great enthusiasm. Secretly, I have been trying out the new moniker, Baby Girl, when she moves, which she does a lot when I am working or eating or teaching. A consistent alarm clock, she wakes me up at 7 a.m. with her hiccups.

As Mitch and I talk, I will Baby Girl to allow my mind the front seat. *Please, do not make my shirt move!* I *think* to her, though evidently you are supposed to *talk* to your "unborn baby." All of the patronizing pregnancy instruction manuals insist you narrate your daily routine to make a baby Einstein in-utero. I just can't speak out loud to a fetus what I do all day: *And now I am cracking an egg. Wow, I just wrote a seven-page syllabus in an hour. What kind of cookies do you want me to order us from the Cookie Jar?* Even worse, months from now, well after the kid is born, I will find a wretched website proposing something called epigenetics,[1] the hatred of women hiding under the rippling banner of science:

> We happen to live in the time where science has more than proven all the detriments of a pessimistic attitude. In another hundred years, every pregnant mom in the world will be consciously cultivating happy joyful thoughts specifically to foster optimal growth for their unborn children.

Now we can label women crappy moms from conception. I embody this label as all of my good preggo oxytocin comes from Chocolate Crinkles; the Faulkner Fetus kicks especially well after some cocoa powdered sugar love.

## Cost: My Synapses

"Faulkner, you should write about this." My friend and co-author, Pam, snorts as we talk on the phone, presumably about a research project, but really she is listening to my litany of pregnancy maladies, urging me to take field notes.

"Baby brain may be the worst at this point. I can't remember the names of objects like *that round ball* that opens the door."

I'm lounging in my office, during office hours, waiting for no-show students, wondering if the few hours I spend in the building each week are suffocating the fetus. After a colleague complained loud enough about our sick building, the Ohio OSHA determined there was indeed mold proliferating in the ceilings and walls, but the colonization was not enough to kill us. This was supposed to be comforting?

I should be writing, doing research, working on my tenure portfolio, prepping teaching—all of the activities I am compensated for under the title assistant professor. What I do with this time lately, though, is obsessively search online for ambivalent pregnant ladies and instant message friends about my bodily annoyances. I can't focus on much except this. Mostly, I find blogs devoted to pregnancy complaints, and the "but it's worth it" qualifier is usually explicitly stated. "I have heartburn so bad it's like a rotten lab experiment, *but it will be worth* it when she/he arrives."

"If I write about this, I will have to add more money to the kid's

## Dear pregnant body

Your floppy joints and loose
ligaments hurt like a hook
screwed into this side of mutton.
Did I remember to tell you?
The forgetting, the pants
Held together with a rubber band.
The parasitic hiccups
begin before noon
before classes of what not
to do. Your restrictions line up
the days into grade school files
on the way to the stinky
cafeteria: coffee will make
a deformed child, cause
me to abort too soon,
cookies are all sugary evil,
crumbs of proof
I'm already a bad mom.
Your only glow I detect
is the stuffy nose
as I heave those hemorrhoids
from bed to couch to itchy
kitchen chair. No. You knock me
down, make me bump into stuff
like a vertiginous seal,
hurtful prickly mound
animal nostrils that discern dinner
at every house as you shamble past
flip those happy myths over
and over and over. (Faulkner, 2009)
(Waiting for Mimi Shawl, 2009-2011)

therapy fund." I say. Pam's laughter makes me snort as I tally up all of the things I am doing wrong, will do wrong, could do wrong: *Daily cookies; bike riding; hand-me-downs; day-care; refusal to allow the kid to wear pink, be a cheerleader.*

⊡

*Relational thinking requires us to step beyond simplistic (yet powerful) dichotomies to recognize a dialectic relationship, a "third space" wherein many possibilities exist for combinations of both/ and. Each woman's life represents a different story with a different combination of desires regarding her private/public lives, and this story evolves over time as different events and opportunities arise.* (Foster, 2005, p. 78)

## Cost: Persona

It is the last two weeks of spring semester. My interpersonal communication students and I are talking about aging and friendship, whether biological age influences the longevity of high school and college relationships. I have a terrible teaching schedule—Monday Tuesday Wednesday night—that feels more than unlucky given my desire to be in bed by 5 p.m. Growing a fetus takes energy, more energy than I've ever needed. Forget recovering from the worst hangover or running a marathon energy. I wear fewer clothes to class, allowing the winter walk from my office to the classroom to slap me awake.

They ask me if I keep in touch with anyone from high school. I tell them I live too many state and moves away. High school was so long ago I even forget to be nostalgic. "In fact, I'm not going to my twenty year highschool reunion in June."

"Why?" more than one student asks.

I have just set myself up for the revelation I avoided all semester. I did not want to be the knocked up professor, to talk about everything baby, to risk being seen as a walking womb, to have my every statement about relationships scrutinized. These were the reasons I did not want to tell my colleagues, either. Of course, that was taken out of my hands when the director of the school asked if she could announce the *good news.* I hesitate because I know what is going to happen next. But I must respond. "I will be seven-and-a-half months pregnant."

The female students burst with questions. "When are you due?" "Why didn't you tell us?" "Are you excited?" I still do not wear maternity clothes at five-and-a-half months, but I thought some of them surely had noticed the looser shirts not tucked in and skirts with stretchy waistbands, the fact that I often sit on the table in the front of the room to teach.

"I am a grumpy pregnant lady. I don't really want to talk about it." But the students need some more explanation and won't let me move on. I try to explain my ambivalence, how I never wanted to be pregnant. Though I never wanted to be married either and that was working.

"What does the word ambivalent mean?" I don't answer and start talking about the next exam.

◧

*Ambivalence is not a very well-understood construct and does not have a standard measurement....Our analysis suggests that disaggregating those women who are ambivalent from the overall group of women with unwanted pregnancies may highlight a group of women who have unique characteristics and risks.* (Mohllajee et al., 2007, p. 679)

## Cost: Certainty

Medical researchers[2] ask pregnant women the question I wrestled with hourly: How do you feel about having a baby now? The ambivalent are characterized as those who accept being pregnant without any enthusiasm, those who change their negative assessment to be positive or accepting, and those with contradictory feelings. Doesn't this typify most pregnant women?[3] Doesn't being pregnant mean you have negative and positive feelings pulling you like a field day tug of war contest? Is one really enthusiastic about funky smells, hemorrhoids, and joints that ache when you breathe? What about the gaping vortex of need, aka an infant?

I get the concern for attitudes given demonstrable research that negativity and ambivalence may be related to undesirable outcomes[4] for mothers and children, such as inconsistent contraception use, congenital abnormalities, low birth rate, vaginal bleeding, prenatal accidents, and pregnancy complications. My question after reading the clinical list of problems is: What about the process of being pregnant?[5] Why all of this need for a nice resolution? What is missing from all of the popular and clinical pregnancy talk is a more sophisticated understanding of ambivalence toward pregnancy[6] than the dichotomous "planned, wanted, or intended" versus "unwanted or accidental." At least, I discovered there is a field of study devoted to unintended pregnancy, those pregnancies that are mistimed or unwanted at conception.[7] However, the *intended* ambivalent pregnancies are the group that does not seem to be well represented. This is, of course, why I did not advertise my ambivalence, just the antipathy toward being pregnant and my pregnant body.[8] Our entire culture participates in the hatred toward the female body; especially a threatening pregnant body, and this hatred translates well into pithy Facebook status updates. *The fetus insists on chocolate, though I can't tie my shoes. Decaf sucks. We love sugar.*

Being pregnant is akin to writing a cost-benefit analysis report with few pros listed on the right hand side of the spreadsheet. In my search for certainty, the unbalanced sheet of costs won't disappear. The ricocheting pro versus con dialogue was not something I mentioned when the nurse practitioner asked me at the office visit to establish the fact of my pregnant body, "Was this a wanted pregnancy?" The answer wasn't an absolute yes. But it also wasn't no. Josh and I both said, "Yes." I could have said *I am committed to a healthy pregnancy.* But then I would have also had to say *what I consider to be a healthy pregnancy.* And this includes coffee, cookies and bitchy skepticism. I know not to react against the happy glowing pregnant lady myth in the obstetrician's office pasted with this dominant discourse. When I sit in the lab room to get blood drawn for iron level and HIV tests, pictures of patients' happy infants thumbtacked to the corkboard stare me silent, as do the Anne Geddes prints hung in every exam room, the flowered wallpaper trim encasing the building, and the box of toys spilling out of the kids' nook in the waiting room.

I remember the previous semester when students in my sexual communication class designed a safer sex campaign for a local service agency. Sara clicked off the costs of a child with a power point slide, and I felt a flutter of, what? Unease? Hypocrisy? I imagined that I was pregnant, and this presentation was for me. I knew even without peeing on a stick. Colin finished the just-say-no talk with why getting pregnant is a poor choice. "Here in Ohio, the first year will cost you $15, 036 and total costs will be like $322, 000. This is true. My sister had a baby last year, and she is always broke." I don't ask them about why they have not considered the myriad of reasons for pregnancy, why they are using the analogies of money and choice. I am the students' collective middle-class fear.

I forget about the students' presentation until the Saturday after Thanksgiving when the family leaves, and I slink to the Walgreens near the house for a pregnancy test. The air is damp with rotten leaf mold, and my face flushes with the secret. Not the chill. I am uncertain why I am doing this alone given that Josh and I agreed to try and conceive. I just need to take the walk. To let the flutters in my chest, a mini-anxiety coaster, work their spasms through my tired system. The utter exhaustion that feels worse than any hangover and the incessant need to pee are the alarms that makes me attend to my body. For the four days we had our parents over the holiday, I assumed that the cocktails and cleaning and cooking and making rules and passive aggressive arguing were the triggers.

⌐

*Would-be-mothers...cannot escape the dictates of their female bodies....They are, despite education and professionalism, simply bodies upon which problematic biological dramas (e.g., infertility, pregnancy, miscarriage, and breastfeeding) are played out. Such tales infiltrate our cultural discourse and the lives of women simultaneously, silencing the possibility for alternate life scripts and locking women into definitions that resist elaboration.* (Foster, 2005, p. 76)

## Cost: Medicalization

The technician has me lift my shirt as she pulls my waistband down, tucking some crinkly white paper into the top of my pants. Josh sits in the chair on the left of the ultra-sound machine that I presume is for audience members because it is oriented toward the screen. He attends every doctor appointment, and he also lets me tell him again and again, "I wish you could be the one pregnant." I scooch down the black pleather covered exam table and rest my hands under my head as the technician dims the lights. She uses warmed conductor gel, so that when she squirts it on my abdomen, I don't flinch. That comes later.

"An alien!" I can't see Josh from my prone angle on the table. He is leaning forward into the shadows of the machine. I smile at his humor, what I think is confirmation.

"It does look like an alien!" I agree with Josh and move my head to get a better view of the dark gray and white sonar image on the ultrasound machine screen. The young technician continues to move the paddle around my mid-section, being careful to keep the cord off the conductor gel, and makes no comment about our observation.

She pushes the paddle down with some pressure in order to register an image. We hear a muffled duh-da duh-da da-da-duh she tells us is a heartbeat. It sounds strange to me, like an uneven rain, a surprise storm tapping on the skylights in our house.

The instrument begins to feel as hot as a lap-top battery on my skin. The technician, whose name I can't remember even though she introduced herself, has her honeyed hair pulled back into a functional pony tale, wears navy scrubs and a pair of pink Crocs. Every one seems younger than me, pregnant at 37. I have been engaging in the guess-their-age game when I encounter any mothers or pregnant women.

"Here's your baby." She hands me the grainy black and white film with three different views of the alien. I tell Josh that we should not put this picture into a baby book because it would give any child nightmares. "It's creepy looking."

"Isn't it an embryo?" I ask the question without pause, thinking about pro-life rhetoric. This talk about unborn babies irritates me, and lately the irritation turns to anger. Everything irritates me in this amped-up hormonal stew that feels like my usual PMS squared. I am an academic. I can, and do, research about gestation, about stages. At eight weeks, I can still decide to abort this embryo. I have no intention to do so, but I know this sack of cells is not an "unborn baby," not viable yet.

"I don't know." The technician tells me I can get up and check out after she hands me a towel to wipe the gel off my midsection. I wonder if these things are being noted in my chart—bad mother, poor attitude, watch with caution.

At the next ultrasound two weeks later, the one I agree to because of my advanced maternal age, the experience is even worse.

"You are here because you're old." The fertility specialist at Toledo Hospital sits behind the clichéd dark wooden desk, his computer rests on one edge, and my chart lies open in the middle. This greeting stuns me. "We used to call you an ugly name, elderly primagravida." I laugh because he expects it. I nod for him to go on. I am not pleased with his tone, and as he talks more, I know he's patronizing me. Josh sits beside me. He does not seem to be reacting, so I remind myself to ask him about it when we leave.

"Your eggs are old—not like when you were 21 and the eggs were fresh, young." The doctor shuffles the papers inside my file as he talks. I want to vocalize the "buts" looping inside my head as his soundtrack keeps going and going. *But I was too busy with school and being a deep adolescent to have a child in my early twenties. I managed to get pregnant in one month on two separate occasions. Clearly age is not affecting my fertility. I have resources. I am middle class enough I can tell a child no. I have more patience, job security, a savings account, a bourgeoisie life style and strong social network.* But, I don't say anything; I just keep nodding. I hope he sees that I will be a better mother. Now.

The doctor slides some pamphlets across the desk. He is talking about amniocenteses and other tests that can be done, the benefits and the risks. "You mean false positives." I am smug. I know the medical term, interrupt him, talk over him, smug until we hear there is no news. The nuchal translucency screening, which I liken to a supersonic 3-D ultrasound, did not provide the measurement of the amount of fluid behind the neck. The damn embryo was 2 cm too short to determine a ratio of Down's risk. We had to make another appointment for the next week when the embryo would transform into the Faulkner Fetus.

*If we consider public and private lives, each with its related sets of constraints and rewards, then the knot of anxiety that accompanies the transition to motherhood for many women begins to unravel—at least conceptually. There is no separation of these experiences of productivity.* (Foster, 2005, p. 78)

## Cost: Waiting    Benefit: Not being Knocked-Up Anymore

Josh wakes up with a snort. It's cold. His neck and right side are stiff. *What's that noise?* He groans when he recognizes the scream of the fetal monitor alarm. The slide-out chair next to the air-conditioning unit was like sleeping on the ground in winter. It was that comfortable. Dr. Bass, the OB who will be on duty when our daughter decides to pop out, asked him what he thought of the chair. She sometimes slept on one in an empty labor/delivery/recovery room and could not tolerate more than one night. He had been sleeping on the rock for almost three weeks. At least he got to steal pudding cups from the OB floor fridge at night while we watched DVDs on my laptop.

I'm untwisting the monitor straps and moving the hot monitor face-plate from side to side on top of my fundus. The machine's constant shrill makes it hard for Josh to hear my muttering. The elastic straps constrict my middle, so I always show him the red circle mark on my skin like a sweat stain from an icy glass whenever I'm freed. The nurse from the day shift had even switched out the previous machine with a newer antepartum monitor from another room on the OB floor. This machine did not work any better, though the nurse claimed the doppler and contraction transducer were more sensitive. "The hospital is still paying it off, but the tech support with this model is terrible." The alarm always went off just when we would fall asleep.

"Sorry! I'm trying to fix it. I'll turn it off." I learned which button could reset the machine after a few nights of the annoying pattern: The alarm would sound. A nurse would stroll down the corridor and through the kitchenette to our room to adjust the monitor straps. We would fall asleep. The alarm would sound. Josh would tell me to push the call button. I would fiddle with the machine myself, because I knew the nurses could hear the monitor in their station. Of course, the nurses never heard the alarm. Or they ignored it. I know that Josh got tired of telling me to reluctantly press the call button by my head. At first, he assumed that something was wrong with Mimi, but the alarm went off anytime I rolled over, the baby hiccupped, the air-conditioning went on, the sheets wrinkled.

And so we wait.

"Unexpected bleeding during pregnancy can be caused by three conditions." Dr. Leggat tells me he is going to give me an obstetrics lecture. He is on hospital duty the next two days, so he scoots past my post at the table with my laptop and lunch tray to sit in the rocker. I know Josh will be irritated he missed this because he usually waited until after the doctor's rounds before going home to feed the rats, pick up the farm share, and do whatever else I had written on the back of envelopes he shoved into his pocket.

I'm thrilled Dr. Leggat is talking to me not as a patient, but in what I consider a smart target audience maneuver, as a student in a lecture! Situation one is placenta previa. However, your placenta is where it should be—not covering the cervix. I nod, clasp my hands at the bottom of my belly, dig my nails in so as not to interrupt as I have for every other talk Dr. Leggat and any medical staff has given me during this pregnancy. I don't even ask about Dr. Bass's hypothesis—that I may have some bleeding uterine cysts that have become more sensitive because of hormonal changes. He continues with his explanation. The second situation is placental abruption where part of the placenta peels away from the uterus before birth. My numerous ultrasounds showed nothing problematic, though it is still a possibility. "We only see 20 percent of all cases that way. You are the third, and worst, category—a mystery." This is why this second stay at what I call the *Spa Wood County* will be an extended one and only end with a birth. "In the past women would stay on bed rest for months with their knitting." *Uh, does he not see the lace merino shawl on the needles in my lap?*

The mystery of this entire thing is what worried Josh. That and my non-concern. *I feel fine. The kid is kicking and hiccupping and enjoying her warm swim.* I felt fine, except for the usual late pregnancy complaints. I almost did not tell Josh about the second bleed, especially because it was 11 p.m. on a Friday night when I noticed. I wanted to go to bed and wake up in spontaneous labor. The "what if" made me grab our packed bag and put on a pair of stretchy pants. Dr. Bass had told us during one of her rounds, "We don't know why women go into labor, what makes it happen. This is why I like obstetrics, there is a lot we don't know about pregnancy. It's an exciting medical specialty."

Josh walks into the room later in the afternoon singing "I tip *my hat* to you. I *tip* my hat to you," my requested "decent coffee" in hand. "Stop it!" I play yell at Josh, though this is one of his funnier songs. He was fascinated with the medical urine hat resting in the bathroom bowl and wondered if the nurses went around singing about them. "Why do they call it a hat?" Another mystery.

My recollection of Leggat's lecture proves we should go nowhere. I know what Josh is thinking: *That damn-hippy doula and her text messages urging my high-risk wife to check out of the hospital.* He laughs at the t-shirt we bought his brother with the picture of a semi-truck grill and the words "Think Fast Hippie." The "but what if" was ever present. There was no more bleeding. There was nothing in the fetal monitor scans. There was a normal picture on the sonograms. *But* the possibility of a bleed out, the quickness with which maternal and fetal mortality was threatened made him hungry to stay and eat the cafeteria's mashed potatoes with extra gravy. Actually, he loved the easy access to cheap gravy three floors down. Other than the hair he once found on a sloppy joe, he relished the high-fat food in Styrofoam containers he carried up to our room on the OB floor.

He had seen the blood all over the sheets, on my hospital gown, on Dr. Bass's hands the first time we rushed from the office to the ER, and Dr. C's hands the second time, spotty on the admitting room floor trailing to the bathroom. Josh hated that they released me the first time after five days, even though I complained that I felt fine. He wanted to stay in the hospital with the monitors, the trained staff, and the equipment in the C-section room we saw during the tour in our childbirth class.

To me the thought of a "rapid operative delivery" was repulsive, was the antithesis of the private hypnobirthing classes I had to hunt down for us to attend. Yet, he was quiet and said nothing about the "fake earth-goddess" instructor or the 20 or 40 or 60 birth videos we watched on her black leather couches that were perfect for napping during the practice hypnosis sessions. He was quiet even though the births made him queasy and certain he could not be near any bloody show.

And so we wait.

When I ask what he remembered about the birth, Josh describes my screaming, the blood, and the moment Mimi shot out like a piece of popcorn. And what a waste of money that doula was, the one who urged a high-risk woman to leave the hospital and who did not show up until the last hour of labor, minutes after my bloody water broke, unassisted.

This was the third induction, the one I consented to because we couldn't take any more of the spa. One overnight Cervidil prostoglandin E2 vaginal insert and a pitocin drip at 39 weeks gestation ended with a run to Jimmy Johns. The Ultimate Porker—what I remember as my first meal—is a magical sandwich filled with bacon and ham and mayonnaise and general grumpiness dissipating goodness that a cup of pudding from the kitchenette was not. The nurse who would chant "pushing is just like taking a big poopie" had not administered the drip properly, irritating everyone in utero and out. The second failed attempt was natural method Monday, a Foley bulb catheter that caused too much bleeding coupled with ineffective nipple stimulation. It was this final pitocin drip that coaxed our daughter out. On her due date and three minutes before dinner, before the midnight hour that Dr. Bass, the nurses, everyone predicted. Mimi did not spend much time being pushed out. I was walking around the halls pulling the IV pole, rolling around on a birthing ball, asking for back rubs during contractions, dragging IV lines into the bathroom to pee, thinking I might actually die from the pain.

Then I'm in bed. There's lots of blood. Josh stays positioned by my head. He hears Dr. Bass's concern about the amount of blood—always the blood—there isn't enough time to do a C-section because the baby's head is crowing. *Now* she rushes to get out. I don't really hear any of this talk. One nurse is pushing an oxygen mask over my face, some other nurse and the doula are holding up my legs. *No*, no mirror, *no* I don't want to feel the baby's head. I just want it to be over. Secretly,

I was in no hurry for the birth because I feared labor, knew the hypno-birthing creed of a "pain-free birth" was like a unicorn jumping over the "rainbow relaxation" chants Josh and I had practiced for months.

"It's just like taking a big poopie." The nurse that should retire is at one foot of the bed, urging me to push. Josh confirms this memory later. My screaming hurts his ears. He feels the entire floor quaking from the noise and wants to put his hands over his ears to protect them from the ringing. And then. Mimi shoots out.

I am supposed to tell you how happy I was, that the birth was my happiest moment ever, that I cried, warbled and shook from joy. Yes, I shook, but the shaking was from exhaustion. And the first two things I said were, "Thank God I'm not pregnant anymore." Then a panicked, "It is a girl?" What I remember is that I was simply stunned. And then relieved for the shower I got to take after the golden colostrum moment, the cord-cutting, weighing and swaddling of the baby. This was the prize for no analgesics, no epidural. Josh tells me he was overwhelmed in that good almost the miracle of birth way, but not quite. He thought, "Ah, she looks like Sandra. No wait, she looks like my father-in-law."

I disclose pieces[9] of the story during the semester I teach a relational communication seminar, relieved—no ecstatic—to end the year of breastfeeding, to be lifted out of the cloying baby fog. The students and I struggle through the latest iteration of Leslie Baxter's relational dialectic theory—RDT 2.0—my favorite interpersonal theory in graduate school. I rolled around in the idea of flux, the way it felt like an epistemological homecoming. We argue about whether we can apply it to our personal experience given the radical idea that relational scholars should use discourse and not *the individual* as a unit of analysis. This shocks me into framing my (and as I understand now, Josh and Mimi's) story as a series of marginalized discourse, in particular ambivalence (versus certainty), bodily knowledge (versus medicalization, versus middle class pregnancy), and flux (versus cost-benefit ratios). The problem is that these marginal/centrifugal discourses are not well represented in the totalizing picture of the *pregnant lady*. The rigidity freezes the alternative script, doesn't allow me to look at my funny, stubborn, watermelon, pot-sticker and dog loving child and say with smirking elaboration "but it was all worth it."

## Questions and Activities for Discussion

1. What does ambivalence mean in the context of family planning? What does ambivalence mean from a relational dialectics perspective (i.e., the idea that relationships are constituted in part through dominant and marginalized discourses)? How does this personal narrative highlight the concept of ambivalence and make it useful for medical personnel and others working with ambivalent pregnant women?

2. Are there any decisions in your life that you feel ambivalent about? What are they, and why do you feel this way? Make a cost and benefit list similar to Faulkner's headings in her narrative.

3. What does the story of an "ambivalent pregnant lady" add to the study of family communication? What ethical issues arise when writing about one's family?

## Notes

1　See www.getfitforbirth.com/thoughts-and-feelings-affect-your-unborn-baby/, which promotes the idea of "get fit for birth" as part of epigenetics (i.e. environmental influences on genetics) and a book, *Discover How Your Thoughts and Feelings Affect Your Unborn Baby: Positive and Negative Thoughts May Affect Baby's Genetics.*

2　Aubrey et al. (2008).

3　Ambivalence about pregnancy is a common, though understudied, experience. In part, this may be because the further away from the pregnancy, the more likely a woman will alter her story (Duck, 2011). Ambivalent women tend to be older, nonwhite, and opposed to abortion. See Bouchard (2005).

4　Laukaran and Berg (1980); Matthias (2010); Mohllajee et al. (2007).

5　Chandra et al. (2005) estimated that about 50 percent of pregnancies in the United States during 2001 were unintended because of mis-timing or being unwanted. The rate of unintended pregnancy continues to be high. For example, see www.TheNationalCampaign.org.

6　Peterson (1987); Trad (1991).

7　Schwarz, Lohr, Gold, & Gerbert (2007).

8　Goldenberg, Goplen, Cox, & Arndt (2007).

9　I have disclosed my birth story, which contains as much about the pregnancy as the birth, more than I anticipated. This telling mirrors many of the impulses individuals in Della Pollock's (1999) study on birth stories recount.

# For Further Reading and Reference

Aubrey, J. S., Click, M. A., Dougherty, D. S., Fine, M. A., Kramer, M. W., Meisenbach, R. J., Olson, L. N., & Smythe, M.J. (2008). We do babies! The trials, tribulations, and triumphs of pregnancy and parenting in the academy. *Women's Studies in Communication, 31*, 186–195.

Bouchard, G. (2005). Adult couples facing a planned or an unplanned pregnancy. *Journal of Family Issues, 26*, 619–637.

Chandra, A., Martinez, G. M., Mosher, W. D., Abma, J. C., & Jones, J. (2005). Fertility, family planning, and reproductive health of U.S. women: Data from the 2002 National Survey of Family Growth, *Vital and Health Statistics, 23*(25).

Duck, S. (2011). *Rethinking relationships.* Thousand Oaks, CA: Sage.

Foster, E. (2005). Desiring dialectical discourse: A feminist ponders the transition to motherhood. *Women's Studies in Communication, 28*, 57–83.

Goldenberg, J. L., Goplen, J., Cox, C. R., & Arndt, J. (2007). "Viewing" pregnancy as an existential threat: The effects of creatureliness on reactions to the media depictions of the pregnant body. *Media Psychology, 10*, 211–230.

Laukaran, L. V., van den Berg, B. J. (1980). The relationship between maternal attitude toward pregnancy outcomes and obstetric complications: A cohort study of unwanted pregnancy. *American Journal of Obstetrics and Gynecology, 136*, 374–390.

Matthias, M. S. (2010). The impact of uncertainty on decision making in prenatal consultations: Obstetricians' and midwives' perspectives. *Health Communication, 25*, 199–211.

Mohllajee, A. P., Curtis, K. M., Morrow, B., & Marchbanks, P. A. (2007). Pregnancy intention and its relationship to birth and maternal outcomes. *Obstetrics & Gynecology, 109*, 678–686.

Peterson, E. E. (1987). The stories of pregnancy: On interpretation of small-group cultures. *Communication Quarterly, 35*, 39–47.

Pollock, D. (1999). *Telling bodies performing birth: Everyday narratives of childbirth.* New York: Columbia University Press.

Schwarz, E. B., Lohr, P. A., Gold, M. A., & Gerbert, B. (2007). Prevalence and correlates of ambivalence towards pregnancy among nonpregnant women. *Contraception, 75*, 305–310.

Trad, P. V. (1991). Adaptation to developmental transformations during the various phases of motherhood. *Journal of the American Academy of Psychoanalysis, 19*, 403–421.

# Chapter 6

# The Social Self

In Chapter 6, the cases detail how others and our social worlds, especially our computer-mediated communication, shape our relationship expectations and experiences. Jenn McKee's blog about an unexpected online encounter highlights the role of framing and expectations in infidelity. Suzanne Berg's chronicle of (in)fertility represents Facebook posts about pregnancy, and conversations with relatives and medical personnel as contributing to feelings of isolation and confusion in her marriage. Ellen Gorsevski details seemingly innocuous daily conversations about parenthood that serve to stigmatize women without children. Our social worlds are not mere abstractions, but realities we confront in our everyday relating. Others' opinions on what being pregnant should feel like, what it means to cheat on a partner, how we should enact the role of friend, and what it means to be an adult woman influence how we talk about these experiences, as well as how we experience them.

Relational expectations at the personal and cultural levels seem relevant to the cases here. Steve Duck (2011) labels these processes personal and social orders: our individual preferences and understandings of society that manifest in our behavior interact with the social order—how society is structured, including power and

*Inside Relationships: A Creative Casebook in Relational Communication*, edited by Sandra L. Faulkner, 177–180. © 2013 Left Coast Press, Inc. All rights reserved.

SANDRA L. FAULKNER

organizational rules. In Chapters 1, 2 and 7 in this book, I discuss the influence of cognitive assessments on our relationships (i.e., schemata, scripts, stereotypes) and continue that discussion in this chapter. These assessments include the questions we ask each other and ourselves about behavior, the situation, and accounts of the situation and behavior (Trenholm & Jensen, 2011). For example, Gorsevski asks in her personal essay why in various situations in which she finds herself, from getting her hair done to going to the dentist to attending an adult academic party, the conversation is supposed to be mother to mother simply because women are present. Cultural ideas that women should have and want to have children and only talk about children permeate the last two case studies here.

We have goals in our interactions, and the accomplishment of these goals entails planning, strategies, and effective reading of social cues (Canary, Cody, & Manusov, 2003). Or in other words, how we manage our personal and social orders in interaction influence our attainment of goals; to obtain our goals, our communication strategies often become routine to be most efficient. Two processes that we use in our routine communication strategies are expectancies and attributions (Canary et al., 2003). *Interpersonal expectancies* reference the expectations we have about our interactions, how we think people will interact with us, and how we think they should interact. McKee in her blog entry, for example, expects that connecting with an old friend from college over Facebook chat would mean appropriate self-disclosure between two former friends and not an inappropriate sexual proposition. And this also demonstrates our deeply ingrained cultural expectations about monogamy. When we try and determine the cause of another's behavior, we are making *attributions*. If we make internal attributions, we consider another's behavior to be because of personal dispositions and characteristics, whereas external attributions manifest in assessments of causation outside of an individual. In satisfied couples, for example, individuals are more apt to make internal attributions for positive behavior from a partner than are those who are dissatisfied with their relationships (Manusov, 1990).

## Social Networks, Online

Many of our interactions have moved online, and some argue that online communication is replacing face-to-face interaction and changing our social worlds (e.g., Lloyd, 2010). Computer Mediated

Communication (CMC) references two or more individuals using networked computers in order to convey messages (Walther & Parks, 2002). Even though some research suggests that students prefer online communication, and text messaging in particular, face-to-face contact is still considered more helpful (Massimini & Peterson, 2009). We can ask if our (online) communication with others is effective, ethical and appropriate. Coyne and colleagues (2011) reported that although many users felt misunderstandings were more likely to occur in text messaging, respondents often preferred to text because they had more time to consider and then articulate what they wanted to say. They also could talk with multiple people simultaneously. Social information processing theory is helpful to consider because it tells us that as we begin to know one another, we use more personal messages in a CMC environment (Walther & Parks, 2002). So, even if we are not as intimate at first online, once we develop a relationship, we use more intimate communication with those we consider to be close. In fact, CMC is useful for maintaining existing friendships because of the availability of constant contact. Further, two studies showed that CMC may facilitate talk about intimate topics, especially for shy or socially anxious individuals, and intimate disclosures result in relationships that are stronger and higher quality (Valkenburg & Peter, 2009a, 2009b).

## References

Canary, D. J., Cody, M. J., & Manusov, V. (2003). Four important cognitive processes. In K. M. Galvin & P. J. Cooper (Eds.), *Making connections: Readings in relational communication* (3rd ed., pp. 42–51). Los Angeles, CA: Roxbury.

Coyne, S. M., Stockdale, L., Busby, D., Iverson, B., & Grant, D. M. (2011). "I luv u:)!": A descriptive study of the media use of individuals in romantic relationships. *Interdisciplinary Journal of Applied Family Studies, 60,* 150–162.

Duck, S. (2011). *Rethinking relationships.* Thousand Oaks, CA: Sage.

Lloyd, M. (2010). There, yet not there: Human relationships with technology. *Journal of Learning Design, 3*(2), 1–13. Retrieved from eprints.qut.edu.au/31187/

Manusov, V. (1990). An application of attribution principles to nonverbal behavior in romantic dyads. *Communication Monographs, 57,* 104–118.

Massimini, M., & Peterson, M. (2009). Information and communication technology: Affects on U.S. college students. *Journal of Psychosocial Research on Cyberspace, 3*(1), 1–12.

Trenhlom, S., & Jensen, A. (2011). *Interpersonal communication* 7th ed. Oxford, UK: Oxford University Press.

Valkenburg, P. M., & Peter, J. (2009a). The effects of instant messaging on the quality of adolescents' existing friendships: A longitudinal study. *Journal of Communication, 59,* 79–97.

Valkenburg, P. M., & Peter, J. (2009b). Social consequences of the internet for adolescents: A decade of research. *Current Directions in Psychological Science, 18*(1), 1–5.

Walther, J. B., & Parks, M. R. (2002). Cues filtered out, cues filtered in: Computer-mediated communication and relationships. In M. L. Knapp & J. A. Daly (Eds.), *Handbook of interpersonal communication* (3rd ed., pp. 529–563). Thousand Oaks, CA: Sage.

# Case 16

# (Not Remotely) Hot Online Action!

## Jenn McKee

*Keywords:* blogging, cmc (computer mediated communication), commitment, cybersex, infidelity, sexual orientation, social network sites

*Jenn McKee's An Adequate Mom Blog*
http://anadequatemom.wordpress.com
**(Not remotely) hot online action!**
March 25, 2010 at 4:09 p.m.

Every once in a while, you get a swift kick to the head to let you know you're not the same person you were at an earlier time in your life.

On a recent Friday night, I was up late working on an AnnArbor.com article about an event that happened earlier that evening when a guy I knew in college began an Instant Message chat with me. This in itself didn't faze me, because he seemed to be a night owl, and we'd exchanged occasional late-night small talk—How was your Christmas? Have you been to this restaurant? Did you see the Michigan game? blah blah blah—via IM a few times previously.

But on this one night, after some typical chit-chat, he wrote,

"Can I ask you something personal?"

"OK."

"Are you bi?"

This is the moment where I should have sniffed out precisely where this was going. And a younger version of myself probably would have. But no matter how educated or semi-worldly we are, marriage and

*Inside Relationships: A Creative Casebook in Relational Communication,* edited by Sandra L. Faulkner, 181–187. © 2013 Left Coast Press, Inc. All rights reserved.

parenthood inevitably jettison us into a completely different mind-space than that of our sex-obsessed, twentysomething selves.

So here was my first thought when I saw this man's question about being bi (and I'm not kidding): "Oh, my God. He's developed an attraction for men, and he's confused by it. He's politically conservative, so the only person he can talk to about this or trust is someone he hasn't seen in eighteen years." So I take the question at face value, thinking I'm empathizing with him, and write,

"No, but I once had a crush on a close female friend in grad school."

"Did you have sex with her?"

Oh, no, I thought. Something already happened between him and another man, and he doesn't know how to process it, or what to do, what it means. So I wrote,

"No. I imagined it occasionally, but if I was ever actually faced with the situation, I'm honestly not sure how I would have reacted."

He wrote,

"You miss the point."

(He didn't know the half of it.) But this baffled me. Here I was, trying to be honest and help him. What else could I do?

Then he wrote,

"Do you remember my wife?"

I wrote that I did, and then I thought, Oh, I've misunderstood and read this all wrong. Maybe this guy's wife was having an affair with a woman, and he's just learned of it? (By my own calculations, I've since determined that I had just fallen off a turnip truck the previous day.)

He wrote,

"Would you ever be involved in a threesome?"

My next stupid thought: Maybe they've just been involved in one and he's confused and feels like he needs to talk about it. So I told him that while I think most people have fantasized about it, I personally think that the reality of it would be way too difficult to live with, and that while it may sound boring, Joe (who this guy knows, too, unbelievably) and I were happy with each other.

Yes, folks, I really, REALLY wasn't getting what was happening here. But I comfort myself now by thinking that I was probably the least satisfying online sex experience this guy ever had.

But wait—I get worse!

He kept urging me to promise discretion, which added to my suspicion that he was struggling to unburden himself about something troubling him, and he asked,

"Are you alone?"

I wrote,

"Yes. No one else is awake at this hour."

"You know what I would do to you alone?"

Ohhhhhhhhhhhh. The light bulb FINALLY went on in my head. He then posted his phone number, just as I was in full-on "ick" mode, and I chided myself for not catching on sooner.

"Do you have permission to play?" he asked.

(What a ridiculous euphemism.)

I suddenly felt so violated and harassed and stupid, and yet I couldn't turn off my reflexive, Midwest politeness. It was like I was holding the door for my mugger. No, please, after you, I insist!

"I've got a deadline to meet and I really, REALLY need to get to work," I wrote.

"This is what married people do."

Not this married person. And what a condescending and skeevy thing to say. This wasn't about being a prude. It was about genuinely having no desire for someone or something else. I'm thankful for every bit of happiness I have in my life, and as the saying goes, I don't want what I haven't got.

"I want to tell you something," he wrote.

"If you want to say it, make it quick,"

I wrote, my curiosity getting the best of me while I was still in shock.

"I wanted to f#ck you."

"Um...back in 1990?"

I was thinking, dude, you were a 21-year-old college student. You wanted to f#ck me and everything else with a vagina, and you haven't seen me in nearly two decades. How flattered could I possibly be by this admission?

"Who's to say I've aged well?" I wrote.

"I do."

Whatever. Still being painfully polite, I pressed my deadlines and insisted that I had to get down to business, leaving it at that and signing off. Ugh.

Later that night, I was lying in bed, feeling gross, and really, really uncomfortable, and confused as to whether or not to tell Joe. There wasn't necessarily anything to be gained by it, and I really didn't know how he'd react; so at first, I thought I wouldn't.

But as the next day wore on, and I chewed on it more, I decided I needed to tell him. I didn't want to have this weird, stupid secret from him, and if we ran into this guy again one day, I wanted Joe to know why I would feel uncomfortable.

So that evening, I shakily told Joe that I needed to tell him something. But as awkward as it was for me to get out the words, Joe pretty much shrugged his shoulders and treated it as a non-event.

I said, "I guess I thought you'd be angry. I'm not saying I'm disappointed that you aren't, it's just—I'm surprised."

"I'm a little pissed off at him," Joe said, "but clearly he's kind of an unhappy guy, and my life is better than his."

Have I mentioned that I adore Joe?

Anyway, in some odd way, my telling Joe about the whole thing made me feel closer to him. And while I initially kept the experience a secret, remembering my promises of discretion (to a guy who abused my trust and goodwill), I've come to realize that my harassment and extreme discomfort trump any pledge I made while thinking that I was helping out an old friend.

One girlfriend of mine mentioned how she kind of missed the occasional ego boost that comes with being hit on, and while I agree with that, this doesn't qualify. If someone who saw and interacted with me now tried it, then at least I could feel flattered. But someone who's getting off on who and what I used to be? Meaningless.

If nothing else, this stupid experience has made me think about how my younger, more free-wheeling dating days were often fun, but I don't at all miss them. At that time in my life, I made some really dumb choices out of vanity; was plagued by self-doubt; and I hurt people I shouldn't have hurt—both through a lack of personal courage and a regrettable tendency toward self-absorption.

That's typical, of course. You're freaking out in your twenties and early thirties, constantly scrambling to figure out and get a career that you can live with while also determining if you're built for solitude or a long-term partnership (and if it's the latter, who that partner might be). But now that I've arrived here, I don't look back.

I tell myself that that's why my thoughts and reactions were so far removed from the basic, obvious thing that was staring me in the face on my laptop that Friday night. I hadn't even intellectually visited my former self since I'd married Joe and later had Lily. And why on earth would I?

I like where I am now. I don't want to go back. I'm good, thanks.

### "Online Action" News
August 21, 2010 at 2:21 am

I thought that those following my ridiculous, but kind of hilarious, online saga—wherein, in March, a college acquaintance started a late-night Facebook chat to try and get me to engage in cybersex, and I REPEATEDLY failed to understand what he was driving at—might be interested in an update.

First, after previously hearing from two men who'd been urged by this same guy—I'll call him PJ, for "Pervy Jackass"—to exchange naked wife photos, and a woman who'd also been directly propositioned, I recently heard from yet another man, who I'll call B, with whom I'd gone to college. (For those keeping score, that brings our current member count for the "I've-been-inappropriately-propositioned-by-PJ-via-Facebook" club up to five—though my guess is there are plenty of others out there who don't know he's doing this TO EVERYONE.)

B reached out to me via FB chat, too—which, admittedly, I'm now wary of, but nonetheless responded to—and he said wanted to talk to me. Now, I hadn't chatted with or seen B in more than ten years, so I was curious as to why. Then he wrote,

"Do you remember PJ?"

"Oh," I thought. "Now I know precisely where we're going."

B had reached a point where he was pretty furious. He'd been fairly close with PJ in college, and considered him a mentor of sorts. Yet here was PJ now, asking B ten times(?!) for photos of his wife. My friend said that he'd politely dodged the issue the first few times, but he was getting progressively angrier.

"Of course you are," I said. "He's disrespecting you and your wife. I got angry, too."

B asked, "Has anyone called him out on it, or just de-friended him?"

I said, "Just the latter, I think. Everyone's so shocked by it in the moment, when it's happening—I know I was—that they just try and get out of the situation as quickly as possible."

I explained to B that I'd just hidden myself from his view, so that he could no longer tell when I was on Facebook (FB).

But after being hidden for months, and writing repeated blog entries (which I promote via FB) about the whole sordid experience, I wondered if PJ had gotten the message somehow. So out of curiosity, I un-hid myself; and I'll be damned if he didn't pretty quickly write this:

"give me your private e-mail."

And then this:

"(no pressure, just having fun with you)"

Blech. I didn't respond. But I thought, "Dude, what are the circumstances of your life that make you this desperate?"

The following night, a "hi" appeared on the screen from him again. Thus began my foray back into hiding. (This guy has a job and a family. How does he have the time to harass everyone I knew at the University of Michigan?)

Of course, an evil part of me briefly considered engaging in a conversation with him, just for the sake of another funny blog post. But ultimately, there's just something too pathetic (and downright creepy) about this man for me to do such a thing.

B wrote that PJ had told him that he'd been trying to talk his wife into a three-way recently; and after B read my blog post, he said PJ had probably been trying to recruit me.

Ewwwwwwwwww. (That can't be the response PJ's looking for.) I think I have to go take a shower or something now...

## Questions and Activities for Discussion

1. How are we influenced by personal style, social convention and awareness of social context? Answer this question using McKee's blog posts as an example.

2. Have you ever been presented with a situation like McKee had? What do you think of her slow reaction to the cybersex request? She wrote, "I suddenly felt so violated and harassed and stupid, and yet I couldn't turn off my reflexive, Midwest politeness. It was like I was holding the door for my mugger. No, please, after you, I insist!"

   What should she have done? Do you think talking to her partner and blogging about the situation helped her contend with the feeling of violation? If so, how?

3. What does it mean to cheat? Does the type of relationship matter when you consider infidelity? What is worse—emotional or sexual infidelity? Why?

## For Further Reading and Reference

Boekhout, B. A., Hendrick, S. S., & Hendrick, C. (1999). Relationship infidelity: A loss perspective. *Journal of Personal & Interpersonal Loss, 4*(2). 97–123.

Brand, R. J., Markey, C. M., Mills, A., & Hodges, S. D. (2007). Sex differences in self-reported infidelity and its correlates. *Sex Roles, 57,* 101–109.

Luo, A., Cartun, M. A., & Snider, A. G. (2010). Assessing extradyadic behavior: A review, a new measure, and two new models. *Personality and Individual Differences, 49,* 155–163.

Muise, A., Christofides, E., & Desmarais, S. (2011). More information than you ever wanted: Does Facebook bring out the green-eyed monster of jealousy? *Cyber Psychology & Behavior, 12(4),* 441–444.

Yarab, P. E., Sensibaugh, C. C., & Allgeier, E. R. (1998). More than just sex: Gender differences in the incidence of self-defined unfaithful behavior in heterosexual dating relationships. *Journal of Psychology and Human Sexuality, 10,* 45–57.

# Case 17

# Thank You for Not Asking
## A Narrative of Infertility

Suzanne V. L. Berg

*Keywords:* infertility, relationship narratives

I gave up smoking in 2005. I gave up meat in 2008. But I held on to drinking, from expensive cocktails in Downtown Minneapolis to solid micro brews from Wisconsin to my own heavy-handed mixed drinks. I loved a glass of red wine after a day of grading, mojitos with home-grown mint in the summer, and the cloying sweet cherries mixed with bitters of a Manhattan. There was one other thing I did not give up: birth control. Then in 2010, Bill and I finally gave up condoms. I began to say goodbye to my alcohol drop by drop, as the rules about pregnancy and drinking were clear; new bottles of gin and whiskey sat on top of my fridge gathering dust. Summer 2011 came, and I did not make a mojito. Fall began and the jar of maraschino cherries sat untouched in the back of the fridge. The only upside to not being pregnant is you can keep drinking, but I lost my taste for it.

For ten months, I noted the date and counted the days between periods. I woke every morning and took the dog out with a thermometer in my mouth. I noted my temperature and went back to bed. During the fertile period of a woman's cycle there is supposed to be a spike in the basal body temperature, which is best measured the second a woman wakes up. For me, though, there was never a significant change. I have no refined scientific knowledge, but I knew it was odd. I tried not to think about it.

*Inside Relationships: A Creative Casebook in Relational Communication,* edited by Sandra L. Faulkner, 188–194. © 2013 Left Coast Press, Inc. All rights reserved.

In June, I went to my annual exam with my typed list of dates of when my period started and ended. I didn't know what true significance *this* list would have, because for me it was just another of my hundreds of lists. In quantitative terms, the frequency of my cycle equaled 35 days and the average length was 32.625 days. The nurse spoke to me in a quiet and professional tone. She said that 35 days between periods meant it was possible that I was not ovulating and told me to buy an over-the-counter ovulation kit and test for two months. I should also work on losing weight because as little as a 20 pound weight loss may improve fertility.

A few days later I talked to my mom. My parents were planning a trip to Ohio in two weeks, and she had just told me. This drives me a little crazy. I am a person who makes lists of things to accomplish that day, that week, that month. I plan a menu for the week and mostly stick to it. I make dinner reservations whenever possible because I do not like wasting time waiting. This obsession with planning is something that gets me into trouble, because when something does not go according to plan, I get inconsolably angry. I decide in this moment to tell Mom about the doctor's appointment, about the 35-day cycle, about ovulation. I was hoping for a loving pep talk from the woman who babysits my best friend's newborn son; who delighted in feeding the toddler daughter of a high school friend during a wedding, and who told me last year for her birthday she wanted a grandchild.

"You just shouldn't try. Focus on your school work." My mom said. I was shocked. Mom was the first of many people who recommended avoidance as the best tactic. But avoiding the problem doesn't make it go away.

A distant acquaintance posted a picture on Facebook of a tiny sandwich—a babewhich—a play on her last name. This picture informs the Facebook world that she and her spouse are expecting. I have seen what seems like hundreds of variations on this theme: a bun in the oven, a chicken nugget, maternity shirts that say "Baby Loading," pictures with "Future Parent" posted over their heads, clever hash tags, blog posts detailing the adorable story, ultra sound shots/videos, and the damn pregnant photo shoot where the parents revel in the full stomach and breasts of the expecting mother. Former students are the worst. They make me feel like nothing has changed in my life since they walked out of my classroom. There is a point where I stop clicking the "like" button on these notifications, because it's a lie. Bill thinks that I'm angry with my pregnant friends and acquaintances. I'm taking it too personally. Their pregnancy is not a referendum on me, my current inability to procreate. But it's not anger; I'm envious. Of their luck. Of their good fortune. Of their progress. One in four people struggle with fertility, and I'm Ringo.

The Question is phrased in a dozen ways: *When are you going to have kids? Do you have kids? Why haven't you had any kids? Are you trying? Are you pregnant? You'd better get started, right?* Many women have no problem asking; it's as if they are asking about the weather. I do know they are asking because they are part of the club. They want to include me, and I want to be a part of it, too. I have witnessed scenes like two mothers who have only just met engage in detailed discussions about infants and growth percentiles. I find women who have no fertility issues the most insufferable, though. I chewed out my sister-in-law for asking me the question on Christmas Eve.

There are about a dozen people to whom I have self-disclosed my infertility status. Some are my closest friends and confidents. Some are people who I disclosed to because it was the right moment to talk. One I sought out because I knew she could provide unique insight. One is my father, who knows because my mom told him. I rarely want to talk, but most people bring it up. I'm sad about the number of times I have to talk about my fertility issues while watching a two year old ripping apart a living room or during infant naps on a long distance phone call.

I get unusually lippy with male family members who ask the questions:

- I yelled at my father-in-law at Thanksgiving for asking if we were doing it right, and I lashed out at my brother-in-law for laughing.

- When my grandfather asked me when my cousin was getting pregnant, I asked him when he was getting pregnant.

- I hung up on my father when he told me that pituitary problems made conception difficult. I hung up on him, because I have a thyroid problem.

- About a month later he took another step too far when he said my weight might be an issue, and then I yelled at him about how I spent five hours a week at the gym and had lost twenty pounds. That earlier that day I had swam a mile in the pool. He told me that he could do ten full pool laps in ten minutes in 1976.

- One of the last things my dad said before Bill and I left for Christmas was that all my problems were stress related and that when I finished my PhD getting pregnant would be easier.

Asking the question is invasive. It is a question about the most intimate details of a couple's life: sex, money, and the future. Asking about pregnancy violates all of the rules about self-disclosure and none of them at the same time. Women who have struggled are more respectful of people's boundaries. I had a long conversation with a former advisor in Jackson Square Park. When I met her ten years ago, she was newly pregnant after a long struggle with unexplained infertility. She had become something of an oracle for young academic women with fertility issues. She waited so patiently for me to bring it up. For a discussion of infertility to happen, the information needs to be volunteered. Asking the question will shut down conversation before it starts.

After some testing and continued weight loss, things seemed better. My doctor was giddy when she saw me in December. I was diagnosed with a low functioning thyroid. I had lost thirty pounds because of my rigorous workouts and diet. But as the months went on, I was still not pregnant. Bill made a doctor's appointment, and we discovered the limits of small town medicine. His doctor had to make three phone calls to find out the process for semen analysis. He could do the test on the hospital grounds or at home, as long as "the sample" was in the lab within a half hour.

I rushed to make an egg salad sandwich because it was time. I told Bill, and when he walked away to go make a sample, I was anxious. Only 30 minutes. I ripped the egg apart and wrapped it in a messy style. I was not ready enough. I hadn't fully packed my bag for class, and I couldn't find the folder with my readings. I was running out of my office when Bill emerged. I did not have a bag to carry it in, so I emptied my office recycling on the floor to find the smallest bag in the house: a brown paper take out container with handles.

I didn't know my heart would race this much. I don't listen to the radio. I don't speak, just drive slightly faster than usual and run a yellow light or two. I keep thinking about the film *Forget Paris*. I park at the hospital and tell the desk attendant "Good Afternoon." He tells me that it is only 11:00 a.m. When I get to the laboratory, I thought I could say, "Good Morning, this is the medical order for my spouse's semen analysis." Instead, I trip over my words and avoid eye contact because I am handing over a container of semen in a brown paper bag.

We live a life of assumed narratives, and the most surreal moments of life are things that do not fit into the narratives. Those things are often unexpected occurrences, like the death of a parent. No one knows how that moment changes that interaction and all of the others that follow. No matter how many lists I write, no matter how solid my marriage is, I am adrift in random acts of circumstance. How did I end up in Wood County Hospital with a bag of semen? The four people I interacted with don't know anything about me, but they know I am a woman who brought semen to the hospital to test for fertility.

There was no way to prepare for this.

Bill and I recently rearranged our apartment so that we each have our own office. (We had been saving the second bedroom for the baby). My office is the smallest room in the apartment and holds a tiny desk, two bookshelves, and the twin bed with the wrought iron frame that I have slept in since childhood. Sometimes, Bill comes and lies on the bed to distract me or to break up his day. When he shuffled into the room, crawled on the bed, and asked me to join him, I knew this was not cuddling to tell me he had donation-grade sperm.

He told me he got the results of the test. This was what we feared: *Low sperm count and low sperm motility.*

We lay there and talked. I cried as that is my default response.

Bill said that there is likely no solution.

I joked that years of computer use have irradiated his sperm. That explained his full head of hair.

I thought having answers would make it easier. We had a legitimate place to start after a year of treading water. But this is nowhere near easier. And this is where the story changes, because the infertility is no longer mine alone. Bill takes full and miserable responsibility for the past two years, though I tell him that it is not so simple. I see his test as a positive sign, because low sperm count is better than no sperm count. A low sperm count can be caused by environmental factors. A zero sperm count is not fixable. However, is low sperm motility fixable, too? If we were still in Minneapolis, we would live next to a hospital with a sexual health clinic. In a town of 20,000 people, we are asking questions that the doctors can't answer. Being far away from family is hard. It often feels like Bill and I are stranded on the island of Ohio. We miss weddings, graduations, and birthdays. Our nieces and nephews are growing up without us.

I also can't talk to people about this anymore, because it is not *my* news to share. Female infertility is one thing; there are loads of resources and people to talk to. But this is different. This is a question of manhood, the latent machismo-based manhood that I am well trained to critique in all contexts but my own. So much research on infertility is focused on the experiences of women. The experiences and expectations of men are unclear. We have always been that couple that does just about everything together without getting on each other's nerves. Early one May morning, Bill and I got up for a bike ride. I wanted to go further and faster, but we came home. Bill logged into his work computer and did three work things before 8:30 a.m. I dragged him back to bed to fold some laundry. Before we sorted the laundry into piles, he pulled me close to him and held me. "All I have ever wanted is to be a dad. I have said for a long time that if we couldn't have kids, you were enough for me because I love you that much. The problem is that I don't love myself that much." I told him what he already knew; I love him that much. We will get through this.

## Activities and Questions for Discussion

1. Does Berg really want a child? How do the social contexts in which people conduct their relationships influence them? React to the idea that having a child is "the next step."

2. Why may Berg have had trouble placing a sperm sample on the counter at the hospital lab? Does this speak to stigma around infertility? What does it mean when Berg wrote that at some point it was not *her* news to share?

3. How does social media play a role in the revelation of good news (e.g., pregnancy, promotion) and bad news (e.g., death)? What do you think of Facebook status updates about pregnancy? Does it matter who is posting? Is *The Question* about children a violation of privacy as Berg contends? What does it mean when Berg claims people ask "because they are part of the club"?

4. Infertility is an unexpected relationship event. Can you list other unexpected relationship events in our lives? What are some good ways of facing these unexpected events? Is there any way to prepare for them? Are there some things that should not be disclosed on social media?

# For Further Reading and Reference

Bute, J. J. (2009) "Nobody thinks twice about asking": Women with a fertility problem and requests for information. *Health Communication, 24*, 725–763.

Pineau, E. (2000). Nursing mother and articulating absence. *Text & Performance Quarterly, 20*(1), 1–19.

Rijken, A. J., & Thomson, E. (2011). Partners' relationship quality and childbearing. *Social Science Research, 40*(2), 485–497.

Savage, D. (2000). *The kid: What happened after my boyfriend and I decided to go get pregnant.* New York: Penguin.

White, L. (2011). The air I breathe. *Text & Performance Quarterly, 31*(4), 430–439.

# Case 18

# Transforming Vignettes of NonBeing into Life Affirming (M)Otherhood

Ellen Gorsevski

*Keywords:* motherhood, infertility, pro-natalism, social expectations

*Nearly one-in-five American women ends her childbearing years without having borne a child, compared with one-in-ten in the 1970s.* (Livingston & Cohn, 2010)

When you are a mother you *are* someone, even if it's a bad mom, like the "OctoMom." Most daytime network television caters to mothers. But what happens, when you've reached that certain, delicate age after your mid-30s and before menopause, if you're *not* a mother? In terms of conversations in everyday situations, it can lead to an ontological state of nullification, of nonbeing: in short, if you are a woman, not being a mother can be a real conversation killer.

The vignettes that follow are presented simply as ruminations over my experiences as a woman without children. I offer these vignettes and my reflections on them as an invitation to begin to create a *new narrative*, a narrative that is more life affirming, a narrative of *being*, rather than one of nonbeing, for women without kids (we'll start with women, and save men's similar but unique issues for another separate rumination some other time).

*Inside Relationships: A Creative Casebook in Relational Communication,* edited by Sandra L. Faulkner, 195–206. © 2013 Left Coast Press, Inc. All rights reserved.

# Hair Salon

I am sitting, hair dripping wet, fully sequestered under the navy blue plastic waterproof canopy at the hair salon. Some hair stylists are chatty, others are more quiet and focused on what to do with the challenge presented by my unruly, wavy, thick head of hair. Today I have the chatty kind.

"So, you have any kids?" she asks me, which in her repertoire is usually probably a very good conversation starter.

"Nope," I reply, "Put it off for too long. Infertility."

"Oooh," she says, "that's too bad. Say! I got pregnant when I was on birth control pills! I've got three kids now."

"Ah, I see," I mumble, wondering if she's attended the latest workshop on 'What Not To Say to Someone with Infertility.'

"Yeah," she goes on, "Nothing could stop my eggs! My kids are great..." she rambles on, and I slink down in my chair, nodding politely and hoping the haircut will go quickly so the noisy blow-drying will limit any further conversation.

*Infertility can be a source of profound grief. Infertile women mourn the loss of the fertile self and their desired children....Part of the work of mourning can be understood as revising the autobiographical narrative in order to accommodate infertility's disruption to the plot of one's life.* (Kirkman, 2003, p. 243)

Kirkman (2003) can tell us that infertility involves grieving, and no doubt for many women it does. But that depressing state of affairs isn't completely accurate for someone like me. I always felt rather iffy about the notion of having kids. I babysat a lot from the time I was about ten years old, up through my senior year of high school, and occasionally, for some quick cash, on into college. Then after that, when my sister and brothers had kids, I became an auntie, and logged many more hours of free kid-sitting for my siblings. I was actually pretty good with kids, so it wasn't that I didn't like kids or that kids didn't like me. We got along pretty well. It was just that I wanted to do so many other things that didn't seem to jibe with having a baby in utero, on board, or on my hip. I wanted to travel the world and ask, "How much is it?" or "Where is the bathroom?" in many languages. I wanted to go to grad school, which, if you include two years for the Master's and three for the PhD, pretty much sucked up the best of my prime ovaries-production years.

I wanted to try all kinds of crazy sports and experience the thrills, and maybe even get a bit injured. I imagined I'd be able to bear scars as tattoos of a life of action, like that scene from the movie, *Mountains of the Moon*, in which the explorers compare their scars and the dramatic ways they got them. In short, I didn't want to wait until my golden years to check off all the items on the kick the bucket list, I wanted to do them while I was full of vim and vigor. And so I did.

Indeed, I went surfing, snowboarding, and horseback riding. I owned and drove a dangerous sports car. Heck, I even jacked it up, got underneath, and changed the oil myself. I also logged a lot of hours as a workaholic, often working from 7 a.m. to 12 midnight, day after day, rinse, repeat. Year after year. My prime egg years were spent doing all of these things. I'd like to think that I'm a fairly content person as a result of fulfilling my key dreams and aspirations. I only wish that other people would *let me be* content.

## Workplace

It is 2005, and I am working on a college campus in an office of international students and scholars. The main task of our unit is to make the experience of F-1 Student Visa holders and J-1 Scholar Visa holders, as visitors to our campus, a productive, safe, and positive experience. We serve about 2,000 constituents, so our office is usually very hectic and full of people. Our physical office space is small and cramped in the basement of an old building on campus. So we have to all try to like each other a lot and to get along, even amidst the stresses of a less than ideal physical office space. We are actually treated by our boss and colleagues more like we are family members than coworkers, which can be a good thing, or not. Our unit is small, tightly knit, and hard working.

We are all dedicated to our jobs. We are all very much alike. I, however, am the only person in the office who does not have children. I have recently made the portentous decision that I do not wish to undergo very painful, time consuming, and expensive medical fertility treatments which only have a 10 to 20 percent chance of working for women in my age demographic. For the people for whom it works, it can often take more than five attempts, at $10,000 per attempt! Most states, including the one in which I now reside, do not cover this as a normal medical expense. It must come out of your own, infertile pockets. But I am not a gambler. Since in this case I only have a 10 to 20 percent chance of winning this particular kind of game into which I must cast ten grand, I figured it was not a good bet. So I am presently mulling over the strange idea of adoption, which I am open to considering, but which my partner is presently resisting while resenting my inability to produce kids the good old fashioned way.

One of my coworkers comes in, and asks, "Hey, we're taking bets, would you like to put some money down on whether or not Lakeesha's baby is going to be a girl or a boy?" Lakeesha is about six months pregnant. How wonderful for her. How wonderful for all the other folks in the office to bond over the impending bundle of joy. How depressing for me, as a nongambler, as a nonparent.

"No thanks," I say, "Betting is not really my cup of tea."

Stunned, taken aback from my unwillingness to participate in what is a normal ritual for office members who go home each night after work to their children, my coworker offers me another chance, "But... uh, are you sure? It's really fun; we did this last time and ..."

"No thanks," I repeat. "I'm not really the gambling type." Seeing the crestfallen look on his face, I summon the best smile I can even though I feel like crying, and I politely lie, "But I look forward to seeing who wins!"

## Dentist

I am sitting in the dentist chair, with excruciating pain shooting up through my rear upper molar and down into my lower jaw. It feels like someone is stabbing me with an ice pick. Over and over. The dental hygienist returns with my X-rays.

"Yep," she says, looking knowingly at the slides and shaking her head, "That's a nasty one. You're going to need a root canal, hon. See that?"

She is pointing to the X-ray slide of a large blurry blob that looks like it has invaded my tooth's root. The dentist comes in, administers the Novocain, and the horrible pain that had attacked the day before and kept me up all night long, finally begins to subside. The dentist informs me he'll return in a few minutes, once the numbing is complete. The dental hygienist, a kindly woman who looks to be in her 40s, starts busily arranging the various drills and drill bits for the dentist.

"So," she says, conversationally, "You have any kids?" Here we go again.

"Nope," I say, through the numbing, although it sounds more like "Ope" since my jaw has started to numb.

"Oh," she says, raising her eyebrows. "Well, the pain you've just felt from that major root decay is much worse than childbirth was for me. Between my root canals and my kids, I think the root canals were way more painful!"

"Really?" I say, genuinely surprised (sounding more like 'Weal-ly?'). From the combination of all the cliché movie scenes of women screaming their way through childbirth, plus all the horror stories I've heard from friends and relatives about the agonies of childbirth over the years, I've never heard anyone admit before that *something else is actually as bad or even worse*. It always seemed to me that childbirth, at least for the women I've known throughout my life, is this pain ritual that women bond over and one-up each other over. It is a form of competition. Child-birthers, it seemed to me, formed an exclusive club, with its chief membership criterion being based on the unique and incomparable pain of having a nine-pound baby pass through a hole that, well, seems like it's meant for somewhat smaller things, like tampons, penises, or their vibrating plastic equivalents, if you're into that sort of thing. In exploding this myth of the exclusivity of child-birth-level pain, the hygienist has given me something to think about. She continues puttering around, humming pleasantly.

"You still in a lot of pain?" she asks.

"No, thank heavens," I say with utter relief, "it's numb now. That was awfully painful before, but it feels fine now." Even reclining and vulnerable to the tiny, doll-sized bottle brush that the dentist is about to jam into the hole he has drilled into my molar, I now feel empowered. Having survived the agonizing pain before the Novocain, even in the absence of being a mother, I realize that I have actually experienced a high threshold of pain, the pain that a dental hygienist and mother of two tells me is on par with, or even exceeds, that of childbirth. Of course, this is just her anecdotal evidence, I tell myself. Still, I feel secretly pleased. I can take pain: I am a *real* woman after all!

*Barriers to narrative revision included cultural and social factors such as the dominance of the motherhood narrative, the absence of a collective narrative of the non-mother, and lack of audience support; as well as more personal factors such as a lack of meaningful alternative goals and the existence of hope.* (Kirkman, 2003, p. 248)

ELLEN GORSEVSKI

# Party of 40-Somethings

I have been invited to a party that I only could have dreamed of when I was in my 20s. A party of some faculty members who teach in other departments across campus, artsy types like those who teach theatre design or screenwriting, some philosophers, a couple scientists, and a few locals who work in the community. These are smart, bright, sensitive people. In my 20s self, I imagine we will exchange witty banter about novels, poetry, and Big Thoughts. But reality is here, my 40s self finds, a half hour into the party.

"So, do you have any kids?" she asks, smiling. Here we go again, *again*.

"No, do you?" I ask; this has become my standard turnabout reply, which, I've learned, shifts the conversation away from my lack and toward someone else's bounty.

"Yes, my daughter just won a scholarship. She's headed for London."

"Oh, that's wonderful," I say, "how exciting for her." My interlocutor then goes on to speak in great detail about the trip, her daughter's incredible qualifications for being able to go, and so forth. I grow quieter, and the conversation shifts to other topics. A couple hours later, one member of our group brings up the recent topic of the woman on the cover of *Time* magazine, who was pictured breastfeeding a child who looks to be about four years old. The women in the group weigh in.

"I think it's gross!" says one woman.

"One of my daughters uses the Attachment Parenting method, they're really into it. Those moms are probably just part of that wave," says another woman.

The men in the group are remaining conveniently out of the conversation. An awkward silence ensues. I feel the idiotic need to rush in and fill it. What to say? I try to think of something that will make everyone feel okay.

"Well," I speak up, "my older brother says he tried not to make the same parenting mistakes that our parents made with us, but he found that he just made different mistakes instead, so I suppose no matter what you do, I guess no parent can be perfect." I thought that came out pretty well.

"Yeah," said the woman whose daughter was headed to London, "But it's hard for people who don't have kids to appreciate how difficult it is to raise kids..." she continued on, turning to talk directly to one of the other moms in the conversation. Ouch! Did I really just hear that?

I'm standing right here. I give my significant other the high sign: it's time for us to head home for the night. Some dream party. More like a déjà vu party.

❏

*The number of childless people in the United States is on the rise, yet in our pronatalist culture, childless people report that their interests and needs are neither recognized nor met.* (Hayden, 2010, p. 133)

Sure, Livingston and Cohn (2010) can tell us, "Over the past few decades, public attitudes toward childlessness have become more accepting" (¶6). However, as Hayden (2010) discovered, such acceptance doesn't always happen, even in educated circles. There seems to be a general lack of an alternative, viable narrative for women without kids. (That is not to say that childless men don't have woes, but sorry, dudes, for the sake of space and focus, we'll save your story for another time.) We, the women of un/non/childed status are variously supposed to be: (1) grieving; or (2) actively seeking ridiculously painful and expensive fertility treatments into our 60s so we can vie for the *Guinness Book of World Records* title of 'The world's oldest woman to give birth'; or (3) we are supposed to be very angry, bitter people who hate folks who have kids (Hayden, 2010); or (4) we are supposed to be focusing on being doting aunties/consumers, buying lots of cool stuff to spoil our nieces and nephews with (Hayden, 2011); or (5) we are supposed to buy into the pop culture fantasy that a little *boy* that we can keep will magically sprout in the backyard, as purveyed through Hollywood's latest infertility themed film, "The Odd Life of Timothy Green"; or, the most obvious option, (6) we are just freaks. Ok, let's replace option #6 with adoption, we are supposed to adopt. Okay, let's try that.

## Dilapidated Medical Center Somewhere in Former Yugoslavia

"Take off your shirt, *and* your bra!" commanded the surly, man, who appeared to be 30ish and quite interested in the results of the disrobing.

"No, I will not." I replied.

"Madame, I have been X-raying women for many, many years, and they all must remove their brassieres. No brassiere removal, no X-ray!" His tone and volume indicated he was indignant that I would dare question his daily, on-the-job breast viewing.

How did I end up in a third world country, in this dilapidated hospital, in a cold, tiled room, with a strange man telling me to get topless? Well, once we'd finished all the paperwork for adoption in the United States in order to qualify to apply for adoption in this tiny Balkan nation that is so small you need a magnifying glass to find it on a world map, we had to redo all the earlier home study paperwork, plus do a whole battery of physical and mental tests. I'm in the throes of the physical tests, and to do a tuberculosis lung X-ray, you need to be topless, otherwise the metal clasps on the bra will interfere with the chest X-ray. In this old, run-down hospital in this tiny, 'economically developing' nation, they do not have the wherewithal to use those fancy paper gowns that we take for granted here in the United States of America, land of medical wonders. Hence, the upper half of the birthday suit is the only option here, or so it seems.

After much commotion, involving me telling my intimate partner, "No, I won't do it! I don't care if they don't let us adopt, I'm not going to show a complete stranger my boobs, even if they are very small, they're still mine!" So my spousal partner, who is originally from this town, called a friend, who then called another friend, who called the chest X-ray technician. The technician was very upset that a woman had questioned his authority, and he had to be calmed down. Collectively, they figured out a workaround. Thank goodness for cell phones! Now the ornery technician would grudgingly allow me take off my bra (in private), but leave my shirt on during the X-ray process, with my dignity more intact.

## Unresolved Conclusions of NonBeing

It is probably a good thing that not everyone can, or wants to, have children. It is probably helpful in enabling human beings to manage the planet's limited resources of space, food and energy (oil, coal), which most experts agree will only get more limited in supply in the future. It is not a very good thing, however, to socially experience the status of being in one's middle-aged years without children. In many daily conversations, I am characterized not by my life's experiences, world travels, and contributions to making the world a better place. Rather, I am often perceived though my status of nonbeing, lacking in parental status. I realize I'm outnumbered. I realize most people probably don't mean to be mean. But I have to say, it does get exhausting after a while. Still, I am not the type to retreat into bitter sarcasm that Hayden

(2010) says is characteristic of people who do not have children. She notes that the non-parenting in many cases find refuge in dark humor, mocking parents, referring to them in livestock terms as 'breeders.'

To be sure, there are multiple kinds of oppressions, differences among people that make my own and other nonparents' experiences of social exclusion, awkwardness, and silent suffering seem less important. As a society, the invisibility of white privilege still causes persons of color continued suffering. Gay dads or lesbian moms in our heteronormative world experience unfortunate incidents of being excluded or treated as inferior to heterosexuals. I agree other social challenges abound, and the urgency of how to relate to nonparented persons is lower on the scale.

At the same time, however, just because the parental status of nonbeing may not be the most urgent form of socially, and often communicatively expressed, exclusion, it still exists, even though it doesn't need to. I leave it up to you to ponder, then, the interpersonal, familial, workplace, and broader social implications for how and why this discrimination is made acceptable, and thus seemingly, at least from my perspective, intractable.

When average persons conceive a child "naturally" through biological means, they are presumed automatically to be 'normal' and to be 'innocent' in terms of their propensity toward things like child abuse. This fact may stem from the parental-normativity of society. Yet when persons with 'infertility' seek to become parents 'unnaturally' through complicated legal and social frameworks of adoption, they are assumed automatically to be deviant weirdoes. Yes, I understand that there are bad people out there who should not, under any circumstances, be allowed anywhere near small children, much less adopt them. Look no further than your local sex offender registry, which exists in just about every town in the United States, whether it is a small town or a big city.

That said, average persons wanting to adopt—normal, decent people like my spouse and me—are treated through the official system as being presumed to be predisposed toward child molestation or abuse. For instance, we have to reapply on a regular basis to the Child Abuse Registry of the State of Ohio to prove that we are *not* on the list. On an annual basis, we have to be finger-printed at the local sheriff's office so our prints can be verified as *not* matching any in the FBI's national database. Annually, we drive to the ghetto of Detroit, to the nearest U.S. Customs and Immigration Office, where we are fingerprinted at an ever rising cost (last time it was $125 per person) in U.S. Homeland

Security's international system, where ours are cross-matched against terrorists' fingerprints, to verify that we are *not* involved in human trafficking or terrorism. In short, we must prove the *negative*, that we are not bad people, which is an expensive, humiliating and time consuming process. For people who do not give birth themselves but who seek to be parents through adoption, it is as if you are presumed first to be a very bad person, indeed.

Therefore, as an exercise in sensitization toward the parental status of NonBeing, I leave you with an open-ended chart. I have already *partially* filled in the left column for you, having left out many requirements plus dollar amounts, which I invite you to Google. I hope you complete the right half of the chart. Once you are done, consider the differences between the columns: what do they suggest to you? What might we be able to do, conversationally, socially, perhaps legally one day, to reduce some of the differences or alleviate some of the challenges these disparities in treatment between groups may pose?

| Legal Requirements Before Adoptive Parenting | Legal Requirements Before Birth Parenting |
|---|---|
| Undergo and pay for extensive and expensive home study interviews conducted by an adoption agency, in which you are asked about everything from your childhood to your views on corporal punishment, to your reactions to infertility, to your use/abuse of drugs and/or alcohol. If married, you are asked to speculate about the viability of your union. | |
| Home inspection by adoption agency representatives on a regular basis, from your sock drawers to bedrooms, to your garage and yard. | |
| Participate in prospective adoptive parenting workshops (6–8 hours in length). | |
| Explain your attitudes toward adopted child's/children's continuing or eventual contact with the birthmother. | |

| Legal Requirements Before Adoptive Parenting | Legal Requirements Before Birth Parenting |
|---|---|
| A local fire marshal must verify your home has one fire extinguisher, plus smoke alarms in every room, and a fire-exit plan. | |
| Be fingerprinted regularly for the state Child Abuse Registry (and if international adoption, also with U.S. Homeland Security). | |
| Have three unrelated persons write extensive support forms and character reference letters supporting your adoption, to be updated regularly. | |
| Have emergency phone numbers, including 911, posted on your refrigerator. | |
| Provide regular bank statements as evidence of financial security. | |
| Provide regular documentary evidence of stable employment. | |
| Provide list of prior arrests, if any. | |
| Provide tax returns for prior five years. | |
| Provide medical evidence of mental and physical stability/soundness. | |

## Questions and Activities for Discussion

1. How does social pressure influence our relationship expectations and desires? Gorsevski describes an increasingly common approach to childbearing (i.e., waiting until one is older), which may lead to fertility issues. How should we talk to those who do not *have* children, either by choice or circumstance?

2. Do you have any children? Would you like to have children someday? Why or why not? Have you heard of a movement called childfree by choice (see, e.g., childfree.net; thechildfreelife.com)? What do you think of support groups for men and women who do not want to have children? How should we talk to those who do not *want* to have children, either by choice or circumstance?

3. The cost of adoption, both material and immaterial, can be prohibitive. Gorsevki asks you to consider the legal requirements of parents who adopt versus parents who give birth. Do the comparison by asking your friends and family members who have children (or yourself if you have kids) to complete the chart she provided. Once you are done, consider the differences between the columns: what do they suggest to you? What might we be able to do, "conversationally, socially, perhaps legally one day," to reduce some of the differences or alleviate some of the challenges these disparities in treatment between groups may pose?

4. What reaction do you have to Gorsevski's experiences? What problems do you see with the following comments made to childfree individuals?

- You're not a fulfilled woman without the experience of having children.
- Even if you don't want them now, you'll want them later.
- When you meet the right guy, you'll want to start a family with him because that's the evidence of true love and unity.
- We're biologically designed to reproduce; why fight it?
- But you'd be a great parent!
- I was just like you before!

## For Further Reading and Reference

Kirkman, M. (2003). Infertile women and the narrative work of mourning: Barriers to the revision of autobiographical narratives of motherhood. *Narrative Inquiry, 13*(1), 243–262.

Livingston, G., & Cohn, D. (2010). More women without children. Pew Research Center. Retrieved from pewresearch.org/pubs/1642/more-women-without-children

Hayden, S. (2010). Lessons from The Baby Boon: "Family-friendly" policies and the ethics of justice and care. *Women's Studies in Communication, 33*(2), 119–137.

Hayden, S. (2011). Constituting savvy aunties: From childless women to child-focused consumers. *Women's Studies in Communication, 34*(1), 1–19.

# Chapter 7

# Gender and Culture

Chapter 7 contains three cases that (de)construct gender and culture in our relationships. Cynthia Nicole maps the tattoos on her body as geographic representations of gender and surviving in close relationships. Manda Hicks muses about culture and gender through a litany of how daily interactions at work and on vacation personalize these concepts. Lisa Hanasono's personal narrative of others' reactions to her being American as a third generation Japanese woman demonstrate the process of how telling one's story can be a form of social support. What all of the cases have in common is the explicit questioning of our use of *stereotypes*, a way of categorizing that relies on simplified and standardized conceptions about the characteristics or expected behavior of members of an identifiable group (e.g., women, tattooed women, Asian Americans). When you stereotype, you perceive a person to possess certain characteristics (e.g., feminine, tough, bitchy, passive) because of perceptions that they belong to a certain group; it goes beyond categorizing to predicting others' behaviors. For example, if you expect an Asian American woman to be passive, then you may be surprised when she calls you out for using an ethnic slur.

We use stereotypes as a kind of mental shortcut; we develop generalized perceptions about any group we come into contact with, and

*Inside Relationships: A Creative Casebook in Relational Communication,* edited by Sandra L. Faulkner, 207–212. © 2013 Left Coast Press, Inc. All rights reserved.

then notice behaviors that fit with the stereotype and ignore those behaviors that deviate (Bodenhausen, Macrae, & Sherman, 1999). This process is fraught with perceptual inaccuracies because it ignores individual differences. I may be a professor who at times is absent-minded and is always bookish, but I'm also a knitter, a runner, and an excellent pie maker. When we use stereotypes as the basis of social interaction, we risk miscommunication and creating hard feelings like we see in Hanasono's and Hicks's experiences below. Sure, stereotypes can function like a script to help us know how to behave in some situations (see Chapter 2 in this volume for a discussion of script theory) or when we want to reduce uncertainty in an interaction, especially initial interactions (for example, uncertainty reduction theory). Many of us are able to move beyond stereotypes and acquire information based on some truth. However, when we do not move beyond these impressions, trouble occurs. It seems that gender and ethnic stereotypes are especially pernicious and long lasting (Wood, 2012).

This can be especially true if you define culture as based on group membership such as gender, race, ethnic background, and relationship status (Baldwin, Faulkner, Hecht, & Lindsley, 2006). Definitions of culture are not universal, though; they are influenced by economic and political forces and climatic and geographic changes, and vary based on whether you emphasize structure (e.g., culture as role dependent), individual goals and purposes (e.g., sense of belonging), lifestyle (e.g., wedding ceremonies), product (e.g., architecture), or cultivation (e.g., civilized vs. savage). Some researchers refuse to define culture because the very act of defining culture is powerful and exclusionary. For our purposes here, let's consider culture to be constituted in communication at the same time that ideas about cultural practices are created and reinforced through interaction (Baldwin et al., 2006). For example, the desire and need to appear moral when discussing and enacting sexuality with a romantic partner was a cultural performance for Latina women in a study on sexual talk in close relationships (Faulkner & Mansfield, 2002). And in the case of Jewish Americans, identity constitutes an ethnic and cultural identity, as well as a religious one. One can answer the question, "Who is a Jew?" by using the matrilineal principle where one's mother must be Jewish, the nonlineal principle of having one Jewish parent and being raised Jewish, and/or relying on cultural indicators such as gastronomy, traditional family, and being involved in a community with the rituals, ceremonies, and frame of reference/communal identity

(Edelman, 2000; Golden et al., 1998). In other words, culture is communication, and communication is culture (Faulkner & Hecht, 2006).

## Communication Theory of Identity

If we focus on interaction and relationships as central in the process of identity formation and negotiation, the Communication Theory of Identity (CTI) provides a useful theoretical framework (Hecht et al., 2004). Faulkner and Hecht (2011), for example, use CTI to frame a study of the processes through which LGBTQ (lesbian, gay, bisexual, transgender, queer) Jewish Americans decide to reveal or conceal their Jewish and sexual minority identities and the relationship between multiple identities given the relational circumstances that influence such decisions. For example, whether one had a Jewish partner, where one lived, and the importance of multiple identities influenced participants' enactment and disclosure of their identities. One participant in our study summed up her process:

> I've underestimated my attachment to being Jewish and my sense of it as a core piece of my identity. I think this is still very much evolving, my sort of understanding what it means to me to be Jewish, because I'm not a very religiously observant Jew... So much of who I am doesn't have anything to do with being gay. But yet it's like how do you take that out of the equation? You can't. It's so a part of who I am, which means it's a hundred percent important to me. And yet in terms of how I live my day or what my dreams are, anything like that, it's not a part of my day. It's such a contradiction...It's so hard to even imagine what it would be to not be either one of those things (bisexual lesbian and Jewish), they're just so pivotal to who I am I can't even think about separating them out or ordering them. (Lydia, 37, bisexual lesbian)

CTI considers identity to consist of four layers or frames—personal, enacted, relational, communal—in which messages are exchanged (Faulkner & Hecht, 2006). The *personal layer* references identity as an individual characteristic (that is, self-concept, self-image, preferred identity label) while the *enacted layer* of identity is embodied in social interactions through an individual's presentation of identity. For example, an individual's view of her/himself (e.g., I am a student, I am a lesbian) falls within the personal layer while the expression of those attributes is the enactment of identity (e.g., attending a lesbian support group on campus). *The relationship layer* frames aspects of identity that are invested in social and personal relationships, as well as the relationships among various identities, including how one contends with ascriptions that others make about one's identities. For example, individuals may see themselves as members of a certain social network (e.g., LGBTQ Synagogue), in relation to a particular other (e.g., girl/boyfriend, Rabbi/congregation member), and experience juxtaposition in their identities (e.g., Jewish and bisexual). Finally, *the communal layer* references the idea of identity as group-based identification. CTI argues that communities hold collective identities in addition to individual identities. For example, these different conceptions of Jewish identity can be seen in a study on how a communal representation of Jewish Americans in the television show *Northern Exposure* influenced participants' personal, enacted, and relational identities (Hecht et al., 2002). The common assumption that all Jews are New Yorkers, expressed at various times during the series, bothered some participants in the study because they felt that many people ascribe a "New York" identity to them because they are Jewish. Some even felt "less Jewish" because they were not from New York. The interpenetration of communal identity (media messages in which only New York Jews are shown) with the relational identity (ascription by others) influenced personal identity (feeling less Jewish).

This layered approach to identity allows a multi-faceted and process oriented understanding because at any one time all four frames are present and, in a sense, a part of one another. The cases in this chapter may be framed from a CTI perspective as well as an intersectional one. Feminist intersectionality theory as articulated by McCall (2005) offers a way of viewing the intersection of layers by focusing attention on the intra-categorical, those places where minority identities cross boundaries, such as sexual, religious, tattooed woman. The process of identity management is more pervasive than ethnic or social identities and a more complex process given the potential gaps between and among various layers. Identity negotiation processes point to areas where individuals feel conflict because of identity gaps, those places where their self-concepts and avowed identities conflict with others' perceptions and understandings, creating dissonance and a need to negotiate the competing and conflicting identities. The implications of these gaps range from alienation to depression to lack of choice in identity enactments (Jung & Hecht, 2004; Jung, Hecht & Wadsworth, 2007). For example, Hecht and Faulkner's (2000) study of Jewish Americans reveals how the interplay between personal (whether Jewish identity was central or peripheral) and relational (whether the person was a stranger, acquaintance or friend) identity frames affected if, how, when, and to whom they chose to reveal their Jewishness. Further, participants in the study described how they dealt with their personal self-concepts as Jews at the same time they contended with others' perceptions of their Jewishness. Another way to see this is to ask you where the intersections of gender, culture, and love occur in the case studies presented in this chapter, and why they matter.

# References

Baldwin, J. R., Faulkner, S. L., Hecht, M. L., & Lindsley, S. L. (Eds.) (2006). *Redefining culture: Perspectives across the disciplines.* Mahwah, NJ: Lawrence Erlbaum.

Bodenhausen, G. V., Macrae, C. N., & Sherman, J. W. (1999). On the dialectics of discrimination: Dual processes in social stereotyping. In S. Chaiken & Y. Trope (Eds.), *Dual process theories in social psychology* (pp. 271–290). New York: Guilford.

Edelman, S. M. (2000). To pass or not to pass, that is the question: Jewish cultural identity in the United States. In M. W. Lustig & J. Koester (Eds.), *Among us: Essays on identity, belonging, and intercultural competence* (pp. 33–40). New York: Longman.

Faulkner, S. L., & Hecht, M. L. (2006). Tides in the ocean: A layered approach to culture and communication. In B. B. Whaley & W. Samter (Eds.), *Explaining communication: Contemporary theories and exemplars* (pp. 383–402). Mahwah, NJ: Lawrence Erlbaum.

Faulkner, S. L., & Hecht, M. L. (2011). The negotiation of closetable identities: A narrative analysis of LGBTQ Jewish identity. *Journal of Social and Personal Relationships, 28*(6), 829–847.

Faulkner, S. L., & Mansfield, P. K. (2002). Reconciling messages: The process of sexual talk for Latinas. *Qualitative Health Research, 12,* 310–328.

Golden, D., Niles, T. A., & Hecht, M. L. (1998). Jewish American identity. In J. N. Martin, T. K. Nakayama, & L. A. Flores (Eds.), *Readings in cultural contexts* (pp. 62–70). Mountain View, CA: Mayfield.

Hecht, M. L., & Faulkner, S. L. (2000). Sometimes Jewish, sometimes not: The closeting of Jewish American identity. *Communication Studies, 51,* 372–387.

Hecht, M. L., Faulkner, S. L., Meyer, C., Niles, T. A., Golden, D., & Cutler, M. (2002). Jewish American identity: A communication theory of identity analysis of the television series Northern Exposure. *Journal of Communication, 52,* 852–869.

Hecht, M. L., Warren, J., Jung, J., & Kreiger, J. (2004). Communication theory of identity. In W.B. Gudykunst (Ed.), *Theorizing about intercultural communication* (pp. 257–278). Newbury Park, CA: Sage.

Jung, E., & Hecht, M. L. (2004). Elaborating the Communication Theory of Identity: Identity gaps and communication outcomes. *Communication Quarterly, 52*, 265–283.

Jung, E., & Hecht, M.L., & Wadsworth, B. C. (2007). The role of identity in international students' psychological well-being in the United States: A model of depression levels, identity gaps, discrimination, and acculturation. *International Journal of Intercultural Relations, 31*, 605–624.

McCall, L. (2005). The complexity of intersectionality. *Signs: Journal of Women in Culture and Society, 30*, 1771–1800.

Wood, J. T. (2012). *Gendered lives: Communication, culture and gender*. Belmont, CA: Wadsworth.

# Case 19

# Seven Tattoos
## A Personal History

Cynthia Nicole

*Keywords:* appearance, body art, cutting, identity, loss

I think most people assume that tattoos are an expression of one's identity, an outward reflection of who the person is deep inside. While this assumption is not entirely incorrect, it's not exactly the truth. Sure, many people get tattoos to mark a significant event in their lives or to adorn their body with symbolic markings of their personality. But almost as much as we inscribe our character into our skin, it can also be said that the ink transforms who we are. In the following piece, I outline a personal history through recalling the designs I had tattooed on my body, the circumstances under which I got my ink, and, perhaps more tellingly, the ways in which each tattoo has led me to redefine both myself and the meaning I ascribe to it.

This small heart on my right hip was my first tattoo. I had wanted one for a while, and after a failed suicide attempt in December 2002, I decided that perhaps I needed a permanent reminder to love myself. I created the design myself because, though I wanted

*Inside Relationships: A Creative Casebook in Relational Communication*, edited by Sandra L. Faulkner, 213–219. © 2013 Left Coast Press, Inc. All rights reserved.

a fairly traditional image—a heart—I stubbornly refused to select from flash art in favor of having something unique. In January 2002 my best friend Sarah came to visit me and talked me into getting it done while she was in town. I got my first tattoo at a small shop in San Marcos, Texas, where I went to college. I vaguely remember it being painful, but nothing a cutter couldn't handle. What I recall most about the experience was the stern reprimand of the tattoo artist when I couldn't manage to sit still because Sarah was making me laugh too much. Other than the disapproval of my parents, this tattoo never got much attention due to its small size and easily hidden location. I don't know if I can say that it ever served its original purpose, but it has always reminded me of a fun time with Sarah.

Sarah died in April 2009. It was unexpected, sort of. She had an addiction to pills, which I knew about, but she always managed to give the illusion that she had the habit under control. I never thought she would accidentally kill herself.

As part of my grieving process and as a way to memorialize my friendship in a medium Sarah loved, I decided to get a tattoo of her favorite flowers—stargazer lilies. I had an artist friend draw the design, then in January 2010 I met with a tattoo artist who had been highly recommended. At our initial consultation she suggested that we break the large design into two sessions, one for the outline and shading and a second for the coloring. Since this was my first tattoo in eight years and a much larger piece than my first tattoo, this seemed like a good idea. As it turned out, the first sitting went so smoothly that my artist could finish the entire tattoo, color and all, in about three hours. She complimented my ability to sit still and endure pain, a physical activity that seemed to mirror my emotional state. And with the catharsis of her needle, I had found myself a new hobby.

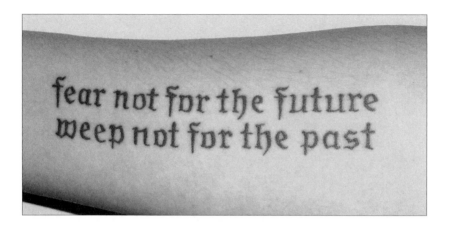

Between Sarah's death and a painfully ill-fated romantic interlude in the summer of 2009, 2010 was a year of dwelling upon the past and being anxious about the future. In March, I went to Las Vegas for Spring Break. The friend I went with really wanted to get a tattoo, but was fearful as she has a low threshold for pain and a strong aversion to needles. As I attempted to assure her that it really wasn't that bad, I somehow talked myself into getting a tattoo with her. It seemed like a requisite move after a week of drunken abandon in Sin City. We made an appointment with a reputable, reasonably priced studio, and I decided upon a quotation to have inked onto my forearm. A line from Percy Bysshe Shelley's "The Revolt of Islam" seemed fitting for this stage in my life, and with a quick Google search to confirm the correctness of my memory, I acquired my third tattoo, which reads "fear not for the future, weep not for the past." Of course, Google isn't a reliable failsafe, and when I revisited the original text upon my return home, I discovered that I had tattooed a common misquotation on my arm. The actual poem reads "Fear not the future, weep not for the past." As a person with obsessive-compulsive disorder, this was kind of my worst tattoo nightmare. I initially felt like one of those jerks you see photos of online with something like "live without regret" tattooed on their backs. But, once it's permanently inked into your flesh, it's best to make peace with your tattoo, particularly when it's in such a visible location. And so, this tattoo taught me a lesson about giving up control.

In the summer of 2010, I finally felt like moving on with my life. Mourning lost relationships was not healthy, and I decided it was time

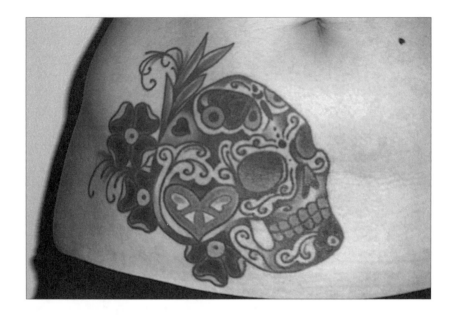

for a rebirth. I was also growing displeased with my first tattoo. Compared to the beautiful lilies, that sad little heart was an eyesore. I still liked the idea of it, but I wanted to incorporate it into a larger and more aesthetically appealing design. I met with the artist who inked my lilies to brainstorm ideas. The first idea I tossed out was a "sugar skull," the type of decorated skull associated with Dia de Los Muertos, one of my favorite holidays. The holiday itself is a celebration of the dead, and the bright floral skulls represent a rebirth. She quickly worked up a design that seamlessly integrated the heart and fit well on my body. In the course of two months, in two sittings, I went through a period of transforming the past, even as I embraced it, and emerged reawakened to life's potential. I got a lot of compliments on the stunning and intricate tattoo, so I also discovered a new passion—the aesthetic redesign of my body through tattoos.

In January 2011, I met again with my tattoo artist to discuss ideas for a new tattoo. I wanted a half sleeve, and I was contemplating something that would express my love of astronomy—a theme that lends itself well to visual arts like tattooing. I had always appreciated the look of old star charts, and when I showed some images of them to my artist, she was excited about the prospects. We decided that selecting a single constellation to feature on my upper arm would allow for an appropriately detailed tattoo. I don't have a favorite constellation, but I'm a Virgo, and it seemed sensible to go with my sign.

I met with my artist a month after our initial consultation and was astounded by her design. Her drawing of Virgo managed to represent the virgin without making her look too angelic or wholesome. The stars in the tattoo design match up clearly with the actual stars in the constellation. And she had incorporated Messier objects (that is, astronomical objects first catalogued by French astronomer Charles Messier in 1771) in their rightful place. This tattoo

marries the aesthetic beauty of traditional tattoo art with an understanding of astronomical objects and their locations.

Though my forearm tattoo is in a visible location, since it's on the inside of my arm, it often goes unseen. However, this half-sleeve is readily visible. With the acquisition of this ink, I became a visibly tattooed woman. I hadn't given it too much thought beforehand, but since undergoing this transformation I realize that people see me and interact with me differently. Some perceive me as tough and rebellious, others start conversations with me for the sole purpose of learning more about my tattoo or the artist who designed it. As I've had to come to terms with this new version of myself, I find that it's altered my self-perception.

The spring of 2011 proved to be a trying one. Two of my grandparents died, I stopped talking to my father, and my academic future was particularly shaky due to a decrease in funding. I had been toying with the idea of a leg tattoo, something to balance out my body now that my left arm was covered. I thought that something floating on the side of my leg would look a little odd, so I began thinking about a semi-traditional

design—a garter. However, I didn't want just a plain garter, and my long-time admiration of Hunter S. Thompson led to the concept of a Gonzo fist sword being tucked into a garter on my thigh. It seemed a perfect way to provide myself with some therapeutic ink after a rough semester and to arm myself for any oncoming battles. My tattoo artist loved the idea, and in the summer of 2011, I went through two long and painful sittings, the result of which is that *I am now a warrior.*

The most recent tattoo I got was really just for fun. In October 2011, I saw the Smashing Pumpkins perform live in Detroit. This band has been one of my favorites since I was in junior high and in some ways I suppose I attribute to their music my getting through the horrors of adolescence. I've always loved their video for "Tonight, Tonight" and the original silent film to which it pays homage, *Le Voyage dans la Lune.* On a whim, I met with a new tattoo artist about a design that would incorporate the style of the music video with a scene from the film. He emailed me a proof later that week, and by the end of October, I had new ink.

After acquiring these seven tattoos from four artists over ten years, I think it's fair to say that I'm becoming a collector. What started out as a means of body adornment and commemoration has become an art form to which I turn for catharsis and transformation. If I want to

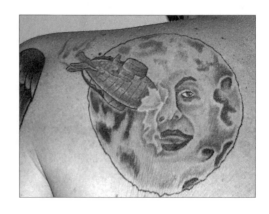

feel beautiful or strong or whimsical, I can use ink to become those things. But because people react to my tattoos and talk to me about them, I understand that I don't have total agency over who I become (then again, who really does?). As I have embraced my tattooed self, I have also switched research topics and moved forward in a project to enmesh this tattooed identity with my work as an academic. And so, yet again, my tattoos have transformed me.

## Questions and Activities for Discussion

1. How can body art, such as tattoos, work as a source of identity and identity transformation? What functions do tattoos serve for Nicole? She wrote, "And with the catharsis of her needle, I had found myself a new hobby." Are the tattoos another form of cutting or something else?

2. How does one's appearance reflect inner states and relationship challenges? Have you ever deliberately altered your appearance to create a feeling you wanted to embody (maybe even gotten a tattoo yourself)? If so, did it work and why? What reactions did you experience from friends or other significant others?

3. What does it mean to be a "visibly tattooed woman"? How do gendered assumptions about feminine appearance influence how one reacts to a tattooed woman? How can appearance transform our expectations about gender (e.g., Suicide Girls)? Find images of visibly tattooed women (e.g., http://ilovetattooedwomen.com) and discuss your reactions.

## For Further Reading and Reference

Atkinson, M. (2002). Pretty in ink: Conformity, resistance, and negotiation in women's tattooing. *Sex Roles, 47*(5/6), 219–235.

Doss, K., & Hubbard, A. S. E. (2009). The communicative value of tattoos: The role of public self-consciousness on tattoo visibility. *Communication Research Reports, 26*(1), 62–74.

Ryan, K., Heath, M., Fischer, L., & Young, E. L. (2008). Superficial self-harm: Perceptions of young women who hurt themselves. *Journal of Mental Health Counseling, 30*(3), 237–254.

Sweetman, P. (1999). Anchoring the (postmodern) self? Body modification, fashion and identity. *Body & Society, 5*(2–3), 51–76.

Vail, D. A. (1999). Tattoos are like potato chips . . . you can't have just one: The process of becoming and being a collector. *Deviant Behavior: An Interdisciplinary Journal, 20*, 253–273.

# Case 20

# The Conversation About Culture and Gender that I Would Have With You

Manda V. Hicks

*Keywords:* culture, definitions of culture and gender, gendered
assumptions

In his strange and soulful little book *Beyond Culture,* Edward Hall
suggests that culture is the external manifestation of the mind.

Whoa.

Right? The way the mind works to create meaning, the processes it
goes through, the limits it bumps against; when we begin to discuss
culture and how it functions, it's pretty much the same as the mind.

Culture is the external manifestation of the mind, and it is an extension of the human and human possibility.

The world is an invention. The way we live our lives and make sense
of things is all a product of culture, and culture is not innate; it is
learned. The way we learn to relate to each other and the way we learn
which expectations to have about each other are all made possible (and
impossible!) through culture.

What does culture make possible and impossible for you? And how
does gender impact that?

Gender and culture are:

The time I was called a cunt in basic training, and the time I was called
a dumb slut when I was a sergeant.

---

*Inside Relationships: A Creative Casebook in Relational Communication,* edited by
Sandra L. Faulkner, 220–224. © 2013 Left Coast Press, Inc. All rights reserved.

When I was called a dumb slut, the thing that bothered me the most was the generic-ness of the slur; the guy hadn't even bothered to identify accurate qualities to defame me. It was like he reached into a bag and pulled out any one of the many standard ways to hate women. His hand moved past "fat cow" and "stupid whore" and settled on "dumb slut." If he'd bothered to sort and categorize his bag, maybe I would have had the pleasure of being called "mean bitch," because that's the one that might have fit the best.

What's in that bag? That bag that gives power and weaponry to hurt and shame? All those words at the ready to help us hate on women and make them feel shitty about themselves?

Bitch.DumbBitch.FatBitch.UglyBitch.StupidBitch.Pig.FatPig. DumbPig.StupidPig.Whore.DumbWhore.FatWhore.StupidWhore. UglyWhore.Cunt.StupidCunt.UglyCunt.Slut.DumbSlut.FatSlut. StupidSlut. BobbleHead.TownBicycle.SpermDumpster.

Even words like FUPA (fat upper pubic area) and muffin top and tramp stamp are used to conjure the female body as something disgusting and deserving of assault.

There are websites and hashtags devoted to describing how ugly vaginas are.

These are some of the resources our culture provides us for making sense of women. Great, right?

Gender and culture is:

When I had worked my way through several tournaments and hours of competition to play poker in a nationally televised tournament, one of the competitors at my table asked me and the other lone female where our husbands were.

My student scrawling "feminist cunts" across a ballot for a debate he had lost, and me having to talk with him about it.

The time at the bar where this guy was buying rounds and pushing shots on me. When I declined and said I needed to keep it together, he said, "Let me guess. You got kids you have to get home to." And I said "Maybe I need to be up early to work in my research laboratory."

Gender and culture is going to graduate school with males that call 60-year-old female faculty members 'bitches' and think its okay to speculate on the oral sex give-and-take between two married faculty members. Gender and culture is going to graduate school with females that think it's okay, too.

Gender and culture is not making sense in public. When I am with my lover who is ten years my junior, it feels like we're on some fucked up game show called "Why Are These Two Together?" The snack guy on Amtrak thinks he's being charming by referring to us as sisters (because I'm *clearly* her mother, and I should enjoy his flattery); the waitress at the sketchy diner decides we must be sisters because we've got "the same small eyes."

I beg your pardon? Come again?

If I'm out in public with another woman, we must be explained. It's obvious when females are fun hot bitches out on the town; or demure professionals taking a mommy break; or chubby office mates indulging in lunch together; or skinny office mates having a coffee. These organizations of women are easy to make sense of, easy to understand. They tell us how to treat them. Hot bitches out on the town are to be treated as such, and chubby office mates? Well, they are to be ignored.

I live in a world in which for MANY males the value of a woman with a high public profile is based on how hard she makes him.

Hillary Clinton? Old ugly bitch.

Lady Gaga? She's got a dick.

It's funny that Lady Gaga, a mainstream artist that caters to a gay gaze more than nearly anyone before her, has a metaphorical dick slapped on her in order to justify that she's not fuckable.

Do you get what I'm saying? Straight men don't like Gaga. They don't like her because she really doesn't craft her imagery for the straight male gaze. Now, because she doesn't do that, she's not hot. And because she's been deemed not hot, there has to be an explanation for her 'not hotness' (notness?).

So...

She gotta dick.

When I go out with a group of girlfriends, I brace myself. I enjoy their company, and I like to hang out and party with my friends, but they are far more comfortable with/receptive to behavior that I shoot down like a UFO-sized clay pigeon.

At a winery the other day, I met up with three female friends that I see about once a year. Among the four of us, we have an above average attractiveness quotient. This is not a boast; this is to clarify that in terms of how we are seen, the women in my group attract positive attention. We sat outside and shared our picnic and got up to take some pictures before going in for the tasting. As we walked in, a middle-aged regular dude came up and announced that he was the birthday boy and that we should take a picture with him to put up on Facebook.

I kept walking.

I kept walking with the belief that some of the people in my party would have been friendly-ish and at least engaged in conversation (if not posed for a photo) before they moved on. But one friend followed my lead into the building and another joined us in the winery and offered that she was too married and pregnant to indulge that kind of stuff anymore, and the last one finished her friendliness obligation and trailed in.

It's not news to say that women are socialized to be friendly, or that they have a burden of making other people feel good about themselves. It's not news to say that men know this and, intentionally or unintentionally, use that to their benefit. It's also not news to say that things do work vice versa, and men are often compromised and made vulnerable by gender dynamics and expectations in our culture. What perhaps IS news is that there is a template out there—a cookie cutter shape that tells people how to make sense of you and how to treat you. And you have to spray on some serious repellant—you have to do a lot of brave work—to deny that template and be made sense of on your own terms.

## Questions and Activities for Discussion

1. What does culture make possible and impossible for you? And how does gender impact that? How does one "spray on some serious repellant" and decide how to write different gender scripts within a culture?

2. What does Hicks suggest about the relationship between gender and culture? How do our ideas about appropriate behavior and roles for women and men influence our cultural understanding? How is Hicks defining culture? Gender?

3. Write your own litany about gender and/or culture. Billy Collins's poem, *Litany,* is a good example.

## For Further Reading and Reference

Blair, C., Browne, J. R., & Baxter, L. A. (1994). Disciplining the feminine. *Quarterly Journal of Speech, 80,* 383–409.

Cohen, C. J. (1997). Punks, bulldaggers, and welfare queens: The radical potential of queer politics? *GLQ: A Journal of Lesbian and Gay Studies, 3,* 437–465.

Hall, E. T. (1976). *Beyond culture.* New York: Anchor Books.

Holland, S. L. (2006). The dangers of playing dress up: Popular representations of Jessica Lynch and the controversy regarding women in combat. *Quarterly Journal of Speech, 92,* 27–50.

# Case 21

# Sticks and Stones
## Dealing with Discrimination

Lisa K. Hanasono

*Keywords:* Asian American, social support, stereotypes

"Where are you from?" To many folks, this question is a classic con-versation starter. However, to me this seemingly innocent question frequently serves as the gateway to frustrating and awkward social interactions. Typically it begins like this: a stranger asks me, "Where are you from?" Without hesitation, I say, "I'm from Indiana." Some-times, my initial answer satisfies the stranger's curiosity, and we move to other topics. However, my response often evokes confusion in my conversational partner. The person looks at my Asian American face and presses further.

"Oh. I mean, where are your *parents* from?" The stranger asks. At this point, I politely smile and respond, "My parents are from Southern Cal-ifornia. They met each other while attending school at the University of California in Los Angeles." The stranger frowns; this was not the answer that he or she had expected. Persistent, the questioner tries again.

"No...Where are your *grandparents* from?" The stranger uncom-fortably waits for my response. My smile widens.

"Originally, my grandparents were from the San Francisco area," I explain. "When they were young adults, they lived in Colorado. After a few years, they moved to Los Angeles to raise their kids."

By this point in the conversation, the stranger seems frustrated or embarrassed. To put the stranger out of his or her misery, I explain,

*Inside Relationships: A Creative Casebook in Relational Communication,* edited by Sandra L. Faulkner, 225–231. © 2013 Left Coast Press, Inc. All rights reserved.

"My *great-grandparents* immigrated to the United States in the late 1800's from Japan. I'm a *yonsei*, which is a fourth generation Japanese American."

Throughout the years, I've had the "where are you from" conversation with dozens of people. Each time, I painstakingly explain my roots and my family's American background *before* disclosing my ethnic identity. I suppose it would be easier to initially say, "I'm a fourth generation Japanese American who was born and raised in Indiana." However, I've come to understand this conversation as an opportunity to educate others about the heterogeneity of Asian American identities and to challenge the assumption that people of Asian descent are perpetual foreigners in the United States.

## Back Home in Indiana

As a child in the 1980's, I grew up in the Indianapolis suburbs. For many years, my family and I were the only ethnic minority members in our neighborhood. Instead of participating in *Obon* and Cherry Blossom Festivals, we went to Colts and Pacers home games and watched Jim Nabors sing "Back Home Again in Indiana" at the Indy 500. My favorite foods were mashed potatoes and fried chicken, and I enjoyed taking horseback riding lessons and performing in dance recitals.

Although I *felt* like a Hoosier (that is, a person who was born in Indiana), many people looked at my racialized body and called me an outsider. In elementary school, some kids would grotesquely slant their eyes at me and recite anti-Asian chants. Others teased me with the nickname "Chicken Chow Mein." (As a Japanese American, I found this particularly strange, because chow mein is a Chinese dish.) One of my playmates wouldn't let me touch her dolls, because she thought I'd get them dirty. Older kids made crude comments that sexually objectified Asian women.

In truth, I didn't know how to deal with their bullying and insensitive behavior. At first, I was surprised by my classmates' remarks and jeers; I didn't realize that I was "different" until they pointed it out to me. After a while, though, I began to feel embarrassed—and then ashamed and hurt. Most of the time, I tried to ignore my feelings. I silenced my anger to make my peers and friends think that their actions didn't bother me. I didn't tell my parents and teachers about these incidents, because I wanted to pretend that the events weren't real. But secretly, I felt ashamed and was painfully aware that I was different from most of my peers.

For the next ten years, I worked to hide my racial and ethnic differences. I didn't want to be treated like an outsider. I wore clothes from J. Crew and the Limited, and I attempted to emulate the hair styles and make up trends that were featured on the glossy pages of popular magazines like *Seventeen, YM,* and *People*. I decided to take French classes (instead of Japanese) in high school, and I joined my school's show choir and dance teams.

Despite my attempts to blend into the social fabric of my hometown, people occasionally singled me out. For example, I remember a bookstore sales associate who said to me after we engaged in some small talk, "You speak English really well!"

Surprised, I paused for a second. I responded, "Thanks. I'm glad that I can speak English, because it's the only language that I know!" This time, it was the sales associate's turn to be surprised.

## Coming Full Circle and Taking a Stand

During college at Miami University, I finally learned to embrace my racial and ethnic identities. I realized that hiding or ignoring my Japanese American heritage was not solving any of my problems. No matter how hard I tried, people inevitably read my body as a racialized text. Instead of attempting to hide my identity, I refocused my energies on learning about my ethnic background and the racialization of Asian Americans. I enrolled in undergraduate and graduate courses that explored key topics like stereotyping, prejudice, discrimination, and social identities. I voraciously read books on Asian American cultures, histories, and media representations. I also joined several Asian American activist groups, such as the Japanese American Citizens League. While pursuing my PhD at Purdue University, I joined a team of faculty, graduate students, undergraduate students, and staff members who worked together to establish a new Asian American Studies Program; I eventually got the opportunity to design and teach an Asian American Studies course. This educational journey was empowering. I finally felt secure and comfortable in my skin, and I had a profound appreciation of my heritage.

Despite these positive changes, a scary encounter made me realize how much I still needed to learn. Several years ago, my then-boyfriend and I decided to go to our favorite local restaurant for dinner. The evening began as anything but extraordinary. We sat at our usual table and ordered a dozen Buffalo wings, a small order of mini corn dogs, and a basket of potato wedges. When we finished our meal and got up to leave, I noticed three White men standing about ten feet from the door. As we approached them, one of the guys stared at me, smirked, and turned to his friends.

"Look at that *chink*," he said, pointing to me.

Surprised, I flushed with embarrassment and anger. *Chink* is a racial epithet that historically referred to Chinese and Chinese Americans. My head started to spin. *What should I do?* A small part of me wanted to yell at him for being ignorant. Another smaller part of me wanted to hide and pretend that nothing had happened. I felt like I couldn't ignore the man's words after taking courses on racial inequalities, prejudice, and stereotyping and after being active in various civil rights organizations; I knew that I needed to take a stand.

I took a deep breath. Perhaps I could engage the man in a healthy dialogue about racial identities and engender feelings of mutual respect and understanding. After all, my professors frequently praised the use of dialogue as a means to resolving conflict. I walked over to him.

"Excuse me," I said calmly, "But I don't appreciate being called that." I used my most polite tone. I paused, waiting for him to either apologize or explain that he didn't know that *chink* was a racially offensive label. He surprised me with an alternative response. His face quickly contorted into a dangerous blend of rage and defensiveness.

"What the hell?!" He growled. "I'm not a fucking racist!" It was clear that we weren't going to have a meaningful dialogue.

"How dare you call me a racist!" Before his friends could respond, the man lunged at me with clenched fists. I jumped out of the way, and he chased me out of the restaurant, screaming obscenities at the top of his lungs.

"You stupid bitch! I'm not racist!" He yelled as I sprinted several feet down the restaurant's front walk and toward the street. "Fuck you!" He moved toward me to beat my 5'3" frame into a pulp. Fortunately, his buddies and my boyfriend caught up to us in time. The man's friends grabbed his arms and held him back as he lurched at me, kicking his legs. My boyfriend positioned his body between the enraged man and me.

"Hey....We're cool. We're cool." My boyfriend said. I could tell that he was frightened, but he held his ground. "Everything's cool."

One of the man's friends attempted to talk him down, too. "Yeah," he said. "We're alright." He looked at his buddy and said, "Dude, you gotta calm down." The angry man's friend pulled him away from us and said softly, "You better get out of here." I didn't argue and left with my boyfriend, feeling utterly defeated and shaken. As a racially conscious person, I believed that it was important to take a stand against prejudice and discrimination. As an academic, I thought that the use of dialogue could solve most interpersonal problems. In this situation, taking a stand—even in a fairly polite manner—nearly landed me in the hospital. Even worse, I had put my significant other in danger and felt guilty. Taking a stand was important to me, but was it worth the price of endangering the people I loved?

On the way home, I apologized to my boyfriend and thanked him for being there. He said, "There's no need to apologize. You have to stand up for what's right. And when you stand up, know that you are not alone."

I was stunned because for the longest time, I thought that I needed to deal with discrimination on my own. It never occurred to me that people in my support network—especially close friends and family members—were ready and willing to take a stand with me.

I learned several lessons that night. First, it's okay to take a stand against prejudice and discrimination, but it's also important to pick your battles and to consider the potential risks of fighting. Moreover, there are different ways to deal with discrimination. In the years to come, there were times when confrontation was necessary. However, numerous alternatives exist, such as ignoring the perpetrator, reporting the incident, or seeking support. Second, I realized the importance of close relationships. Although I certainly don't want to ever put my loved ones at risk, it's comforting to know that they have my back—and that I have theirs.

## Where Are *You* From, and Where Are *We* Going?

People have continued to make racially insensitive remarks and operate on faulty stereotypes. After telling strangers I'm from Indiana, some still ask, "No, where are you *really* from?" (I usually tell them that I'm *really* from Indiana.) A few friends have asked me if I have ever eaten dog meat. (For the record, I've never eaten dog meat. My family pet was a Shetland Sheepdog named Chip, but we didn't eat him.) One of my ex-boyfriends told me that he didn't feel comfortable introducing me to his family, because they were not used to interacting with people of Asian descent. While attending university orientation programs, staff members frequently instructed me to attend special sessions designed for international students (even though I'm a U.S. citizen) and asked me about my visa. (At first, I thought they were asking to see my credit card! As you can imagine, this led to more awkward interactions.)

Instead of feeling ashamed or defeated by these social encounters, I now consider them to be "hopeful learning moments." While most of the people that I've met embrace the ideals of social equality and diversity, I know that there are malicious people who still harbor dangerous prejudice against people of Asian descent. Hate speech, cyber bullying, and violent acts continue to target racial minority members, including Asian Americans. It's important to take a stand against prejudice, and targets of discrimination shouldn't have to cope alone.

On a brighter note, I have found that *most* people are well-intentioned and do not mean to say or do racially offensive things. Sometimes, people aren't aware of common Asian American stereotypes. Other times, people do not realize that their comments or behaviors could be interpreted as racially insensitive. As an educator, friend, Hoosier, and Japanese American, I feel responsible for teaching others about the multiplicity of Asian American identities, histories, cultures, and perspectives and to help those who are dealing with discrimination.

## Questions and Activities for Discussion

1. Have you ever been excluded and/or called out because of difference? What was the difference, perceived or real? How did you react to the situation? Was your reaction helpful? If not, what did you learn from the situation? How important is it to call others out about ignorance, discrimination and prejudice?

2. Why do you think it took so long for Hanasono to learn to speak out against prejudice and discrimination? What role does social support play in dealing with the fear of difference?

3. Make a list of your important identities. Do you have any racial and ethnic identities in your list? How are these identities important to you? How do these identities function in your close relationships?

## For Further Reading and Reference

Burleson, B. R., & Hanasono, L. K. (2010). Explaining cultural and sex differences in responses to supportive communication: A dual process approach. In J. Davila & K. Sullivan (Eds.), *Support processes in intimate relationships* (pp. 291–317). New York: Oxford University Press.

Hanasono, L. K. (in press). Discrimination against Asian Americans. In L. Dong (Ed.), *Encyclopedia of Asian American culture.* Santa Barbara, CA: ABC-CLIO.

Hanasono, L. K., & Chen, L. (2012). Identifying communities in need: Examining the impact of acculturation on perceived discrimination, social support, and coping amongst racial minority members. Paper presented at the annual meeting of the National Communication Association. Orlando, Florida.

Miller, C. T., & Kaiser, C. R. (2001). A theoretical perspective on coping with stigma. *Journal of Social Issues, 57,* 73–92.

Pascoe, E. A., & Richman, L. S. (2009). Perceived discrimination and health: A meta-analytic review. *Psychological Bulletin, 135,* 531–554.

Takaki, R. (1998). *Strangers from a different shore: A history of Asian Americans.* Boston: Back Bay Books.

# Chapter 8

# Relationship Maintenance

The authors in Chapter 8 use poetic and visual representations to demonstrate how we maintain our relationships. Camille-Yvette Welsch wrote a poem about her aunt's cancer to ask if lying to a dying loved one, as a form of comfort, is justifiable. Paul Ruby visualizes a dialogue between a romantic couple about meanings of love, lust and romance in a photo-poem, and Abigail Lea Van Vlerah uses a diagram of frustrations about communication with a lover to demonstrate the importance of talking about interaction expectations. *Relational maintenance* involves those behaviors we enact to keep our relationships going, to keep them in existence in a desired state (Canary & Stafford, 1994). We can argue that most of our relational lives are spent maintaining relationships, so a focus on effective behaviors to keep our relationships in a satisfactory condition or state of repair (depending on how you view the idea of maintenance) is a good thing. Spending time attending to our relationships and their fluctuations over time can lead to more satisfying ones and contribute to liking, commitment and love (Stafford, 2011). *Relationship satisfaction* can be defined as pleasure and enjoyment that we get from our relationships (Vangelisti & Huston, 1994).

*Inside Relationships: A Creative Casebook in Relational Communication,* edited by Sandra L. Faulkner, 233–236. © 2013 Left Coast Press, Inc. All rights reserved.

Common behaviors we use to maintain our relationships include being positive and cheerful (e.g., I love date night.), being open and self-disclosing (e.g., You always give me good advice.), providing assurances (e.g., You are the sexiest person in this room.), demonstrating love and faithfulness, sharing tasks (e.g., doing the dishes), doing activities together (e.g., grocery shopping, playing badminton), being sexually intimate and expressing affection, and being spontaneous (Canary & Stafford, 1994). The types of relationships we have influence our maintenance behaviors. Acquaintances and Facebook friends may not merit as much care as best friends, romantic partners and family members. For example, some research suggests that those involved in on-off again relationships use fewer maintenance behaviors compared with those in steady ones (Dailey, Hampel & Roberts, 2010). These individuals are less likely to see positive outcomes such as love and understanding and more likely to see negative outcomes like uncertainty and communication problems. Also, relationship stage and commitment can predict maintenance (Ogolsky, 2009). In the beginning stages of relationships, we may be more attuned to our partner's maintenance behaviors, which can lead to relational commitment. In more established relationships, the commitment we feel for another may be the motivation for us to engage in maintenance behaviors regardless of whether they began online, are primarily face-to face, or exist only online (Rabby, 2007). Koerner and Fitzpatrick (2002) argue that decoding nonverbal communication is important for satisfying marriages. "Identifying correctly what the partner experiences as positive in the relationship allows spouses to do more of the same and to be satisfied for having a positive impact on an intimate partner" (p. 48). This appears to be more important than encoding. In friendships, the ideal standards we have can probably only be met up to a point, and then we experience disappointment (Hall, Kiley & Watts, 2011). Research indicates that best friends are able to fulfill these standards better than causal friends, though. Fehr (1996) suggests that openness, supportiveness, and positivity are important for maintaining friendships.

The maintenance behaviors we enact can also be classified as pro-social, dependent on channel, and strategic or routine (Guerrero, Andersen & Afifi, 2011). We engage in some behaviors on a routine basis, such as making a weekly phone call to mom and a weekly date night, while others are more strategic, like calling a friend after an argument. The fact is that we also use anti-social behaviors to maintain relationships, from making a partner jealous, being unfaithful to show we have alternatives to the current relationship, or spying, to avoiding topics because that could damage a relationship. The use of negative behaviors can be strategic and keep a relationship in existence, even one someone is dissatisfied being in. Goodboy and Myers (2010) studied relationship quality indicators—relationship satisfaction, commitment, control mutuality, liking, respect—to predict the types of maintenance behaviors individuals used. Not surprisingly, low quality relationships were marked with the use of more negative maintenance behaviors (i.e., jealousy induction, avoidance, spying, infidelity, destructive conflict). Further, the researchers found that love styles mattered; ludus (game-playing) and mania (possessive) lovers were more likely to enact negative maintenance behaviors. Hendrick and Hendrick (1986) characterize love as passionate (eros), game-playing (ludus), friendship-based (storge), logical (pragma), possessive (mania), and selfless (agape). What love styles and maintenance behaviors do you see present in the cases that follow?

## References

Canary, D. J., & Stafford, L. (1994). *Communication and relational maintenance.* San Diego, CA: Academic Press.

Dailey, R. M., Hampel, A. D., & Roberts, J. B. (2010). Relational maintenance in on-again/off-again relationships: An assessment of how relational maintenance, uncertainty, and commitment vary by relationship type and status. *Communication Monographs, 77*(1), 75–101.

Fehr, B. (1996). *Friendship processes.* Thousand Oaks, CA: Sage.

Goodboy, A. K., & Myers, S. A. (2010). Relational quality indicators and love styles as predictors of negative relational maintenance behaviors in romantic relationships. *Communication Reports, 23*(2), 65–78.

Guerrero, L. K., Andersen, P. A., & Afifi, W. A. (2011). *Close encounters: Communication in relationships* (3rd ed.). Thousand Oaks, CA: Sage.

Hall, J. A., Kiley, A. L., & Watts, A. (2011). Satisfying friendship maintenance expectations: The role of friendship standards and biological sex. *Human Communication Research, 37,* 529–552.

Hendrick, C., & Hendrick, S. (1986). A theory and method of love. *Journal of Personality and Social Psychology, 50,* 392–402.

Koerner A. F., & Fitzpatrick, M. A. (2002). Nonverbal communication and marital adjustment and satisfaction: The role of decoding relationship relevant and relationship irrelevant affect. *Communication Monographs, 69,* 33–51.

Ogolsky, B. G. (2009). Deconstructing the association between relationship maintenance and commitment: Testing two competing models. *Personal Relationships, 16*(1), 99–115.

Rabby, M. K. (2007). Relational maintenance and the influence of commitment in online and offline relationships. *Communication Studies, 58,* 315–337.

Stafford, L. (2011). Measuring relationship maintenance behaviors: Critique and development of the revised relationship maintenance behavior scale. *Journal of Social and Personal Relationships, 28*(2), 278–303.

Vangelisti, A. L., & Huston, T. L. (1994). Maintaining satisfaction and love. In D. J. Canary & L. Stafford (Eds.), *Communication and relational maintenance* (pp. 165–186). San Diego, CA: Academic Press.

# Case 22

# Comfort

## Camille-Yvette Welsch

*Keywords*: death and dying, grief, illness, social support, therapeutic writing

## Comfort

The resurrection was short.
A few hours. The bones in the bed trembled
and turned when we lifted the weighty blankets.
She stared back at us, her eyes widening
hollows in the gaunt face. The wig was gone now,
her only ornament disease, ridges of tumor
buttoned down her back. When she turned,
suddenly demure, she pulled
her nightgown down, fought that last little
battle of the body, keeping it hidden
even when the most terrible secret made
its way out. In stuttering breaths, she said
she felt better, that we would go to the movies
and the beach, back to summers at the lake.
And we all sat, locked together, nodding.

*Inside Relationships: A Creative Casebook in Relational Communication,* edited by
Sandra L. Faulkner, 237–238. © 2013 Left Coast Press, Inc. All rights reserved.

## Questions and Activities for Discussion

1. Have you ever written a poem, story or letter about a sick family member? How does writing about illness help one contend with difficult feelings? Did you ever share such writing with anyone in the family? Why or why not?

2. Welsch asks how much honesty do we owe each other? Is it right to lie if you believe that it will help the person? What factors dictate when we lie to the sick, to loved ones? Can we trust our own assumptions about their needs? That is one of the big questions that the poem asks for her: Am I lying for her or for me?

3. How does caring for a sick family member contribute to a sense of family identity? How could you consider social support an act of relationship maintenance?

## For Further Reading and Reference

Bosticco, C., & Thompson, T. L. (2005). An examination of the role of narratives and storytelling in bereavement. In L. M. Harter, P. M. Japp, & C. S. Beck (Eds.), *Narratives, health, and healing: Communication theory, research and practice* (pp. 391–411). Mahwah, NJ: Lawrence Erlbaum.

Harris, J., Bowen, D. J., Badr, H., Hannon, P., Hay, J., & Regan, S. K. (2009). Family communication during the cancer experience. *Journal of Health Communication, Supplement 1*(14), 76–84.

Heinz, D. (1999). *The last passage.* New York: Oxford University Press.

Pennebaker, J. W. (1993). Putting stress into words: Health, linguistic, and therapeutic implications. *Behavior Research and Therapy, 31,* 539–548.

# Case 23

# Tell Me About Love

## Paul D. Ruby

*Keywords:* attraction, love, relationship dialogue

**Tell me about love.**

**How does it feel?**

*Inside Relationships: A Creative Casebook in Relational Communication,* edited by
Sandra L. Faulkner, 239–241. © 2013 Left Coast Press, Inc. All rights reserved.

Tell me about love.
*What is it that you want to know?*

How does it feel?
*Biologically, I feel nothing.*

Nothing?
*Not a thing, but I do feel something, I feel loved.*

What does that feel like?
*Read my book.*

You're writing a book about love?
*Chapter one. Others are about attraction and communication.*

What about attraction?
*Read my book.*

I can't read it, you haven't written it yet. What about me do you find attractive?
*Your ass is attractive.*

And?
*You have a nice ass.*

Is that it?
*Every time I tell you something you put it in a damn poem. It's embarrassing.*

Tell me.
*No. I told you before.*
*I like you because you like me like I am, stubborn and bitchy.*

And communication? Don't say read my book.
*Read my book. See, I told you!*

Congratulations. Do you fall in love in your book?
*Yes.*

How does your book end?
*I haven't written the ending. How do you want it to end?*

I want you to show me how love feels.
*Okay.*

Okay, you will love me?
*Come over here. I want to feel your ass.*

## Questions and Activities for Discussion

1. Select a song that deals with the topic of the photo-poem (that is, relational conversations about love and attraction and implicitly relationship maintenance). Analyze how the song examines love, attraction and maintenance through the interaction described in the lyrics.

2. How does the photo-poem function as meta-talk about a couple's relationship? How would you describe the couple's relationship based on the dialogue? What ideas about love and attraction are presented? Is this about a same-sex couple? Did you make gendered assumptions about the speakers in the poem? If so, why?

3. Create your own photo-poem. 1) Select a photo of a loved one. 2) Answer the following questions about the photo: What themes do you see? Note these parts of the image. What do these themes feel, smell, and taste like? How can you describe these themes using more than one sense, especially if it is a sense you usually ignore? 3) Write a poem based on the answers in part two. 4) What does your photo-poem depict about the relationship?

## For Further Reading and Reference

Dailey, R. M., Hampel, A. D., & Roberts, J. B. (2010). Relational maintenance in on-again/off-again relationships: An assessment of how relational maintenance, uncertainty, and commitment vary by relationship type and status. *Communication Monographs, 77*(1), 75–101.

Goodboy, A. K., & Myers, S. A. (2010). Relational quality indicators and love styles as predictors of negative relational maintenance behaviors in romantic relationships. *Communication Reports, 23*(2), 65–78.

Jostman, N. B., Karremans, J., & Finenauer, C. (2011). When love is not blind: Rumination impairs affect regulation in response to romantic relationships threat. *Cognition & Emotion, 25*(3), 506–518.

Ogolsky, B. G. (2009). Deconstructing the association between relationship maintenance and commitment: Testing two competing models. *Personal Relationships, 16*(1), 99–115.

Slotter, E. B., & Gardner, W. L. (2012). How needing you changes me: The influence of attachment on self-concept malleability in romantic relationships. *Self & Identity, 11*(3), 386–408.

# Case 24

# The Onion

### Abigail Lea Van Vlerah

*Keywords:* demand-withdrawal cycle, divorce, emotions,
relationship maintenance

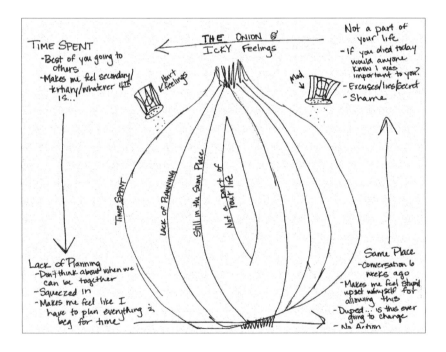

---

*Inside Relationships: A Creative Casebook in Relational Communication,* edited by
Sandra L. Faulkner, 242–245. © 2013 Left Coast Press, Inc. All rights reserved.

# The Story

He was going through the Big D—DIVORCE. Which meant we were in the closet. I didn't particularly enjoy not being official, not telling people that we were together, but I wanted him to be 100 percent comfortable with us before we came out. So, there we remained. The secret romance was kind of fun at first—intimate moments in his office, stolen kisses when no one was looking—but eventually the luster wore off, and we were left in a cycle of unrest. Part of our problem was our many miscommunications. We were both becoming easily upset by things the other couldn't understand. One night after a disagreement, I was particularly sad (and crying) and unable to sleep, so I made *The Onion*.

I needed to sort out my thoughts and convey to him that I wasn't happy with our status quo. I chose an onion first because they have layers, second because I know he hates onions, and third because they make you cry. I diagramed the way I felt. That night the problem started with him being out at the bar WITH his friends and WITHOUT me. But it wasn't just about him having fun without me, the problem reached much deeper into our relationship. That night, instead of just being honest about how I felt, I turned into a passive aggressive (or maybe outwardly aggressive) bitch. We had done this upset/passive aggressive cycle so many times we even had a code word for when we were starting to feel it—salt and pepper. "I felt salt and peppered tonight," I finally texted him. His reply: "Me, too, but I don't know why." We had a lengthy text and phone conversation about how the night played out; the cycle needed to be broken. I was so tired of fighting with him and just wanted to get at the heart of why we'd been bickering so often. We decided to talk through the issue the next day, but I still couldn't sleep.

I'd never made anything like *The Onion* before. I'm not into journaling or keeping diaries or talking about my feelings. I'm into internalizing issues then running away from the source of the problem. In fact, I'd never even cared enough about someone else to try working things out in a relationship. But this one was different. We were both too stubborn to accept losing our best friend. As I drew, I intentionally added personal touches that I knew would impact him—the salt and pepper shakers (our code words for when we're upset with one another), the sad face in the O, and most importantly, the truth about the way I felt. After I finished drawing *The Onion*, I was able to fall asleep and felt much better having (I thought) figured out the problem.

The next day, we met to have ANOTHER talk about our clandestine relationship. "We're not crying today, ok? I cried last night. It's time to fix this!" I told him. I brought out *The Onion*. He took some time to look at it. He allowed me to explain it to him. He was quiet.

He cried a little and said, "I know, I'm not supposed to cry, but I didn't cry last night." I told him it was okay, that he was allowed to cry. "This one hurts the most," he said pointing to the part of *The Onion* reading, "If you died today would anyone know I was important to you?" After we finished talking about it, we hugged for a long time and tried to move forward. *The Onion* seemed to have worked for the moment. I don't know why, but I found out later that he carried *The Onion* with him in his backpack for months. For me, that's the most endearing part of the story.

## Questions and Activities for Discussion

1. How does the model here serve as a metaphor for the relationship? Why do metaphors about relationships matter? What do they convey? What is their significance in everyday relating? Why do people often complain that their relationship "is not going anywhere"?

2. Think about a problem in a past and/or current romantic relationship that you were unable to articulate verbally. Draw a model like *The Onion* to describe the problem and include interaction patterns, private language, and emotions.

3. The demand/withdrawal pattern in relationships references a communication cycle where one partner makes demands (perhaps because of feeling powerless) and the other becomes defensive and retreats. How do you see that represented in the model? How did *The Onion* and the subsequent dialogue between the partners help break the cycle?

## For Further Reading and Reference

Caughlin, J. P. (2002). The demand/withdrawal pattern in communication as a predictor of marital satisfaction over time: Unresolved issues and future directions. *Human Communication Research, 28,* 49–85.

Cui, M., Fincham, F. D., Ddurtschi, J. A. (2011). The effect of parental divorce on young adults' romantic relationship dissolution: What makes a difference? *Personal Relationships, 18*(3), 410–426.

Houser, M. L., Fleuriet, C., & Estrada, D. (2012). The cyber factor: An analysis of relational maintenance through the use of computer-mediated communication. *Communication Research Reports, 29*(1), 34–43.

Sandfield, A. (2006). Talking divorce: The role of divorce in women's constructions of relationship status. *Feminism & Psychology, 16*(2), 155–173.

# Chapter 9

# The Dark Side
## Conflict, Dissolution and Other
## Difficult Conversations

This chapter highlights cases with darker concepts like mental illness, verbal and physical abuse, and the breakdown of relationships. Dessa Anderson's personal essay on multi-generational abuse in her family reveals the normalization of verbal and physical violence in families. Sandra Faulkner's performance poetry piece shows the breaking down process of romantic relationships and friendships. In a series of poems about being institutionalized for mental illness, Wonda Baugh describes how social support from family and friends helped her with healing and the sting of stigma. The necessity of *social support* for dealing effectively with difficult relational challenges is a key concept woven through all of these cases. Social support means we engage in supportive communication, the use of verbal and nonverbal behaviors intended to provide or seek help (Burleson & MacGeorge, 2002).

How we enact support means more or less explicit communicative efforts by one person to improve the well being of another who is perceived as in need or under stress. These stressors include the topics in this chapter's case studies (and others chapters')—abuse, mental illness, breaking up, health, and relationship transitions. What you will notice about this definition is that communication centers the process of social support. There exists a direct connection between our

*Inside Relationships: A Creative Casebook in Relational Communication*, edited by Sandra L. Faulkner, 247–253. © 2013 Left Coast Press, Inc. All rights reserved.

well-being and how we communicate with one another. For instance, research suggests that the quality and quantity of social interaction contributes to healing and adjustment for those dealing with severe and persistent mental illness (Eklund & Hansson, 2007). This is more than a sociological focus on our roles and social networks or just a psychological focus on a person having others who are supportive. What is important for us to recognize is the role of communication, including the importance of goal setting and strategically enacting supportive behavior.

Social support arises in our interactions and is not something that is delivered like a commodity or resource. When we provide social support, we must determine what the other person needs and how we can enact appropriate behavior. Do they need a ride to the doctor? Do they need a hug? Do they need some advice? The question is whether our behavior achieves the primary goals of social, material, or psychological support. In a study on deployment, communication with loved ones, and post-traumatic stress disorder (PTSD), researchers discovered that having more secure interpersonal relationships, more community support, and ways to deal with worry contributed to helping soldiers with PTSD (Tsai et al., 2012). The use of person-centered messages, nonverbal immediacy, and emotional support constitute important behaviors that contribute to short and long term relationship health (Jones, 2004; Metts, 1997).

*Highly person-centered comforting messages* recognize and legitimize the other's feelings by helping the other articulate and elaborate about his or her feelings as well as assisting the other in seeing a broader context. *Nonverbal immediacy* means we show attentiveness through touch (e.g., hugs, pats); close proximity (e.g., leaning in and/or sitting closer to a person); eye contact; or looking concerned, sad, or empathetic. *Emotional support* entails making another feel better without necessarily giving advice or trying to "fix" a problem. In other words, we should match our messages to the stressor, paying attention to *subjective, affective, and relational* aspects of communicative contexts. For example, if you found out that your friend's father just had an emergency leg amputation because of an aneurism, a highly person-centered and immediate message could be the following: "I'm sorry to hear about your dad. It must be difficult to help him with the adjustment, though I'm glad he's okay. I bet your mother and father are both relieved that the amputation was the worse thing that happened given the seriousness of aneurisms."

How we provide social support matters for maintaining the health of our relationships, and inadequate social support can contribute to relational decline.

## Breaking Up

One explanation for why relationships end is Steve Duck's (2011) *Relationship Breakdown Model*. This model consists of five phases that focus on the relationship between cognition and communication during the dissolution process and includes the dyad's social networks and their communication. I prefer Duck's explanation to others, such as Knapp and Vangelisti's (2005) model of relational dissolution, because of the focus on communication in and as relational processes. This focus on communication between the dyad and social network is a major strength of the model given the importance of the break-up story (Kellas & Manusov, 2003) and the idea that communication is relational; action is the basis of our relationships (Duck, 2011). In other words, we do relationships. And we also tell different stories about our breakups and relationships to different people. These stories likely change over time as well. The audience influences our story telling strategies. We want to appear likable, and definitely datable, in the future!

The dissolution process begins when there is communication breakdown and dissatisfaction with the relationship (Duck, 2011). The *intrapsychic processes* occur when individuals ruminate about the cost of the relationship and a partner's faults; feelings of resentment may be present. A person often considers alternatives to the current relationship (for example, being with other people, not being in a relationship). The decline of a relationship often begins with the realization that you are working more, putting more into it than a partner (Goodfriend & Agnew, 2008). Differing investments in terms of material and nonmaterial resources mean one person may be over-benefited and another may be under-benefited. Recognition of this often begins with intrapersonal dialogue. You feel angry. You deserve to feel this way. Another way to think of this is through the dialectic of autonomy and connection, the fact that partners may experience different needs for closeness and independence; thus they struggle to figure out what to do (Sahlstein & Dun, 2008).

*Dyadic processes* begin when individuals decide they would be justified in withdrawing from the relationship. Partners may discuss their unhappiness with one another, and those in one's social network may express disapproval (for example, a belief that divorce is bad). Individuals may withdraw from social contact or decide starting a new relationship is best. Engaging with others in the social world may cause stress, which is part of the pain of breaking up. Of course, people also end relationships suddenly because of a critical incident or traumatic event according to catastrophe theory. Say a partner cheats or you discover that you have different values or fundamental beliefs (Felmlee, Sprecher, & Bassin, 1990). Maybe you can't deal with cultural differences, or perhaps, even, someone dies (Baxter, 1984; 1986). Catastrophe accounts for about 25 percent of our relational endings (Rawlins, 2009). A relationship may not gradually go through stages of decline or follow an ordered cultural script of progression from lack of communication, avoidance, assessing the situation, arguments, trying to work things out, to dating other people and breaking up (Battaglia, Richard, Datteri & Lord, 1998). Though, many relational endings do follow ordered scripts. Sometimes, however, we are clueless and dense about signs of trouble until too late (Vaughn, 1986).

The next stage entails *social processes* of going public by seeking advice or support. Accounts of the relationship are subject to social scrutiny at this point. An individual attempts to have his or her personal order validated with public critique of the partner and by building alliances. Duck's model of relationship dissolution focuses on the importance of social networks. We tell our break-up stories in these networks. Support from family, friends and peers influences relationship longevity (Lehmiller & Agnew, 2007; Sprecher & Felmlee, 1992). This seems to matter even more than larger cultural scripts. Some factors that contribute to breaking up include the amount of time spent with a partner, social network support, and whether the relationship was marginalized because of being interracial, same-sex, or partners having a large age gap.

*Grave dressing processes* occur when individuals transform the relationship history into a story that is plausible to others. An individual needs to present himself or herself to others as a good person for new relationships. Most decisions to break up are unilateral; bilateral dissolution is rare, which explains some of the pain of breakups (Tashiro & Frazier, 2003). One partner may experience guilt for breaking up while the other partner wishes the relationship would continue. Everyone wants to smell good in the formulation of an account, though. Relational processes are similar for heterosexual couples and homosexual and lesbian couples; the biggest differences occur because same sex couples lack social network support (Gottman et al., 2003; Kurdek, 1991). Transforming a romantic relationship into a friendship depends on how we broke up, whether we get something out of being friends, how we handle the transition, and again, whether our social network supports us (Busboom, Collins, Givertz & Levin, 2002; Kellas, Bean, Cunningham & Chen, 2008).

Finally, during the *resurrection processes* an individual recreates a sense of social value through the presentation of the self as a desirable relational partner with the story of "what I learned and how things will be different" (Duck, 2011, p. 190). Having different values, attitudes, and beliefs than one's partner is one of the reasons that individuals report ending a relationship (Baxter, 1986). Sexual incompatibility, including values, can cause relational partners to recognize they have incompatible love styles and conceptions of romantic relationships. When the relationship has been transformed into something other than a romantic one, we must provide an account about the relationship. We need to justify the self to others. A complete and sequential narrative of terminated relationships aids adjustment, as does writing about them (Kellas & Manusov, 2003; Lewandowski, 2009). What a good reason for you to write some poetry.

## References

Battaglia, D. M., Richard, F. D., Datteri, D. L., & Lord, C. G. (1998). DO: A script for the dissolution of close relationships. *Journal of Social and Personal Relationships, 15*(6), 829–845.

Baxter, L. A. (1984). Trajectories of relationship disengagement. *Journal of Social and Personal Relationships, 1,* 29–48.

Baxter, L. A. (1986). Gender differences in the heterosexual relationship rules embedded in breakup accounts. *Journal of Social and Personal Relationships, 3,* 289–306.

Burleson, B. R., & MacGeorge, E. L. (2002). Supportive communication. In M. L. Knapp & J. A. Daly (Eds.), *Handbook of interpersonal communication* (3rd ed., pp. 374–422). Thousand Oaks, CA: Sage.

Busboom, A. L., Collins, D. M., Givertz, M. D., & Levin, L. A. (2002). Can we still be friends? Resources and barriers to friendship quality after romantic dissolution. *Personal Relationships, 9,* 215–223.

Duck, S. (2011). *Rethinking relationships.* Thousand Oaks, CA: Sage.

Eklund, M., & Hansson, L. (2007). Social network among people with persistent mental illness: Associations with sociodemographic, clinical, and health-related factors. *International Journal of Social Psychiatry, 53*(4), 293–305.

Felmlee, D. H., Sprecher, S., & Bassin, E. (1990). The dissolution of intimate relationships: A hazard model. *Social Psychology Quarterly, 53*, 13–30.

Goodfriend, W., & Agnew, C. R. (2008). Sunken costs and desired plans: Examining different types of investments in close relationships. *Personality and Social Psychology Bulletin, 34*, 1639–1652.

Gottman, J. M., Levenson, R.W., Gross, J., Frederickson, B. L., McCoy, K., Rosenthal, L., & Yoshimoto, D. (2003). Correlates of gay and lesbian couples' relationships satisfaction and relationship dissolution. *Journal of Homosexuality, 41*, 23–43.

Jones, S. M. (2004). Putting the person into person-centered and immediate emotional support: Emotional change and perceived helper competence as outcomes of comforting in helping situations. *Communication Research, 33*, 338–360.

Kellas, J. K., & Manusov, V. (2003). What's in a story? The relationship between narrative completeness and adjustment to relationship dissolution. *Journal of Social and Personal Relationships, 20*(3), 451–466.

Kellas, J. K., Bean, D., Cunningham, C., & Chen, K. Y. (2008). The ex-files: Trajectories, turning points, and adjustment in the development of post-dissolutional relationships. *Journal of Social and Personal Relationships, 25,*23–50.

Knapp, M. L., & Vangelisti, A. L. (2005). *Interpersonal communication and human relationships* (5th ed.). Boston: Allyn & Bacon.

Kurdek, L. A. (1991). The dissolution of gay and lesbian couples. *Journal of Social and Personal Relationships, 8*, 265–278.

Lehmiller, J. J., & Agnew, C. R. (2007). Perceived marginalization and the prediction of romantic relationship stability. *Journal of Marriage and the Family, 69*, 1036–1049.

Lewandowski, G. W. (2009). Promoting positive emotions following relationship dissolution through writing. *The Journal of Positive Psychology, 4*, 21–31.

Metts, S. (1997). Face and facework: Implications for the study of personal relationships. *Handbook of personal relationships* (2nd ed., pp. 373–390). New York: John Wiley & Sons.

Rawlins, W. (2009). *The compass of friendship: Narratives, identities, and dialogues.* Thousand Oaks, CA: Sage.

Salhstein, E., & Dun, T. (2008). "I wanted time to myself and he wanted to be together all of the time": Constructing breakups as managing autonomy-connection. *Qualitative Research Reports in Communication, 9*, 37–45.

Sprecher, S., & Felmlee, B. (1992). The influence of parents and friends on the quality and stability of romantic relationships: A three wave longitudinal investigation. *Journal of Marriage and the Family, 54*, 888–900.

Tashiro, T., & Frazier, P. (2003). I'll never be in a relationship like that again: Personal growth following romantic relationship breakups. *Personal Relationships, 10,* 113–138.

Tsai, J., Harpaz-Rotem, I., Pietrzak, R. H., & Southwick, S. M. (2012). The role of coping, resilience, and social support in mediating the relation between PTSD and social functioning in veterans returning from Iraq and Afghanistan. *Psychiatry: Interpersonal & Biological Processes, 75*(2), 135–149.

Vaughn, D. (1986). *Uncoupling: Turning points in intimate relationships.* New York: Oxford University Press.

Yan, L. J., Hammen, C., Cohen, A. N., Daley, S. E., & Henry, R. M. (2004). Expressed emotion versus relationship quality variables in the prediction of recurrence in bipolar patients. *Journal of Affective Disorders, 83*(2/3), 199–206.

# Case 25

# Falling Spell/Spelling Fail
## Examining a History of Physical and Emotional Abuse

Dessa Anderson

*Keywords:* physical abuse, relational dialectics, verbal abuse

Relational Dialectics Theory (RDT) allows us to understand meaning making within relationships by examining how our contradictory needs, such as privacy and openness, are represented in discourses (Baxter, 2011). I use RDT to frame my personal narrative detailing a history with physical abuse through a discussion of the competing discourses of family love and support and abuse. I explore how tangled the dialectics become through words, action, and silence within a family unit and organize the essay by four dialectics that define my relationships of abuse: dominant/marginal, organization/chaos, privileged/marginalized, and daughter/spouse.

## Dominant/Marginal
### *Misplleled*[1]

I moved around a lot as a kid; by the time I was thirteen I had moved five times. The only way I can locate the memories of childhood is by houses. I can separate memories from the house on Madison by the first time we lived there and the second time we lived there. I know the difference between a memory from the first house in Vermillion and the second house in Vermillion (the key here is heat; all of my memories from the first house swelter, no matter the season). Moving is such a part of my identity that I make many decisions based on conditional

*Inside Relationships: A Creative Casebook in Relational Communication,* edited by Sandra L. Faulkner, 254–262. © 2013 Left Coast Press, Inc. All rights reserved.

time with an exit strategy. The places I have lived and the others, which will inevitably follow this, all mark time. The houses of Sioux Falls are marked differently. I entered Sioux Falls a child, and I left it as an adult.

I was in fifth grade, and we had just moved to the house on Huntington. I was struggling with spelling. There are theories about why I am bad at spelling. My parent's blame the Vermillion public schools, which used my first grade class as a guinea pig for the Whole Word Language system instead of phonetics. I can't sound out words, and I struggle with pronunciation. But I can't believe that every child who had first grade in Vermillion circa 1988 struggles with spelling. Dad is a natural speller, which is a point of pride. We sat in the office in the Huntington house and ran spelling words for hours.

### *Ineveitalbe, Veener, Prividlege*

He would get angry.

We went through the list six, seven, eleven times a night. I had other homework, but I never got to it. He tried to tell me that spelling was the easiest to pass because the answers were always the same, and I knew what words were on the list beforehand.

### *Orgainzation, Anixieity*

Dad was yelling, the kind of yelling that people save for customer service personnel or the police. But I was a ten-year-old girl who couldn't spell.

My memory fails here, because I don't know if it happened once or dozens of times. But I know how it feels, and I know how it feels now as I am writing about it.

He hit me so hard that I fell backward out of the chair.

It was only a foot, maybe two.

Any unexpected fall is unnerving. The sinking feeling of imbalance in your stomach, the helplessness, and anxiety of the fall, which ends with the crash against the floor: that is what spelling feels like. I lay there on the floor crying, out of fear instead of frustration. The worst part about that fall is not hitting the floor in tears and a collapse of limbs, not being slapped across the face. The worst part is that I still don't know how to spell.

### *Contexulizing*

Tina Pierce Braun is the matriarch of our family, a force of nature, and I am lucky to have her as my grandmother. She turned 75 in 2009, and to celebrate, my father orchestrated a family cruise. Twenty members of my family ranging in age from 17 to 75, farmers, bureaucrats, nurses, lawyers, and academics, all cruised through the Caribbean over Christmas.

What brought my family together was not the holiday spirit, the weather, or swimming, but trivia contests. Three to four times a day, trivia contests were held in bars throughout the ship. We gathered, spread out into evenly matched teams, and made up silly names like "the Legitness." My cousin Anne proved her knowledge of movie trivia (e.g., *Fight Club* was made in 1999). Greg, Quincy, and Peter rocked an extensive knowledge of sports trivia (e.g., the Atlanta Braves were formerly the Milwaukee and Boston Braves). My mother insisted upon singing every song in the TV theme trivia (e.g., "Suicide is Painless" is the theme to *M\*A\*S\*H*). This family of history nerds pummeled questions about the U.S. presidents and wars (e.g., James is the most common name for a U.S. president). I knew random things nobody should know (e.g., pigs were the primary livestock that Columbus brought to the Caribbean). We wanted to prove to each other how smart we were and to crush the other families in attendance. We won eleven trivia contests over the course of the cruise. Our reward was bragging rights and dozens of branded passport wallets and hats.

On Christmas Day, my dad slapped my mom in the food line with the twenty members of my family as witnesses. I did not see it happen. Aunt Remy asked me what happened, and I had to ask my spouse. I sat down across the table from my dad and tried to talk to him. I told him this was unacceptable behavior, and I hated having this conversation again—*London 1999, Rapid City 2001, Mom's 50th birthday*—

Dad looked at me with his dark brown eyes, without a hint of guilt, and asked a question when I told him that slapping my mom was bad behavior. "What about how I feel? What about me? I am the victim here." I was dumbfounded. The quiet man I married raised his voice, "John, you hit your wife; you don't get a vote."

We finished the vacation and put on pretty faces. I cried desperately at the Ft. Lauderdale airport, because I had no idea when I would see my family again. I briefly talked with my dad upon their return, but the word *victim* prevented me from calling him. Critical scholars take the term *victim* seriously. There is victimhood, victim feminism, victims of atrocities, victims without voices, and victims are people who need saving. My dad is not a victim. The idea that he thinks he is one disgusts me.

# Organization/Chaos

*"Something will come from all of this, and it will be me."* [2]

**September 13, 2010, 11:36 AM, a Facebook conversation with my spouse**

Me: I was up half the night last night considering what my relational paper should be...And I need you to talk me out of it.

Him: 'Kay

Me: Remember the paragraph personal narrative I wrote last spring?

Him: Vaguely

Me: I am thinking of working on a personal narrative performance off of that dealing with relational dialectics theory.

Him: I don't know what any of that means.

Me: Write about my family history of abuse and the tensions that surround accepting and hiding it. How terrible of an idea is this?

Him: It's not.

Me: Why? Other than my silence as a tacit acceptance of a history of abuse.

Him: It might be a bad idea for you personally, but that has nothing to do with the paper itself.

Me: Why personally—the emotional issue, the public issue, or the family issue?

Him: You have next to no control over your emotions for such things.

Me: Could this help?

Him: I have no idea. It could make it worse.

I did not speak to my father for five months after our family vacation. When I told my mom that I was not speaking to my father, she was furious with me because she thought it was cruel to place blame. This history goes much deeper (as the cycle of abuse does). This essay was my attempt to organize the chaos inside me. I was outraged, and my aggression was focused in unprofessional places. I shut down and avoided other people. I focused on school, which was its own place of chaos. I had lost the ability to speak, which I have been told is common for PhD students who are attempting to process the full content of what they are doing. Not speaking to Dad did not help me resolve any chaos. In fact, not talking to him hurt, because he understood what I was going through at school. With two advanced degrees, he sympathizes with the work of academic life. However, he likes to remind me that law school is harder and more competitive than any PhD program.

### Mainting

Not long after we moved into the house on Huntington I asked my dad if I could rearrange his books. The books lived in the basement office on tall shelves. So in the office where I spent my time studying for school and working through spelling tests, I moved the books how I wanted. I studied in that room for another four years, until we moved again. I still screwed up spelling tests, I still got knocked out of chairs, but the books were in order. I controlled what I could control.

## Privileged/Marginalized

I spent two years teaching in the general education program of a culinary school. I taught students who were victims of their circumstances—medical issues and learning disabilities. Others suffered from trauma—like Iraq War veterans, recovering drug addicts and alcoholics, and ex-cons. Many of them blamed their past for their present circumstance. I felt sympathetic for those who were trying to be better, trying to succeed despite their setbacks. But others made me angry when they wore their past like a banner that anyone could see, when they allowed their past to control their present and blamed it for their current mistakes. When meeting a new community of people, a person cannot pretend to be fundamentally different, but he or she can choose to interact differently. Our history is only pertinent if we make it part of the present.

### Detrimined

Why do I insist on devaluing my own experience? Although I have written my story for a class, presented it at a conference, and published it in this book, I am still hiding. I changed the names in this essay, including mine, to protect whom? Unlike my former students, I don't like to lead with what is wrong with me. If I am silent, the memories are saved in a spot in me where I rarely go. I can believe that allowing the past to control who and what we can become is limiting. I can pretend not to understand why people choose to be victims of what happened to them. I had distanced myself to the point where I could pretend the abuse hadn't happened. I told myself that part of growing up is the emotional and physical distance from tragic events.

But that's the problem: I was taught to never talk about it. This abuse is multigenerational, but my family is silent. Dad and I got into an argument on the streets of London over tube stops, and he slapped and bruised my eye. Later, Grandma Tina brought me white tulips to keep in our flat. She is a survivor of over twenty years of verbal, emotional, and physical abuse from my grandfather.[3] Instead of solving the issue or discussing it, she bought me flowers. I learned that night the best way to cover bruises around the eye is not with purple eye make-up but green.

On the cruise, she was with Greg, Dad, and me at the table during our terse argument. I thought she was going to settle this issue once and for all; my feminist role model was going to defuse 50 years of history with one sentence. She talked about the shore excursion instead and said nothing about the conflict. What was I thinking? She could not stop abuse for herself; how could she stop this force from her three children, her beloved daughter-in-law or her grandchildren? I am left with the passive-aggressive thesis of my family: *being civil is more important than being right.*

## Daughter/Spouse

When I consider the most important people in my life, the women who impact me stand together en masse. They talk with each other and laugh because they can relate to each other's experiences. These women affect and change me as a group. The men who profoundly changed me stand apart from each other, because their influence happened individually.[4]

My father and spouse are alike in small ways, which is something Greg hates to hear. They are both know-it-alls, both excellent editors and spellers, and both love me. Greg knew early on about my father's abuse. I am a terrible liar when asked direct questions.

The first time Greg met my parents, my dad threw a phone book across the room. Greg jumped. Mom and I didn't blink.

When I ask my dad to spell a word, he does it so quickly that I have to ask him to repeat it several times, which makes him angry. When I ask Greg to spell a word, he goes slowly and will repeat it as many times as I need. Greg understands that my inability to spell is not about him; it is about me. Dad and Greg are like dialectics of each other: Dark/

Fair, Loud/Quiet, and Boastful/Humble. If these two men met at a party, they would immediately dislike each other. I am the one thing that connects them together.

## *Compleicated*

**December 2008**

I told my parents a few days before Thanksgiving that I was applying to PhD programs, and that it was probable that Greg and I would be moving within the year. Dad called a few weeks later to chat about the cruise that was only in the planning stages. I told Dad that Greg and I would not be on the cruise because all of our savings were invested in moving to where ever I was accepted. Dad paused for a moment.

"Well, it is a tough year, so who knows what will happen."

I ended the call quickly and turned to my spouse, "I think dad just told me that I'm dumb." Greg and I laughed about this, but he knew that I was hurt. Dad is not un-supportive of my ventures; he just does not think hope is a good idea.

## *Asthedically*

October is my favorite time of year because I love playoff baseball. We were watching a game, and it was almost midnight when we decided to cut Greg's hair. His last haircut had been before the cruise in December. There is an intimacy about this work. We say very little as I do my best not to cut his scalp or my fingers. My scissors are too big, and the angles are all wrong. But layer after layer we remove Greg's hair. He finds his beard trimmer, and we try to get a closer cut. I slowly uncover the face of the man I love, and he looks like the eighteen-year-old that I met over twelve years ago. We met by accident, and he was kind of a jerk. But he was funny, and I liked the way he smiled. He was too shy to make the first move, so I had to do it. Twelve years, and this man loves me enough to have me cut his hair at midnight on a Wednesday when we both have to work in the morning. We hold each other together.

## *Emergenceies*

My oldest memories are of intimate hugs of the four members of my immediate family. My parents would pick Fiona and me up off the floor, and the four of us would hug as hard as we could. I think of the love I felt, three feet off the ground hugging my whole family. My father is not a villain, and he is not a bad father. I cannot stop being the daughter of

John Braun, so I have no answers about what all of this means. What I do know is that I am over thirty years old, in the waning hours of my doctoral work, and I still can't spell. I have learned to cover well. When I teach, I prepare thoroughly and make special notes of words I know I have to write on the board. I spend hours editing and sitting in our campus writing center. I have a dictionary downloaded on to my phone for spelling emergencies (which happen often). I carefully spell check emails to avoid public embarrassment. Even with all these safeguards in place, between Greg and me it is different. My spelling issues are a joke that we alone can tell. Every week, I find new and unique ways to spell "lettuce" on our grocery list.

## Questions and Activities for Discussion

1. Ellis (1995) writes that "in evocative storytelling, the story's validity can be judged by whether it evokes in you, the reader, a feeling that the experience described is authentic, that it is believable and possible; the story's generalizability can be judged by whether it speaks to you the reader, about your experiences" (p. 318). How does this narrative speak to you as a reader? Is it an evocative story? Why? How can a personal narrative speak to and perhaps break a cycle of abuse?

2. In many ways, family violence is normalized, which makes it difficult to discuss. Anderson wrote, "I had distanced myself to the point where I could pretend the abuse hadn't happened. I told myself that part of growing up is the emotional and physical distance from tragic events." How are competing discourses represented in this narrative? Do you find the narrative effective at highlighting the normalization of abuse in order to disrupt it? Why?

3. React to Anderson's statement: "When meeting a new community of people a person cannot pretend to be fundamentally different, but he or she can choose to interact differently. Our history is only pertinent if we make it part of the present." Is this a privileged position? Is this idea born out in her essay or part of a dialectic she writes about? How?

# Notes

1   These headings are from a list of words I spelled incorrectly within the preparation of this essay. They serve as transitions within the narrative and between academic ideas.

2   This quotation comes from a print (a perspective shot of a barn) that a friend bought me several years ago. The quotation rings true of my life. I also included this phrase in the dedication to my grandparents on the dedication page of my Master's thesis.

3   The specter of this man, who died from his vices over a decade ago, in the late nineties, haunts my family as the possible source of this abuse. But that is the easy way out.

4   It might be anti-feminist to spotlight the men, especially my father and my spouse, but that is all part of the dialectic. I cannot deny the influence of the men in my life who have formed me.

# For Further Reading and Reference

Baxter, L. A. (2011). *Voicing relationships: A dialogic perspective.* Los Angeles: Sage.

Ellis, C. (1995). *Final negotiations.* Philadelphia: Temple University Press.

Gardner, S. (2009). Teaching about domestic violence: strategies for empowerment. In R. Crabtree, D. Sapp, & A. Licona (Eds.), *Feminist pedagogy: Looking back to move forward* (pp. 150–158). Baltimore, MD: Johns Hopkins University Press.

Poulos, C. N. (2009). *Accidental ethnography.* Walnut Creek, CA: Left Coast Press, Inc.

Wood, J. (2001). The normalization of violence in heterosexual romantic relationships: Women's narratives of love and violence. *Journal of Social and Personal Relationships, 18*(2), 239–261.

# Case 26

# FROGGING IT
## A Poetic Analysis of Relationship Dissolution

### Sandra L. Faulkner

*Keywords:* poetic inquiry, relational dialectics, relationship dissolution

Themes in work and life intertwine, often without conscious process-ing. I recognized that a cadre of poems I had written and revised over the course of many years were of a relational theme—relationship dis-solution, breaking up, calling it quits—only after sorting through them for a poetry editing workshop. These poems showed the breakdown of relationships through the erosion of intimacy in my life and in the lives of my close friends, interview participants, and students. I had used life experiences to craft what some would label autoethnographic poetry because of the focus on the researcher's voice and the systematic study of cultural understanding of the self directly and indirectly connected to others (Faulkner, 2009). The fact that these poems were about close relationships and their inherent challenges was not surprising to me given that I teach courses on and research about relationship process-es. This is my lexicon. The poems I present here concern romantic and friendship dissolution and the aspects of identity creation and loss this entails. I wanted to juxtapose the need for stories about our relational endings with the theoretical literature, so I conducted a poetic analysis of the poems/ providing another lens with which to view relationship dissolution. *Poetic analysis,* a technique of using poems as data for qual-itative analysis, helps me make explicit connections between poetry and

*Inside Relationships: A Creative Casebook in Relational Communication,* edited by Sandra L. Faulkner, 263–275. © 2013 Left Coast Press, Inc. All rights reserved.

interpersonal relationship dissolution through the creation of a poetry performance of relationship break down. This analysis and subsequent representation serve as an exemplar of how poetry offers interpersonal communication practitioners an explicit demonstration of individuals' needs to poeticize their everyday relational challenges (Pelias, 2011). As Baxter (1982) notes, "The breaking up of a relationship is a phenomenon known to most and dreaded by all. It accounts for some of our most intense and painful social experiences" (p. 223). We need to tell the stories of our relationship breakdowns, and sometimes these stories take the form of poems (Duck, 2011; Kellas & Manusov, 2003).

## The Relationship Break Down Process

As indicated in the introduction to this chapter, Steve Duck (2011) offered a pedagogical theoretical model of relationship breakdown that I prefer over other explanations, such as Knapp and Vangelisti's (2005) model of relational dissolution, because of the focus on communication in and as relational processes. This model consists of five phases (that is, intrapsychic, dyadic, social, grave dressing, resurrection) presented in the performance poem below. The phases focus on the relationship between cognition and communication during the dissolution process and include the dyad's social networks and their communication. This focus on communication between the dyad and social network is a major strength of the model given the importance of the break-up story (Kellas & Manusov, 2003) and the idea that communication is relational; action is the basis of our relationships (Duck, 2011).

Breaking up is not just the ending of a relationship, and the use of the term "ending" or "dissolution" may be a misnomer; relationships alter forms as partners disengage from the idea of being a couple (Baxter, 1982; Duck, 2011). Ex-partners still exist as a presence in future relationships because of material things, such as children and mortgages, and immaterial ideas of stories and preferences and assumptions about relationships. The knitting term "frogging" references a process of unraveling or ripping back knitting to fix a mistake or recycle a project; a frog says "rip it, rip it." This seems an apt metaphor for the breakdown of personal relationships and one that I employ to contextualize the dissolution process.

# FROG IT

Frogging: to "rip it, rip it"; the unraveling of knitting mistakes.

### *In this breaking up dream*

your right foot sticks in a flaming
suitcase, orange and red sparks
burn the base of our bed, rented
in some Victorian on University Hill.
I fall off a decrepit chair
mid-lecture, clutch your spitting
pet parrot who has always hated me,
notice charred clothes and consonants
transform into constant aches when magic
markers refuse to write on your skin
or dry erase boards made of hamster pelts.
You can't help me get unstuck,
even the coffee steamed in my cup
as I start the week can't take
the black soot smell away
make me grateful for your love notes
tucked away in my computer annex.

### Break-Down Process

"When your relationships turn bad,
they disturb your epistemic and personal order."[1]

ravel—1580s, 'to untangle, unwind,' also 'to become tangled or confused,' from Du[tch]. *ravelen* 'to tangle, fray, unweave,' from *rafel* 'frayed thread.'

Ravel the relationship
between thought and talk
talk/thought/talk—
all that space filled with stories
knit together from your memories
of thought/talk/thought about fault
unravel your honesty into a new skein

rival the paparazzi of relational failure
start here
unhappy:
      I can't stand it

## I. Intrapsychic Phase

**Subject: Resend**

*The art of poetry is the abolition of doubt....We must somehow learn to be careless.* (Revell, 2007, p. 14)

What do you want? I don't do that. Do you see? You love me? How did we get on this train? How dare you make me feel. Am I being too clinical? Hot? Need I tell you about marriage and what doesn't work? He couldn't get into your pants with a pry bar. I get scared of waking up, realizing I hate this person in my house. What went wrong? I don't dwell on it. The problem is my own problem. How come she can't love me anymore? You can't take it back. It is too late. Why did you say that? Did god tell you to say that? J, K, V and I are part of you. You will go to his wedding. He will come to yours.

How can you be free to love if you are oppressed? He was always trying to change me into something. More palatable. But isn't connection where it is at? Can you ever relax? You need to hear how smart you are. Often. How do you take from someone else and not be a dope? How pretty you are. How can you integrate a life with someone and still be yourself? My old girlfriend used to take her diaphragm home on the weekend. Can you do this and still be strong? Am I being wrong when I say you can only rely on yourself? Who said you are inauthentic? Sometimes I am able to compensate. But this morning it stung. Should I fight for her? Does that sound like a hallmark card? It is my duty (per your instructions and phd) to tell you what I need. Am I bad? How do you take from someone else and not be a dope? What attracted me to you was getting nailed for saying something stupid in poetry class. A peanut butter cookie in my mouth.

Already I am sitting here shaking. Hold on, it's you. Take a deep breath. Put your face right in it. What I wanted to say but couldn't. If you want me to go away you better stop. I wonder if you understand what I am saying? If you understand what you make me feel like? This is what is Real to me. I am spinning in a circle with my head bent over backwards. Why is she burning for me? The fan fails. Forget fears. I want to sink into you like the wake of a boat:

| | | | |
|---|---|---|---|
| tough | ashes | | shaking |
| juices | | sweat | drown |
| | | tough | |
| protect | sentiment | | |

I'd be justified in withdrawing

## II. Dyadic Phase

### *Subject: date/ Should I bring a 6 pack of bud?*

From: pdruby
To: SF
8/16/01
09:07 AM

i have a cooler. don't dare
ask for tofu, my heart or hummus
at the snack stand.

watch me. feel that I want you.
want you like you are. what
does this have to do with sandra?

From: SFaulkner
To: pdruby
Subject: Re: bud?

The vile watered down
horse piss enigma
most people like, my
your tongue becomes numb
when you drink. I am bad.
I shamed my roommate out
of drinking BUD light,
so Don't call me girl.

From: pdruby
To: SF
Re: ooo

you are a dream girl, the phd lady?
the one that tells lesbian jokes—
firegirl—whiskey straight from the bottle.
yes i remember. tsk tsk tsk

bud isn't a beer like ferrari isn't a car,
it is a personal thing
with all the grease monkeys and votech fans.
it takes me to automotive places of comfort.

i like spam and pouilly-fuisse
buying into annhauser busch
chivas and key memories:
bring a 6 pack

To: pdruby
From: Dr. Faulkner
11:36 AM

I know symbols,
dislike bud as a reminder
that my latte will implode.

I work with clean hands,
hands that move
when my mind commands,
no automotive places of comfort.

My assignments: interview people about love,
not roses like impressionistic paintings
what reminds me to throw up.

## Millicent's Opera Glasses

*We can't lie and say we have somewhere to go tomorrow, so we'll be
here all night....We're not leaving here until I finish this bottle of wine.*

> —Eddie Vedder, Pearl Jam Concert, State College,
> Pennsylvania, May 3, 2003

CASE 26: FROGGING IT

I. Act One
I focus in on my altar, collect stares
from the college males as I use
the mother of pearl and brass
scroll-work opera glasses.
You complain about the seats
too far away from the stage
while they pretend not to watch me
watch them spit liquor off
our choir seats, wipe the wetness off
chins with torn cuffs like small kids.
Great grandmother Millie must
have used these glasses cum binoculars
between her own classical piano tours.
I dream she snuck in sherry or vermouth,
calculated modified stage dives off
upper box seats into a writhing unctuous crowd.

II. Act Two
I smile at the not so secret smoke
handed around. Security stops and scolds
the ones who just now found the art
of being bad. We exchange high fives
that just miss, hit me in the gut.
Millie's glasses passed hand to hand
like a flask, I wonder if she craved
the crowds and claps she surrendered
for the Scottish salesman and the wife-
tour through blue collar Philly,
gas refineries and electric pole climbing.
You play the petulant partner now
as I surrender our apartment
for my new job somewhere else,
without you.

III. Act Three
I lost my best friend last tour, wet
on a split garbage bag, cheap grass seats
suspended in some half-way zone,
Trenton or Philly? We sipped free beer

tabled for a good tip. "Your white friends
treat me like a fresh-air fund kid."
Ed flaunts green jeans, worked-out biceps,
all we feel is sex, and hear is sex,
when he rolls up his sleeves.
Sing with me he purrs; *teachers leave those kids alone,*
*but kids, don't leave those politicians alone.*
I'm the teacher who needs to lick the sweat
that pools like the Susquehanna in the hollow
of his throat; I grip the binoculars, drown
like a randy pirate who worships lust.

I mean it

### III. The Social Phase

*Relational Therapy*

My friend makes me imagine dating myself
so I know what my exes know:

I could fuck and not make
a relational statement. My network

of one would never require a plan,
no dates to mark on the calendar,

no need for talk
about talk or apologies.

The day we ended it I lit up
the secret pack of smokes

to feel young and angry. If I were my own
lover, I could remain silent about feelings

because I would know what I intended to say
would be. If I were my own lover, I could

ignore the sighs and gripes about young girls
whose tastes shift like smoke rings in the wind.

At the end, she took her bed from the basement
but not me, orange rust framed my hands,

but if I were my own lover, I would
breathe words in without tasting blood

I would make all the rules. I would
make all of the rules.

It's now inevitable

## IV. Grave-Dressing Phase

### *How to Write a Break-Up (#2)*

Pretend you don't notice
the ink of her new tattoo or
the thud of his terry cloth shorts

as he drops them in front of you
on the floor of the new studio
you visit because you're friends now,

and friends undress in front of friends.

Take note of the names hurled
at you because you quit it, the jilter-
fake-lesbian-couscous-eater

little girl, ruined by feminism, fallen.
Spill your red wine on their white carpet
while making large gestures.

Always be the one to break it off:
leave him for her and then her for him,
be a non-discriminate leaver.

Sing the break-up story
with the malice of righteousness,
no more limping and wilted words—

you ended the tired thing
with your own words
because they wouldn't.

Forget the scars from sledding
accidents, the curve of ass
the taste of sweat like half-sour pickles

parts you traced with intimate fingers.

Rip up the fed-exed note
delivered to work in front of friends
declaring you better than a Pearl Jam song.

### How to Write a Break-Up (#3)

She writes what she remembers.

You're like a tiny tumor, spontaneous growth
that inveigles her academic persona

makes her skip the prescreening of poor personality,
the cataloged essay of relational observations.

Instead she rides wedged into your crevice
without a helmet, eats fries sans ketchup,

you both smashed together
on the same side of the booth.

She writes of you, forgets the others—
a series of bad choices listed on paper.

She pretends the play worked, love
hung, rose uncontained by labels.

She misses still what she can't write;

how the fun became like the longest
and most boring February.

Time to get a new life

## V. Resurrection Processes

### How to Date Catholic Boys

Talk about premarital sex
like a summer baseball game
to attract the devout.
Paste lipstick kisses on
his stomach instead of Hail Marys.
Use confession to exorcise your
body out of his holy virgin thoughts.
Genuflect over cheap beer in bars
where men wear ties to play pool
and seduce women with alcohol and arguments,
rituals polished like communion cups.
Use left-over cell minutes to break it
off because you want to be the whore.
Memorize these rituals with practice.
Repeat. Order another beer
and touch his knee. Repeat.

### RearViewMirror

—After RVM by Pearl Jam and with a line from Kim Addonizio

Once you airmailed me a jar of jam from the yard
where we had lived together when I believed

in the lilies blooming in the black vase,
once I saw those Pennsylvania blackberries, jarred

in a Madrid café when I was months married
to the man you anticipated I would screw

and who would not suffer for desperate love like us,
I imagined we had lasted, our faces flushed,

sweat like fear, sticking us to the seats in your blue van.
I saw things, saw things clearer when eating

dry toast, starved after sex in some other rented room.
How could you know I saw you in the rear view mirror?

## Questions and Activities for Discussion

1. Faulkner wrote, "Ex-partners still exist as a presence in future relationships because of material things such as children and mortgages
and immaterial ideas of stories and preferences and assumptions about
relationships." How do you see past partners reflected in the poetry
presented? How does poetic inquiry help our understanding of relational breakdowns? Have you ever written a poem about breaking up?
Why or why not? What did the poem help you do, think, or feel?

2. What metaphors do you think describe the breaking down of relationships? How do the metaphors you use influence your understanding of
relationship dissolution?

3. What songs do you have in your playlist/i-pod that are about breaking
up? Choose three songs and compare and contrast the lyrics. What
do they tell you about breaking up? What are the predominant metaphors? What lessons are the songs trying to teach?

4. The poem describes five phases in Duck's Break Down Model. What
themes do you see in the poems presented in each phase?

## Note

1  Duck, S. (2011, p. 187). *Rethinking relationships.* Thousand Oaks, CA: Sage

## For Further Reading and Reference

Baxter, L. A. (1982). *Strategies for ending relationships: Two studies. Western Journal of Speech Communication, 46*, 223–241.

Duck, S. (2011). *Rethinking relationships.* Thousand Oaks, CA: Sage.

Faulkner, S. L. (2009). *Poetry as method: Reporting research through verse.* Walnut
Creek, CA: Left Coast Press, Inc.

Goodfriend, W., & Agnew, C. R. (2008). Sunken costs and desired plans: Examining different types of investments in close relationships. *Personality and
Social Psychology Bulletin, 34*, 1639–1652.

Gottman, J. M., Levenson, R.W., Gross, J., Frederickson, B. L., McCoy, K., Rosenthal, L., &Yoshimoto, D. (2003). Correlates of gay and lesbian couples' relationships satisfaction and relationship dissolution. *Journal of Homosexuality,
41*, 23–43.

Kellas, J. K., & Manusov, V. (2003). What's in a story? The relationship between narrative completeness and adjustment to relationship dissolution. *Journal of Social and Personal Relationships, 20*(3), 451–466.

Knapp, M. A., & Vangelisti, A. L. (2005). *Interpersonal communication and human relationships* (5th ed.). Boston: Allyn & Bacon.

Kurdek, L. A. (1991). The dissolution of gay and lesbian couples. *Journal of Social and Personal Relationships, 8,* 265–278.

Parini, J. (2008). *Why poetry matters.* New Haven, CT: Yale University Press.

Pelias, R. J. (2011). *Leaning: A poetics of personal relations.* Walnut Creek, CA: Left Coast Press, Inc.

Revell, D. (2007). *The art of attention: A poet's eye.* Minneapolis, MN: Graywolf Press.

# Case 27

# Institutionalized

## Wonda Baugh

*Keywords:* family, mental illness, social support, stigma

## My Story

My interest in mental illness and social support is deeply personal on several levels. As a teenager, I was institutionalized on more than one occasion for what was thought at the time to be my inability to get along socially in both school and in my family. My parents thought I had a behavior problem because I refused to attend school, and I was cutting myself. Being in the hospital was stigmatizing and not particularly helpful. With the support of friends and family, I somehow muddled through until I left home at seventeen. I suffered without any treatment or medication and struggled another few years before having a full psychotic break followed by a three-month long institutionalization. In that three-month period, several different medications and diagnoses were tested before the doctors decided that I had Bipolar I Disorder. I continued to go in and out of mental hospitals for the next few years.

During the last major psychotic episode, I lost everything that was important to me: my home, my career, many relationships, and certainly my dignity. I was homeless on the streets of San Francisco for over a month, seeing and hearing things that were not there, lost and unable to understand how to help myself. I lost thirty pounds in about thirty days and terrified my loved ones who could not find me and

*Inside Relationships: A Creative Casebook in Relational Communication,* edited by Sandra L. Faulkner, 272–282. © 2013 Left Coast Press, Inc. All rights reserved.

had no idea if I was even alive. Once I was capable of getting help and seeing things slightly more clearly, it became apparent that there were only two important things in my life—my health and my relationships. I understood then that I could lose my relationships if I decided not to commit to my own mental health, and that is how I found the strength to recover. I made an internal vow that I would continue treatment and that I would work as hard as I could with all my intention to stay sane, because I was loved and because I love. My life continued to be difficult until I found the right combination of medication, and counseling, but it was through my relationships that I found true peace and freedom from my circumstances.

Beyond not being homeless anymore, this right combination of factors has allowed me to gain more than I ever had and to become successful despite the odds. I have been able to reintegrate into life. I have sanity, I have an education, and I have healthy relationships. I am no longer tortured by mental illness. I accept that I have a chronic, lifelong illness that requires treatment to which I willingly comply. So far I have been blessed by thirteen psychoses free years, and for the last seven years, I have been a full-time college student.

## The Poems

I wrote the first three fictionalized poems (*Institutionalized, Stuck,* and *Four Point Restraints*) remembering what it was like to be a teenage girl institutionalized for depression against her will. They are written in a teenage voice with a young adult audience in mind. Writing these served two purposes: writing helps me with the healing process, and sharing the poetry allows me to help people understand the feelings of both being mentally ill and having your freedom taken away.

### Institutionalized

Isolated in a parade of
bee sting blood draws,
invisible yet surveyed
by thugs dressed in white
with name badges and dead eyes,
word salad shoots
out of my mouth
like an auctioneer of mismatched
words Fasterandfaster

my voice malfunctions
like a machine gun
slaughtering innocents.

*Stuck* is about what it is like to sit in a mental ward where the orderlies ignore you, and your symptoms are out of your control. The people who work at the hospital watch from a desk behind glass, while the patients are corralled in a large room to interact with one another, shielded from mainstream society. Sitting inside a building being watched is supposed to have health benefits, but the patient feels like the only thing that is happening is that she is being banished to a room. This poem is about the dehumanization that she experiences as part of the intake process. She is forced to give up her clothing. She was in handcuffs when she arrived. The place smells badly. She is injected with medication that robs her of her ability to move and speak. She is "here" indefinitely.

**Stuck**

Here, cold
    goosepimples and nipples
    erect, clothes stolen.
Here, kidnapped
    stashed in shackles
    removed from my kin.
Here, bared
    forced to disrobe with
    privates exposed.
Here, blocked
    nostrils congested with
    urine covered in bleach
Here, violated
    with needle
    stung into submission
Here.

*Four Point Restraints* is the last in the series. This is about being tied down to a table against your will. The girl feels like a criminal whose only crime is holding secrets. She is humiliated and violated, and this experience does not match her understanding of humane and just treatment.

## Four Point Restraints

Unrelenting and stiff.
I am fettered
by locks from tiny diaries
holding down pubescent secrets.
Spread eagle, tethered
unrelenting and stiff,
wrists out—humiliated
like with the period
stain on my six grade skirt.
This restraint is a corset
truncating my freedom,
it's a pit bull's jaw
Unrelenting and stiff.

Mentally ill people are often feared, misunderstood and marginalized. They are represented in the media as dangerous, and incompetent. The stigma surrounding mental illness is great. It often remains a family secret. This secrecy allows for misrepresentation of the mentally ill as well as the creation of undue pressure on family systems. The last two poems concern stigma and how a person deals with this in personal relationships. There is a lack of resources for the loved ones of people with mental illnesses, and stigma gets in the way of people reaching out to help one another in these tough times. Because mental illness manifests itself as a problem that is easily conflated with behavioral problems, families' parenting skills are scrutinized in a way they are not when a child has a physical illness. This helps create the very isolation in which mental illness becomes its most dangerous; isolation is the enemy of mental health healing. It is inside social networks and with social support that people can begin to heal. With my work, I show how social support has helped me and that families and friends have an important role in healing.

*Phone Call with Mother* is about a daughter trying to heal herself. She craves her mother's approval and love, but the mother wants the child to understand that she will always have the upper hand, be more powerful. The adult child stands up, trying to forge her own way in the world, while the mother wants the child to follow the path she provides. This is a poem about human development and growth—the painful steps a woman must take to be mentally healthy—steps away

from her family of origin. This poem is about how sometimes it hurts
to pull away from your parents.

### Phone Call with Mother

Verbal uppercut
quick and efficient
leaves me gasping.

Roundhouse of judgment
knocks me down
sweating my spirit.

Prying palm to my insecurity
forces me to lose my
balance and self-confidence.

Today on spaghetti legs
I got back up, in close and
blocked your passive aggression.

Back up, shaky,
bruised, yellow, black and blue.
Overconfident and proud.

Until your outmaneuvering—
"I love you"—
kicks me behind the knee,

leaves me wondering
how I got on the floor.
Again.

Summer Lov'n is a poem about sex. It is written from the perspective
of a person whose partner has been hurt in the past, both physically and
emotionally. She is brave enough to share her scars. And because of that
courage, the lovemaking has the potential for healing and for joy that
she did not know existed. This is about the sex after being abused in the
hospital. This is about the fact that joy is possible after depression.

**Summer Lov'n**

Raised textured speed bump
extends past the small of your back.
Gash sewn with
no concern for vanity
lifts up for a healing tongue bath.
Tiny hairs tickle my lips,
your flesh taut beneath my teeth.
Juices flood my breasts
so happy to finally be free
of the too tight summer skin.

## Questions and Activities for Discussion

1. What does the use of poetry for representing stigma and mental illness allow Baugh to accomplish that other forms of writing may not?

2. Create a found investigative poem: 1) Make a list (transcript) of all of the stereotypes and negative portrayals of individuals and families with mental illness. Think of movies and other forms of popular culture. 2) Read your "transcript" and highlight words and passages that represent the experience. 3) Arrange your highlighted passages in a poem that illustrates a theme, idea, or situation. Consider how line-breaks and enjambment can help the tension and sense of poetic language. 4) Connect the poem to a larger political context to show the personal and the historical intersection. This connection may be shown through the poem title or epigraph.

3. Baugh wrote, "I understood then that I could lose my relationships if I decided not to commit to my own mental health, and that is how I found the strength to recover." What role should family play in the recovery from mental illness? What does social support mean in this context?

## For Further Reading and Reference

Baker, C. (2012). *This fragile life: A mother's story of a bipolar son.* Chicago: Lawrence Hill Books.

Gowland, S. (2011). Enabling people to give feedback about their health care. *Learning Disability Practice, 14*(8), 32–36.

Eklund, M., & Hansson, L. (2007). Social network among people with persistent mental illness: Associations with sociodemographic, clinical, and health-related factors. *International Journal of Social Psychiatry, 53*(4), 293–305.

Hartnett, S. J. (2003). *Incarceration nation: Investigative prison poems of hope and terror.* Walnut Creek, CA: AltaMira Press.

Jamison, K. R. (1995). *An unquiet mind.* New York: A.A. Knopf.

Yan, L. J., Hammen, C., Cohen, A. N., Daley, S. E., & Henry, R. M. (2004). Expressed emotion versus relationship quality variables in the prediction of recurrence in bipolar patients. *Journal of Affective Disorders, 83*(2/3), 199–206.

# Index

**A**

Abuse, 27, 133–134, 137–149, 184,
203–204, 247, 280
  Abuser, 139–140, 144,
  146–147, 205
  Child, 203, 205
  Domestic, 137–149
  Emotional, 133, 137, 254
  Mental, 144
  Physical, 138, 145, 247,
  254–261
  Relationships, 146
  Verbal, 137–149, 247, 254–261
Academic Research, 55, 161
Acceptance, 19, 92–94, 106, 128,
156, 201, 257
Adoption, 134, 198, 201–, 205
Affection, 26, 32, 106, 117, 135,
234
Affection Exchange Theory, 135
African American, 57
Aggression, 27, 257, 280
Aging, 29–34
Allen, Mike, 75
Alternative Ways of Knowing, 16
Ambivalence, 20–21, 161–174
Anticipatory Grief, 52

Anxiety, 83, 119, 134, 142, 161,
168, 170, 255
Appearance, 117, 128, 213–219
Army, 220
Art Therapy, 80–84
Arts Based Research (ABR),
15–16, 107
Asexual, 66
Asian American, 207, 225–230
Attachment Parenting, 200
Attraction, 107–115, 117, 182,
239–240
Aunt, 196, 201, 233, 256

**B**

Baby, 20, 32, 34, 80–82, 154, 159,
161–174, 166, 189, 190, 192, 196,
198–199
Baxter, Leslie A., 18, 174, 264
Best Friend, 26, 55, 71, 87, 90, 103,
114, 116, 158, 189, 214, 234, 243
Birthday, 29, 51, 116, 154, 189,
202, 223, 256
Bisexual, 76, 209–210, 181–182
Body Art/Tattoo, 197, 207, 210,
213–219, 271
Body Image, 25, 29–34

Boyfriend, 44, 66, 70–71, 107, 116–117, 119– 120, 210, 227–229

Blog/Blogging, 29–30, 55, 65, 75, 80, 163, 177–178, 181–186, 189

Braithwaite, Dawn O., 18

Breaking Up, 18, 56, 104, 109–110, 247, 249–250, 263–265

Breastfeeding, 168, 174, 200

Buddhism, 88, 90

Bullying, 226
  Cyber Bullying, 230

**C**

Celibacy, 67

Cheating, 105, 109, 111, 177, 181–186, 205

Childhood Memories, 142, 145, 148, 226–227, 254–255

Child/Childhood/Children, 12, 26–27, 32–33, 49, 52, 55, 57–58, 63, 69, 72, 84, 93, 118, 120, 126, 134–135, 137, 139–142, 145–146, 148, 154, 161–174, 177–178, 189–190, 192, 195–205, 221, 225–226, 254–255, 259, 264, 279

Chinese American, 228

Christian, 70, 137–149

Christian Culture, 137–138, 145–146, 148

Christmas, 181, 190–191, 256

Close Relationships, 15, 20, 25, 48, 54–55, 75, 77, 97, 104, 207–208, 229, 263

Cohn, D'Vera, 201

College, 32, 41, 44, 71, 107–117, 119, 123, 138, 144, 165, 178, 181, 183, 185, 196–197, 214, 227, 268–269, 277

Coming Out, 86–95

Commitment, 65, 104, 119, 135, 181–186, 233–235

Communication Privacy Management, 77–78, 123–132, 134

Communication Theory of Identity (CTI), 209–210
  Communal Layer, 210
  Enacted Layer, 209–210
  Personal Layer, 209–210
  Relationship Layer, 209–210

Computer Mediated Communication (CMC), 177–178, 181–186

Coping, 123–131

Creative Nonfiction, 19–21

Critical (paradigm), 18–19, 256

Culture, 21, 27, 49, 53, 57, 63, 65, 76, 78, 93, 104, 137–138, 145–146, 148, 167, 178, 207–211, 220–223, 227, 230

Cultural Narratives, 57

Cutting, 213–219, 276

Cybersex, 181–186

**D**

Dad/Father, 55, 62–63, 86, 116, 137–149, 157, 159, 174, 190–191, 193, 203, 217, 248, 255–260

Dating Relationships, 26, 111, 184

Daughter, 200

Death and Dying, 18, 25, 31, 33, 48–54, 213–214, 217, 237–238

Decision-Making, 133
  Definitions of Culture and Gender, 220–223

Demand-Withdrawal Cycle, 242–244

Denzin, Norman K., 17

Denial, 52

Dia de Los Muertos, 216
Dialectics, 133
Difficult Conversations, 48–54,
247
    Experiences, 15
    Topics, 133
Dinda, Kathryn, 75
Disclosure, 75–77, 104, 126, 134,
190, 209
    Outcomes, 97–99
    Rules, 134
Disordered Eating, 135, 151–159
Discrimination, 93, 203, 225–230
Dissolution, 26, 116–121, 247–
250, 263–264
Diversity, 230
Divorce, 27, 31, 242–244, 250
Duck, Steven W., 177

E
Embodied Knowledge, 15, 20, 174
Emotions, 51, 53, 71, 242–244,
257
Empowerment, 17, 148
Endings, 117, 120, 250, 263
Ethical Practices, 105
Ethnicity, 155, 208, 210, 226–227
Ethnography, 17, 21
    Accidental Ethnography,
    133–134, 137, 151, 254
    Autoethnography, 86, 137,
    151, 161, 188, 225, 254, 263
Expectations, 26, 32, 56–57,
66–67, 75–76, 107–115, 118,
162, 117, 178, 193, 220, 223, 233

F
Face-Work, 107–115
Fact/Fiction Dialectic, 19

Family, 26, 30, 40, 49–51, 55,
57–58, 62–63, 69, 72, 78, 86,
93, 103, 110, 112–114, 116, 129,
130–131, 133–135, 137–149,
151–159, 167, 186, 190, 192, 197,
208, 226, 229, 234, 247, 250,
254–260, 276–281
    Roles, 61–63
    Secrets, 134
Family Communication, 58,
61–63, 69–72, 133, 151–159,
Family Conversation, 58
Family Relationships, 55,
Family Systems, 137–149
Fantasies, 57
Faulkner, Sandra, 104, 209–210
Fertility, 80–84, 169–170, 177,
189–192, 197, 201
Fiction, 15–21, 36
Fiction is Qualitative, 21
Fictional Narrative, 19
Field Experience, 17
Final Conversations, 25, 48–54
Fitzpatrick, Mary Anne, 58
Forgiveness, 75, 80–84
Form, 17
Foster, Elissa, 165, 168, 170
Fraternity, 108, 111–113
Friendship, 16, 26, 66–67, 78,
103–106, 107–115, 117–121,
123–124, 130–131, 165, 179,
185, 214, 234–235, 247, 251, 263
Friendship Development, 123–132

G
Gendered Assumptions, 220–223
Gender Equality, 147
Girlfriend, 61–63, 66, 108,
111–112, 119–120, 153, 184,
222, 266

Goals, 178
Goodall, H. L., 21
Google, 215
Grad School, 51, 174, 182, 191, 196, 221–222
Grandchild, 189
Grandparents, 25, 48, 50–53, 90, 190, 217, 225–226, 259, 269
Grief, 52, 80, 82, 121, 142, 196, 201, 214, 237–238
Grieving, 201
Gutkind, Lee, 20

**H**
Hall, Edward, 220
Harassed, 183
Healing, 119
Hecht, Michael L., 209–210
Heteronormativity, 93, 203, 250
Heterosexual, 66, 203
High School, 70, 114, 116, 165, 189, 196, 227
History, 26
Holidays, 56, 116
Homophobia, 91, 93
Human Trafficking, 204
Husband, 52, 63, 66, 80, 83, 124, 140, 144, 146–148, 221

**I**
Identity, 15, 18, 29–34, 75–78, 105, 119, 134–135, 208–211, 213–219, 226–227, 230, 254, 263
Identity Management, 76, 210
Illness, 48, 103, 117, 123–131, 237, 277, 279
Individual and Cultural Expectations, 26
Infidelity, 181–186
Infertility, 75, 177, 188–193,

195–205
Injury, 120
In-Law(s), 97–99, 163, 190
Instant Message (IM), 181–183, 186
Interpersonal Expectancies, 178
Interpersonal Power, 27
Interpersonal Relationships, 27, 248
Interpretive (paradigm), 18–19
Intimacy, 25–26, 36–46, 67, 76, 103, 260, 263
Intimacy Readiness, 36–46
Invisible Gender Socialization, 15

**J**
Japanese American, 207, 226–227, 230
Jewish Americans, 76, 208, 210–211

**K**
Kirkman, Maggie, 196, 199
Koerner, Ascan F., 58
Kubler-Ross, Elizabeth, 51
Krizek, Robert L., 21

**L**
Language, 17
Latinas/Latinos, 57, 76
LGBTQ, 76, 134, 203, 209, 251, 268, 271
    Relationships, 65–68
Lifespan Communication, 20, 25, 48–54
Livingston, Gretchen, 201
Logic, 118
Loss, 18–19, 31, 44, 51–52, 75, 80–81, 121, 124, 196, 213–219, 263

Love, 29, 32, 37–38, 42, 51–53,
55–56, 63, 65–67, 71–72, 91–92,
98–99, 109–112, 123–124, 128,
131, 135, 140–142, 155–159,
162, 193, 211, 213–214, 229,
233–235, 239–240, 248, 251,
254, 259–260, 265–266, 268,
272–273, 276–277, 279–280

**M**
Male Domination, 57
Male Gaze, 222
Manipulation, 142
Marginalization, 93
Marginalized Discourse, 20, 174
Marriage, 25–27, 36, 57, 70, 112,
121, 134–135, 137–149, 162,
166, 177, 181–185, 192, 204, 221,
223, 234, 256, 266, 273
Marriage Proposal, 25, 36–46
Material Circumstances, 26
McAdams, Dan P., 18
McCall, Leslie, 210
Medicalization, 20, 161–174, 188,
191
Meditation, 116–121
Memories, 53, 117, 133, 142, 145,
148, 153, 155, 159, 254, 258,
260, 265, 268
Mental Illness, 18, 276–281
Metaphors, 55
Method of Inquiry, 16
Middle-Class, 20, 167, 170, 174
Mindfulness, 75, 86–95
Miscarriage, 80, 168
Mixed-Raced, 66
Mom/Mother, 20, 30, 37, 40,
44, 48, 52–53, 55, 57–58, 63,
69–72, 78, 80–82, 84, 90, 105,

109, 116, 133, 135, 138–145,
154–155–159, 163–164, 166,
168–170, 173, 178, 181, 189–190,
195, 199–200, 203–204, 208,
222, 234, 248, 255–257, 259,
269, 279–280
Motherhood, 20, 195–205
Mother's Day, 53
Multi-Voiced, 19

**N**
Narrative(s), 15, 17–21, 31, 57, 78,
87, 130, 133, 137–138, 142–146,
148–149, 188, 192, 195–196,
199, 201, 207, 251, 254, 257
Narrative Inquiry, 15
Narrative Fragment, 87
Reflexive Writing, 94
Nephew/Niece, 192, 201
Nonparent, 198, 203–204
Nonsexual Communication, 58
Norland, Carey M., 58, 69
Nostalgia, 31

**O**
Objectified, 226
Obsessive-Compulsive Disorder,
215
Online, 178
Ontological, 19, 195
Oppressive Discourse, 20
O'Sullivan, Lucia F., 58

**P**
Painting, 75, 81–82, 268
Parent(s), 15, 25, 29–30, 38, 42,
48, 52–53, 57–58, 62–63, 69–70,
90, 131, 134, 137–138, 140, 144,
146–148, 153, 155–159, 168, 177,

182, 189, 192, 200, 202–204,
208, 214, 217, 225–226, 255,
259–260, 276, 279–280
Parent Communication, 57
Parental Control, 58
Partner, 18, 26–27, 56, 58, 66–67,
76, 78, 91, 105, 108, 118, 126,
134, 146, 177–178, 184, 198,
202, 208–209, 225, 234–235,
249–251, 264, 269, 280
Patterns of Interaction, 134
Peer Influence, 151–159
Pelias, Ronald J., 17, 19
Performative Writing, 17–18
   Text, 20
Personal Experiences, 17
Personal Narrative, 21, 48, 61, 69,
116, 123, 133, 161–174, 195, 213,
220, 242
Personal Order, 18, 177
Personal Relationships, 16
Poetry, 15–20, 25, 29–33, 80, 164,
237, 239, 263, 276
Poetic Inquiry, 16, 263–273
Pop Culture, 55, 65–68, 201
Post-Positivist (paradigm), 18
Poulus, Christopher, 133, 134,
153, 154
Power, 104
Pregnancy, 20, 29, 33, 52, 84, 133,
161–174, 188–191, 196
Premarital Sex, 69–72
Prenatal, 166, 188–189
Prendergast, Monica, 18
Privacy, 77, 119, 138,
Pro-Natalism, 195–205

**Q**
Qualitative, 21
Queer Identities, 61–63

**R**
Race, 227–230
Racial Epithet, 228–229
Radical Specificity, 20
Rawlins, William K., 103, 105–106
Real and Ideal Self, 18
Relational Dialectics Theory, 20,
104, 161–174, 254–261, 263–273
Relational Dissolution, 18,
263–273
Relational Health, 20, 133
   Hurt, 20
   Secrets, 151–159
   Stories, 86–95
Relational Lives, 55
Relational Messages, 135
Relational Uncertainty, 77
Relationships, 15, 17–20, 25–27,
33, 49, 51, 53, 55–56, 65–67,
70–71, 76–77, 87, 89–91, 93–95,
97, 103–104, 107–110, 114–115,
117, 135, 152–153, 165, 177–179,
207, 209–210, 215, 233–235,
247–251, 254, 263–265, 276–
277, 279
Relationship Expectations, 65–68,
76, 97–99, 177
Relationship Dialogue, 239–240
Relationship Forms, 61–63
Relationship History, 25, 36
Relationship Maintenance,
242–244
Relationship Metaphors, 56
Relationship Narratives, 188–193
Relationship Processes, 16, 18, 21,
56, 76, 263
Relationship Rituals, 65–68,
116–121
Relationship Research, 25
Relationship Schemas, 26–27

Relationship Trajectories, 36–46
Religion, 137–149
Religious Values, 55, 69–72
Rejection, 36–46
Representation, 19
Romance, 65–68
Romantic Relationships, 25–26,
    55, 67, 76, 107–115
Respect, 26

S
Same Sex, 66
Scripts, 56–57, 103, 116–121
    Sexual Scripts, 56
Secrets, 133
Self and Society, 18
Self-Concept, 25–26, 135
Self-Doubt, 184
Self-Disclosure, 26, 75, 97–99, 191
Self-Esteem, 151–159
Self-Image, 29–34
Self-Help, 86–95
Self-Love, 92
Self-Perception, 217
Sexual Activity, 25, 55, 71, 57–58
Sexual Communication, 57–58,
    69–72
Sexual Decision–Making, 69–72
Sexuality, 29–34, 58, 104–105
Sexual Interactions, 57
Sexual Identity, 78
Sexual Health, 105
Sexually Transmitted Disease, 75
Sexual Orientation, 77, 134,
    181–186
Sexual Partners, 58
Sexual Talk, 25, 29–34, 69, 76, 208
Sibling, 69, 196
Sibling Relationships, 137–149

Silence, 18
Simic, Charles, 17
Similarities, 26
Singles, 65–68
Sister, 29, 65–66, 70, 90, 112, 139,
    144–145, 148, 167, 190, 196, 222
Situation, 27
Social Constructions, 134
Social Order, 18, 177
Social Expectations, 195–205
Social Exchange Theory, 56
Social Information Processing
    Theory, 179
Social Networks, 18, 51, 77, 105,
    170, 178, 248–251, 264, 279
Social Networking Sites, 181–186
    Facebook, 104, 110, 167,
    185–186, 189, 223, 257
Social Norms, 57
Social Reality, 104
Social Science, 19
Social Support, 77, 103, 123–132,
    225–230, 237–238, 276–281
Social Worlds, 18
Son, 61
Sorority, 114
Sotirin, Patty, 20
Spouse, 63, 126, 146–147, 189,
    191, 203, 234, 254, 256–257,
    259–260
Stagnation, 119
Straight, 222
Stereotypes, 207, 225–230
Stigma, 66, 75, 133, 159, 177, 247,
    276–281
Stigmatized Identities, 76, 133
Suicide, 213–214
Subjugated Perspectives, 15

**T**

Teenager, 70
Terrorism, 203–204
Text Messages, 75, 97
Therapeutic Writing, 80–84,
    237–238
Topic Avoidance Taboo Topic, 134
Transcripts, 20
Transformation, 217–218
Trust, 26, 75–76, 94, 103, 105, 114,
    117, 157, 182, 184
TRUTH (Capital T), 19
Turning Point, 157

**U**

Uncertainty/Certainty, 20, 75, 166
Unconscious, 133

**V**

Valentine's Day, 55–56, 65–67
Validity, 19
Virginity, 57, 76, 69–72, 76, 217,
    273
Visual Arts, 15

**W**

Watson, Cate, 19
Wife, 51, 66, 117, 146–147, 172,
    182, 185–186, 256, 269
Women without Kids, 195,
    201–202
Work-Life Issues, 133, 161–174
Workplace, 197

# About the Authors

**Dessa Anderson** is a pseudonym. The author uses rhetorical criticism to study new media.

**Marne Austin** is a doctoral candidate and Dissertation Fellow in the School of Media and Communication at Bowling Green State University. Her research focuses on intercultural and relational communication among marginalized groups. She primarily uses (auto)ethnographic methods in her research on Muslim women, eating disorders in families, and women who sleep with women.

**Tiffani Baldwin** is currently a PhD candidate at the University of Denver. She first became fascinated with interpersonal relationships as a young girl and started studying them academically during her undergraduate education at Arizona State University. Tiffani's area of emphasis is family communication with special interests in gender, aging, and identity. She is especially passionate about teaching communication courses in these areas.

**Meg Barker** is a Senior Lecturer in Psychology at the Open University and a sex and relationship therapist. She has researched and written extensively on relationships, gender and sexuality (particularly on bisexuality, BDSM, and polyamory), co-edits the journal *Psychology & Sexuality*, and co-organizes the Critical Sexology seminar series. Her book *Rewriting the Rules* (Routledge, 2012) is an exploration of the common rules of romantic relationships and the various ways in which these are currently being rewritten.

**Wonda Baugh** is a doctoral candidate in the American Culture Studies Department of Bowling Green State University. She has an MA in Women's, Gender and Sexuality Studies from the University of Cincinnati and a BA in Interdisciplinary Studies with concentrations in women and gender studies and history. Her research interests include disability studies, ethnic studies, and gender studies. Her hobbies include mixed martial arts and spoken word poetry.

**Suzanne V. L. Berg** received her MA in Speech Communication from Minnesota State University, Mankato, and is working on her PhD in Media and Communication from Bowling Green State University. Her research program focuses on the intersections of critical rhetorical criticism and intellectual property law.

**Keith Berry** is an Associate Professor in the Department of Communication at the University of South Florida, and Immediate Past Chair of NCA's Ethnography Division. His work uses phenomenology and ethnographic methods to examine intersections of interaction, culture and identity, particularly the constitution of subjectivity across diverse relational scenes. He has published in journals such as *Cultural Studies ↔ Critical Methodologies* and *Qualitative Inquiry,* and in books such as *Identity Research and Communication: Intercultural Reflections and Future Directions.*

**Lindsey Boyd** is a graduate of Bowling Green State University with a degree in Public Relations and Communication. At Bowling Green, she had the opportunity to work closely with the Children's Miracle Network and Mercy Children's Hospital through the Dance Marathon organization. This nonprofit work instilled a passion for helping people that ultimately led to her current position with the Crohn's and Colitis Foundation of America in Cleveland. Helping people by day and sports enthusiast by night, she is still adjusting to big city life.

**Kimberly Dark** is a writer, mother, performer and professor. She is the author of five award-winning solo performance scripts, and her poetry and prose appear in a number of popular and academic publications. For more than fifteen years, Kimberly has inspired audiences in fancy theaters, esteemed universities, and fabulous festivals. She tours widely in North America, Australia and Europe—anywhere an audience loves a well-told story. Find out more about her work at www.kimberlydark.com.

**Ashley Duggan** (PhD, University of California, Santa Barbara, 2003) is Associate Professor at Boston College. Her main research interests include nonverbal, relational, and health communication. She examines interpersonal control tactics, emotional experience in provider-patient contexts, nonverbal communication behaviors in conversations about physical and mental health, and family communication surrounding illness. Her work can be found in communication, relational, and medical conferences and associated academic journals. Outside the office, she enjoys ballet and tap classes, good food, and laughing with friends.

**Sandra L. Faulkner** (PhD, Pennsylvania State University) is Associate Professor of Communication at Bowling Green State University. Her teaching and research interests include qualitative methodology, poetic inquiry, and the relationships between culture, ethnic/sexual identities, and sexual talk in close relationships. She has published research in journals such as *Qualitative Health Research* and *Journal of Social and Personal Relationships*, and the book *Poetry as Method: Reporting Research through Verse* with Left Coast Press, Inc.. Her poetry has appeared in *Qualitative Inquiry, Women & Language, Storm Cellar*, and *Northwoods*, and her chapbook, *Hello Kitty Goes to College*, was published by dancing girl press. She lives in Northwest Ohio with her partner, their warrior girl, and a rescue mutt.

**Julia A. Galbus** is Associate Professor and Associate Chair of English at the University of Southern Indiana, where she teaches composition, American literature, autobiography, and literary theory. She has published articles about Susan Glaspell and Edith Wharton, as well as contemporary writers E. Ethelbert Miller, A. Van Jordan, and Charles Johnson.

**Ellen Gorsevski** (PhD, Pennsylvania State University) researches contemporary rhetoric of peacebuilding, especially communication practices and artifacts of social justice movement leaders. Her publications span international rhetoric, politics, media criticism and propaganda, and nonviolent conflict communication. She teaches at Bowling Green State University. Her publications include *Peaceful Persuasion: The Geopolitics of Nonviolent Rhetoric* (SUNY Press, 2004), and *Dangerous Women: The Rhetoric of the Women Nobel Peace Laureates* (Troubador, 2013).

**Lisa K. Hanasono** (PhD, Purdue University) is an Assistant Professor of Communication at Bowling Green State University. Her research and teaching interests focus on prejudice, discrimination, and interpersonal coping. She has published in journals such as *Human Communication Research, Communication Quarterly*, and *Sex Roles*. She has taught a variety of college courses, including relational communication, interviewing, communication theory, interpersonal communication, Asian American studies, and health communication. When she is not teaching or working on research projects, she enjoys spending time with her family, cooking comfort food, and horseback riding.

**Manda Hicks** (PhD, Bowling Green State University) is the Director of Forensics at Boise State University. She is a U.S. Army veteran. Her research interests include gender, intercultural communication, feminist theory, qualitative methods, and military culture. She believes that war does strange things.

**Ellen Leslie** is an Assistant Professor at Siena Heights University and researches domestic abuse in religious cultures.

**Kate Magsamen-Conrad** (PhD, Rutgers University, 2012) researches the role of communication in interpersonal relationships, in particular disclosure and privacy and adolescents' processing of prevention messages. She is especially interested in health related disclosure decision-making and the mechanisms through which researchers can apply theory in order to improve health. Her work focuses on the development and implementation of interpersonal and persuasion theory-based health interventions—for example, a Brief Disclosure Intervention for HIV+ individuals stemming from her dissertation research.

**Jenn McKee** (MFA, Pennsylvania State University) is a staff theater critic/entertainment writer for AnnArbor.com. Joyce Carol Oates selected one of her stories, "Under the Influence," for the anthology *Best New American Voices 2003*. She hopes her travel memoir about driving a stranger around the country for a book tour gets published, but until then, she's blogging and neurotically obsessing in her brightly-painted home, which she shares with her lovely husband Joe and two daughters, Lily and Neve.

**Cynthia Nicole** completed her BA and MA in Communication Studies at Texas State University–San Marcos, with minors in Popular Culture and Sociology. After working for four years on her PhD at Bowling Green State University, Cynthia has decided to leave academia and pursue other interests. In some ways, the self-discovery that came along with acquiring tattoos helped free her to make this decision. As soon as she settles into a new career, she plans to commemorate the transition from one chapter of life to the next with a new tattoo.

**Malorie Palma** is a graduate of Bowling Green State University (BGSU). She earned a BA in Communication with a Marketing minor. At BGSU, she was involved in numerous campus organizations, including a sorority that she is still active in today. She has a passion for helping other people and intends to excel in a career where she can influence and impact the lives of many. With college conquered and the world at her fingertips, there is no telling what she will do next.

**Paul D. Ruby** is a graduate of Pennsylvania State University with a degree in Electrical Engineering. He has taught photographic art and poetry classes at Saint Bonaventure University, Pittsburgh Plan for the Arts, private workshops, Olean Public Library, and Schlow Library. He has been in more than 50 photography exhibits, and has won numerous awards. He lives in State College, Pennsylvania, with his parakeets, Wendy and Jimmy.

**Sherry R. Shepler** (PhD, Wayne State University, 2002) studies the intersection of community conflict, ethnicity and communication. She has examined the rhetoric of Jane Addams and how Addams's decision to support peace efforts during World War I led to her public popularity decline. Also, she investigates how ethnicity is portrayed in the media and perceived by those in the Crown Heights neighborhood of Brooklyn, New York. At Saint Anselm, she serves as the Coordinator of the Communication Program and Director of Internships, housed within the English Department.

**Frances Spaulding** is a masters degree candidate at Michigan State University. She has worked at a domestic violence shelter in several capacities and has experience working with domestic violence survivors.

**Sheila Squillante** is a poet and essayist living in Western Pennsylvania. She is the author of four poetry chapbooks: *A Woman Traces the Shoreline* (dancing girl press, 2011); *Women Who Pawn Their Jewelry* (Finishing Line Press, 2012); *Another Beginning* (Kattywompus Press, 2012), and *In This Dream of My Father* (Seven Kitchens Press, forthcoming). Her work has appeared widely in print and online venues like *No Tell Motel, MiPOesias, Phoebe, Quarterly West, Prairie Schooner, Waccamaw, Literary Mama,* and *PANK.* Her essays have been nominated for *Best American Essays* and Dzanc's *Best of the Web,* her poetry for the Pushcart Prize.

**Abagail Van Vlerah** is a doctoral student at Bowling Green State University majoring in American Culture Studies and Women's Gender and Sexuality Studies. She is a graduate of the University of Wyoming and Saint Mary's College, Notre Dame, Indiana. She is miserable with relationships and spends most of her free time riding motorcycles and running marathons.

**Camille-Yvette Welsch** teaches literature, creative writing, and composition and rhetoric at The Pennsylvania State University. Her work has appeared in *Indiana Review, Mid-American Review, The Writer's Chronicle, Barrow Street, From the Fishouse*, and other journals. She is the author of a biography of the young adult writer, Meg Cabot, as well as the author/editor of numerous books of literary criticism. She lives in Central Pennsylvania with her husband and son.

**Gabriel Welsch** has published more than 40 stories in journals, including Southern Review, New Letters, Ascent, PANK, Georgia Review, Cutbank, Mid-American Review, Chautauqua, and The Collagist. He is also a recipient of a Pennsylvania Arts Council Individual Artist's Fellowship for Literature in Fiction. Welsch's four poetry books are: *Four Horsepersons of a Disappointing Apocalypse* (Steel Toe Books, 2013), *The Death of Flying Things* (WordTech Editions, 2012), *An Eye Fluent in Gray* (2010), and *Dirt and All Its Dense Labor* (WordTech Editions, 2006). He lives in Huntingdon, Pennsylvania, with his wife and daughters, and is a Vice President at Juniata College.

**Erin K. Willer** is an Assistant Professor of Communication Studies at the University of Denver. Her research focuses on the communicative management of identity and relational difficulty. As such, she studies such management vis-à-vis social aggression and issues related to reproductive health. Her research also focuses on types of communicative management strategies, such as storylistening and perspective-taking. Using quantitative, qualitative, and visual methods, she wants her work to increase individual and relational health, and understanding and acceptance of outgroup members. She is also an artist, runner, and possibilitarian.